CONTOURS OF CONFLICT
THE MAKING & REMAKING OF SRI LANKA

Democracy at Gunpoint: Sri Lanka's Struggle for Stability
(1948-2024)

COMPILED BY:

TUAN B. KAMISS

This book is dedicated to *the dreamers, dissenters, and doers*—to every citizen who braved injustice, every youth who demanded better, and every soul who believed that democracy is not given but grown.

Copyrights

Disclaimer

This book is a work of nonfiction based on publicly available sources, historical records, and journalistic accounts. While every effort has been made to ensure accuracy, the author does not claim to provide definitive legal or investigative conclusions. All statements regarding individuals or groups are presented for informational purposes only and should not be construed as accusations or endorsements.

The author and publisher are not liable for any misinterpretation of content and make no representations concerning ongoing legal proceedings or government actions. Readers are encouraged to consult official documents, legal judgments, and primary sources for a more comprehensive understanding of the subject matter.

The views and interpretations expressed in this book are those of the author and do not necessarily reflect those of affiliated organizations, publishers, or contributors. Any resemblance to actual persons or entities outside of cited sources is coincidental and unintended.

TABLE OF CONTENTS

1

Introduction

A Testament to Truth, A Plea for Justice

I did not walk the marbled halls of power, nor did I dine at the tables where futures are bartered and boundaries redrawn. I am no politician—not in title, not in allegiance. But I have watched the machinery of influence grind down communities, and I've felt the tremors of decisions made in shadow. This book is my reckoning. Not as an architect of policy, but as a witness to the storm that brews behind closed doors.

Politicians are often praised as servants of the people, builders of progress, defenders of principle. But strip away the gloss, and another truth emerges—raw, unsparing. Many are driven less by vision than by a hunger to belong to the ruling order, to win at any cost. That hunger breeds betrayal, silences conscience, and feeds a cycle where survival outranks sincerity.

This book is not a parade of polished narratives. It is a descent into the unlit passages of Sri Lankan politics—where ambition often eclipses compassion, and where loyalty is traded like currency. It unmasks the quiet deals, the backroom compromises, and the systemic erasures that have scarred this island's soul.

Sri Lanka, beautiful and broken, has long danced to the rhythm of political expediency. The chapters that follow do not seek your applause. They seek your attention. They hold up a mirror to communal exploitation, especially the suffering of Tamil and Muslim minorities under the guise of governance. These are not allegations. They are lived truths.

I write not out of bitterness, but out of a burning hope—that the youth of today will read, reflect, and reject the politics of division. That they will rise with empathy, reclaim unity, and shape a future rooted in coexistence and shared dignity.

Do not read these words as a sermon. Read them as a cry—from someone who once called Sri Lanka home. Who still carries its wounds. Who will not stay silent while silence enables injustice.

TUAN B. KAMISS (Author)
Calgary
Canada
September 2025

Sri Lanka: 1948 to 1953

Birth of a Nation

My journey into Sri Lankan politics began not through ambition, but through sorrow. I was only eight years old in **August 1953**, when I lost my beloved mother. Our home was filled with mourning, yet amidst the grief, something else stirred—a sense of unrest, confusion, and urgency. I remember my father and relatives, their eyes red from tears, also glued to the pages of *The Times of Ceylon*. Though I could barely read, one image stood out: **a burning train engine on the front page**. That was my first glimpse of politics—not in speeches or slogans, but in smoke and silence.

*Later I came to know that this was the **Hartal of 1953**, the first major political uprising in post-independence Sri Lanka, which was still called **Ceylon** at the time.*

The Dawn of Independence

Sri Lanka gained independence from British colonial rule on **February 4, 1948**, becoming a **Dominion of the British Commonwealth**. The country retained the **British monarch** as head of state, and **Don Stephen Senanayake** became **the first Prime Minister**. The new government adopted a parliamentary system, but it was largely led by Western-educated elites who were disconnected from the everyday struggles of the common people.

The early years of independence were filled with hope, but also with hidden tensions. The economy was fragile, heavily dependent on exports like **tea, rubber, and coconut**. The government promised stability, but cracks began to show.

(Above: The first Board of Ministers in the 1952 Parliament)

Prime Minister Don Stephen Senanayake, Sri Lanka's first Prime Minister, also called Father of the Nation, died on **March 22, 1952**, following a tragic accident. On the morning of **March 21**, while riding his horse along **Galle Face Green** in Colombo—a routine he enjoyed—he was **thrown from the horse**, reportedly due to a sudden stroke that caused him to lose control.

He was found unconscious, bleeding from the nose, and was rushed to hospital. Despite medical efforts, he passed away **33 hours later**, at the age of 67.

His death sent shockwaves across the nation. Mourners from all walks of life gathered to pay their respects, and tributes poured in from world leaders, including heartfelt words from **Jawaharlal Nehru**, who called him a symbol of Asia's transition to freedom.

He was succeeded by his son, **Dudley Senanayake**, who became Prime Minister on **March 26, 1952**. Dudley continued his father's legacy but resigned in **October 1953** following the political fallout from the Hartal uprising.

Below: (Seated) D.S. Senanayake with his son Dudley Senanayake

The Rice Subsidy Crisis

One of the most critical issues was the **Rice Subsidy**, a legacy from World War II rationing. Rice was the staple food, and the government had long subsidized its price to keep it affordable. In the **1952 election**, the ruling **United National Party (UNP)** promised to maintain the rice price at **25 cents per measure**.

But after winning the election, the government reversed its promise. In **July 1953**, the rice subsidy was cut, and the price jumped to **70 cents per measure**—nearly triple. This decision was influenced by:

- **Mounting budget deficits**: Food subsidies consumed nearly **20% of government spending**.
- **Pressure from the World Bank and Central Bank of Ceylon**: These institutions urged the government to reduce welfare spending and focus on economic development.
- **Internal divisions**: Finance Minister **J.R. Jayewardene** pushed for austerity, while others hesitated.

Alongside the rice hike, the government also:

- Increased **rail fares and postal rates**
- Withdrew **free school meals**
- Raised **taxes on basic goods**

These measures hit the poor hardest and sparked widespread anger.

The Hartal of 1953

Above: LSSP leader NM Perera addressing a mass protest in Colombo's Galle Face Green in opposition to a UNP (budget. Source: World Socialist Website

On **August 12, 1953**, leftist parties including the **Lanka Sama Samaja Party (LSSP)** and **Communist Party** organized a nationwide **hartal**—a general strike and civil disobedience campaign. It was the first time the masses rose against an elected government.

The protests were intense:

- **Trains were sabotaged**, including the one I saw burning in the newspaper
- **Roads were blocked**, and **telegraph lines cut**
- **Shops and offices closed**, and **transport halted**
- **21 people were killed**, and the government declared a **state of emergency**

For a brief period Dudley Senanayake "ran away" to India, giving the reins to Sir Joh Kotelawala. The Prime Minister, **Dudley Senanayake**, was so shaken that he later resigned in **October 1953**.

My Awakening

That burning train was not just a symbol of chaos—it was a spark. It lit a fire of curiosity and reflection that grew with time. I was not a politician, but I became a witness indirectly. And this book is my testimony.

From the hopeful dawn of independence to the fiery reckoning of 1953, Sri Lanka's political journey began with both promise and pain. The Hartal was not just a protest—it was a turning point. It revealed the deep disconnect between the ruling elite and the working class. It showed that politics was not confined to parliament—it lived in the streets, in the homes, and in the hearts of the people.

Dudley Senanayake's Resignation and Retreat: A Turning Point in Sri Lankan Politics

The aftermath of the **1953 Hartal** left Prime Minister **Dudley Senanayake** physically and emotionally drained. The mass uprising, triggered by the government's decision to cut the rice subsidy and other welfare measures, had shaken the foundations of the newly independent nation. Though the Hartal lasted only a day, its impact was profound—**21 people were killed**, infrastructure was sabotaged, and the government was forced to declare a **state of emergency**.

Senanayake, already burdened by the sudden death of his father **D.S. Senanayake** in 1952, had taken on the premiership reluctantly. The Hartal exposed deep divisions within the ruling **United National Party (UNP)** and revealed the growing disconnect between the government and the working class. Dudley, who had campaigned on maintaining the rice subsidy, now faced public outrage for reversing that promise.

A Quiet Escape to India

Following the Hartal, Dudley Senanayake's health deteriorated. He was reportedly **gravely ill** during the crisis and **retreated to India** for a brief period to recover. This move was seen by many as a symbolic withdrawal—not just from the political spotlight, but from the pressures of leadership itself. While in India, he remained out of public view, leaving the reins of government in the hands of **Sir John Kotelawala**, his cousin and Minister of Transport and Works.

This temporary absence gave rise to speculation. Some believed Dudley was contemplating **leaving politics permanently**, and there were even rumors that he might become a **Buddhist monk**. Though these claims were never confirmed, they reflected the depth of his disillusionment.

The Resignation

On **12 October 1953**, Dudley Senanayake officially **resigned as Prime Minister**, citing **ill health** and the need for a leader "unhampered by any ailment". In his resignation statement, he wrote:

"I have endeavoured to fulfil the heavy responsibilities of the important charge entrusted to my care with all the conscientiousness that is possible to a human being... But I take my leave of you with firm faith that our Party and our new Government will work in unison for the welfare and happiness of Sri Lanka."

His departure marked the **first voluntary resignation of a head of government** in independent Sri Lanka. The Governor General, **Lord Soulbury**, then invited **Sir John Kotelawala** to form a new government, which he accepted.

Legacy of the Resignation

Dudley's resignation was not just a political event—it was a moment of reckoning. It highlighted the fragility of post-independence governance and the emotional toll of leadership. His decision to step down, rather than cling to power, earned him a reputation as a **reluctant yet principled politician**.

Though he remained a **backbencher** until 1956, Dudley would later return to lead the UNP and serve as Prime Minister again in **1960** and **1965–1970**, proving that his retreat was not the end—but a pause in a remarkable political journey.

To understand Sri Lanka's Constitution during the time, we need to go back to events before Independence.

3

Sri Lanka's Peaceful Revolution

(Old Parliament building in Galle Face, Colombo)

Before the world knew Sri Lanka as a free nation, it was called **Ceylon**—a pearl in the Indian Ocean, rich in culture, beauty, and history. But for more than **400 years**, this island was ruled by foreign powers: first the **Portuguese**, then the **Dutch**, and finally the **British**. Each left their mark, but it was the British who stayed the longest, shaping the island's politics, economy, and society.

The Colonial Grip

In **1815**, the British took full control of the island after signing the **Kandyan Convention**, ending the rule of the last native king of Kandy. From then on, Ceylon became a **British Crown Colony**, and the people were governed by laws made in London. The British built roads, railways, and tea plantations—but they also took land from villagers and gave power to a small elite class.

Despite this, there was no major armed rebellion after 1848. Unlike India, which fought for freedom through mass movements and sacrifice, Ceylon's path to independence was **quiet, strategic, and political**.

The Rise of Reformers

In the early 1900s, a new generation of educated Ceylonese began to speak out. They were lawyers, journalists, and teachers—men like **Sir James Peiris**, **E.W. Perera**, **F.R. Senanayake**, and **D.S. Senanayake**. These leaders didn't raise swords—they raised their voices. They demanded **constitutional reforms**, **equal rights**, and **self-rule**.

One dramatic moment came in **1915**, during the **Sinhalese-Muslim riots**. The British arrested many Sinhalese leaders without trial. In response, E.W. Perera secretly carried a petition to London—**hidden in the sole of his shoe**—to expose the injustice. This act of bravery helped turn British opinion and led to changes in governance.

The First Steps Toward Freedom

In **1931**, the British introduced the **Donoughmore Constitution**, giving Ceylon **universal adult franchise**—the right for all adults to vote. This was revolutionary. Even in Britain, not everyone had that right at the time. But the people wanted more.

By the **1940s**, the demand for full independence grew louder. **D.S. Senanayake**, a respected statesman, led negotiations with the British. He didn't ask for freedom with fire—he asked with facts, diplomacy, and dignity. He argued that Ceylon had supported Britain during **World War II**, and now deserved its own place in the world.

Independence Without Bloodshed

Finally, on **February 4, 1948**, Ceylon became an **independent Dominion** within the British Commonwealth. There were no battles, no martyrs, no rivers of blood. The transition was peaceful, a rare achievement in a world torn by war and revolution.

D.S. Senanayake became the first **Prime Minister**, and the country began its journey as a free nation. The British flag was lowered, and the lion flag of Sri Lanka rose again.

A Legacy of Peaceful Struggle

Sri Lanka's independence was not won by violence—it was earned through **patience, unity, and political wisdom**. The leaders who shaped it believed in negotiation, not confrontation. They proved that freedom could be achieved without war, if the people stood together and spoke with one voice.

*Sri Lanka's independence movement was shaped not only by the Sinhalese majority but also by influential leaders from minority communities—particularly **Tamil**, **Muslim**, and **Burgher** groups—who played key roles in shaping the island's political future.*

Tamil Leaders and Their Contributions

Sir Ponnambalam Ramanathan

- A prominent Tamil lawyer and statesman in the early 20th century.
- Advocated for constitutional reforms and civil rights under British rule.
- Though conservative in some views, he was respected across ethnic lines for his intellect and oratory.

Sir Ponnambalam Arunachalam

- Brother of Ramanathan and a key figure in founding the **Ceylon National Congress** in 1919.
- Worked toward uniting all communities under a common national identity.
- His early efforts laid the groundwork for multiethnic cooperation in the independence movement.

Muslim Leaders and Their Influence

Tuan Burhanudeen Jayah

- A respected educator and politician from the Muslim community.
- Played a major role in securing Muslim representation in the legislature.
- Advocated for communal harmony and was part of the delegation that negotiated independence terms with the British.

Burgher Community Contributions

Eugene Wilfred Jayewardene

- A member of the Burgher community and father of future President J.R. Jayewardene.
- Served as a Supreme Court judge and was involved in legal reforms during the colonial period.
- Though not a political activist, his legal legacy influenced the shaping of post-independence governance.

Why Their Roles Mattered

- These minority leaders **challenged colonial policies** that favored division and inequality.
- They **advocated for inclusive governance**, even when communal tensions were rising.

- Their presence in early political institutions helped **legitimize the independence movement** as a national—not just ethnic—struggle.

Governors During Independence (Pre-1948)

Before independence, **Ceylon** was governed by British-appointed officials. The **last colonial Governor** was:

Sir Henry Monck-Mason Moore

- Served as Governor of Ceylon from **1944 to 1948**
- Oversaw the final years of British rule and the peaceful transition to independence

First Three Governor-Generals of Ceylon (Post-1948)

After independence on **February 4, 1948**, the role of Governor was replaced by the **Governor-General**, who represented the British monarch in the Dominion of Ceylon:

NAME	TERM OF OFFICE	NOTEES
Sir Henry Monck-Mason Moore	1948-1949	Transitioned from colonial Governor to first Governor-General
Lord Soulbury	1949 – 1954	Headed the Soulbury Commission; oversaw early constitutional reforms
Sir Oliver Goonetilleke	1954 – 1962	First Ceylonese to hold the post; played key roles in civil defense

Key Government Leaders (1948–1952)

During this formative period, the country was led by:

Don Stephen Senanayake

- **Prime Minister** from **1947 until his death in March 1952**
- Widely regarded as the **Father of the Nation**
- Led the **United National Party (UNP)**
- Focused on agricultural development, national unity, and gradual reforms

Dudley Senanayake

- Succeeded his father as **Prime Minister** in **March 1952**
- Continued UNP leadership until **October 1953**, when he resigned after the Hartal uprising

Before I go back to political transformation in Sri Lanka through my eyes, the following is a summary of Sri Lanka's early political transformation during the years 1947 to 1954 for easy understanding.

Visual Timeline Summary: Sri Lanka's Early Political Transformation (1947–1954)

1947	First general elections under British colonial rule	Don Stephen Senanayake becomes Ceylon's first Prime Minister Ceylon becomes a Dominion in the British
1948	**Independence on February 4**	**Commonwealth under PM D.S. Senanayake; Sir Henry Monck-Mason Moore continues as Governor-General**
1949	**Lord Soulbury** appointed Governor-General	Commonwealth under PM D.S. Senanayake; Sir Henry Monck-Mason Moore continues as Governor-General
1952	D.S. Senanayake dies suddenly on March 22	Died after falling from a horse following a suspected stroke at Galle Face
1952	**Dudley Senanayake** becomes PM	Continuation of father's legacy; elected after general election victory
1953	**Hartal uprising on August 12**	Protest against rice subsidy cuts; 21+ people killed; State of Emergency declared
1953	Dudley resigns on October 12	Brief retreat to India due to illness and political strain
1954	**Sir John Kotelawala** appointed PM	Took office after Dudley's resignation, strong personality and military background
1954	**Sir Oliver Goonetilleke** becomes Governor-General	First native Ceylonese to hold the post; served until 1962

4

The First Educational Reforms in Ceylon in the 1950s and Their Effects

A New Beginning After Independence

Ceylon, now called Sri Lanka, gained independence from British rule in 1948. After becoming a free country, its leaders wanted to make changes that would help build a stronger and fairer nation. One of the biggest areas they focused on was education. They believed that education could help reduce poverty, create equal opportunities, and build a proud national identity.

Before independence, the education system was mostly in English and was often only available to children from wealthy families. Poorer children, especially those from rural areas, were left out. The government knew they had to fix this unfair system.

Starting the Reform Movement

Although the push for change began in the 1940s, the real action happened during the 1950s. A key figure behind these changes was **C.W.W. Kannangara**, known as the "**Father of Free Education**" in Sri Lanka. His Special Committee on Education proposed bold ideas that would make education free and fair for all.

C. W. W. Kannangara - Sunday Observer

In 1950, the **Education (Amendment) Act No. 5** helped turn these ideas into reality. The main goals were:

Making education free from primary school to university
Teaching in Sinhala and Tamil instead of English
Creating different paths in secondary school—academic, practical, and vocational

What Changed in the 1950s?

1. **Free Education for Everyone**

Children no longer had to pay fees to attend school. This opened education to thousands of families who couldn't afford it before.

2. **Learning in Local Languages**

   Schools stopped using English as the main teaching language. Instead, students learned in their mother tongue—**Sinhala or Tamil.** This helped many children understand lessons better and feel more connected to their culture.

3. **Different Education Paths**

   Not all children wanted to go to university. So, the government created schools that focused on job skills, like farming and mechanics, along with academic subjects. These schools were called **Senior Practical Schools**.

4. **Building More Schools**

   To support the new system, many schools were built all over the country, especially in remote and rural areas. Old schools were brought into the free education system as well.

What Happened Because of These Changes?

Good Outcomes

More Children in School
School enrollment increased a lot. Children from poor families and villages finally got a chance to learn and succeed.

- **Stronger National Identity**

  Learning in Sinhala and Tamil helped people feel proud of their language and culture. It gave a sense of unity and belonging.

- **Better Job Opportunities**

  Free education allowed children from all backgrounds to become doctors, teachers, engineers, and more. It gave them a way to improve their lives and their families' futures.

Challenges and Problems

- **Not Enough Qualified Teachers**

  Many teachers had been trained to teach in English. Switching to Sinhala or Tamil was hard, and there weren't enough new teachers ready to help.

- **Some Schools Lacked Resources**

Practical and vocational schools didn't always have the tools or funding they needed. Students sometimes didn't get the training that was promised.

- **Ethnic Tensions**

   Language changes later became political. Some groups felt unfairly treated, which led to ethnic tensions in the decades that followed.

Personal Reflections on Education and Division in Sri Lanka

The educational reforms introduced in Sri Lanka during the 1950s marked a turning point in the nation's history. They laid the groundwork for an impressive rise in literacy rates and cultivated a strong national belief in accessible education for all—no longer reserved for a privileged few. Subsequent governments built upon these foundations through the 1970s and 1990s, further expanding the reach and impact of education.

I vividly recall my own experience as a Grade 2 student. My classroom was a vibrant tapestry of ethnic backgrounds: Tamil, Sinhala, and myself, a Malay. We came together to learn English, united in curiosity and the joy of shared learning. At that age, there were no racial or language barriers—we simply saw classmates and friends.

But that unity was abruptly disrupted with the implementation of the Swabasha policy, which mandated instruction in native languages. We were split into separate classes based on ethnicity and language. It was a moment that left a lasting impression on me. What had once been a harmonious space quickly became divided. That segregation, in my view, planted the seeds of future conflict.

Without a common language to bridge our differences, people became increasingly isolated from one another. This separation based on race and language gradually eroded the sense of national unity. Tragically, these divisions contributed to one of the most violent and painful chapters in Sri Lanka's history in the decades that followed.

5

Leftist Politics and the Birth of Sinhala Nationalism

The Boy in the Back Row

I first encountered politics not in the newspapers or on television, but in a modest classroom during my sixth-grade year. A new teacher had arrived—a man with sharp eyes and a soft-spoken demeanor—and he taught us History and Civics with a passion that felt unusual, almost revolutionary. On his very first day, he broke the ice with a question none of us had ever heard asked aloud:

"Students, which political party do you like?"

We were stunned. It felt more like a question meant for grown-ups around a dinner table, not children in their school uniforms. We looked at each other, hesitant and wide-eyed, until someone shouted "**UNP!**" And then, as if a switch had been flipped, the rest of us echoed it in a chorus. UNP, of course. The party we overheard our parents discussing, perhaps while sipping tea or debating during the evening news. It was the only political name many of us even knew.

But then came a small voice from the back of the classroom.

"I like the **Samasamajists**," he said.

There was a palpable silence. Heads turned. Brows furrowed. Who was this boy who dared to say something different? His voice was firm but calm, and unlike the rest of us, he didn't look around for approval. It didn't take long to learn that his father was a staunch member of the **Lanka Sama Samaja Party**—one of the oldest and most ideologically committed Leftist parties in Sri Lanka.

To me, at the time, that party had a dark cloud over it. The grown-ups in my life—my father especially—spoke of the Left as if it were a reckless force, the kind that threatened tradition, prosperity, and authority. The idea of siding with the working class or challenging the upper echelons of society wasn't just alien to us—it was something close to forbidden.

But that moment in class stuck with me. The courage of that boy to speak his mind planted a seed of curiosity. Years later, as I learned more—about socialism, labor rights, revolution, and the colonial legacies that bred such movements—I found myself peeling away the layers of misconception. These were not the villains I had been warned about. In fact, they were thinkers, fighters, and dreamers who envisioned a fairer future.

This chapter opens the story of Sri Lanka's Leftist movement—a story often silenced or ridiculed, especially by the wealthy and those who clung to hierarchy, like my father. But within it lies struggle, sacrifice, and a vision for dignity and justice that still echoes through the island.

Setting the Stage: Post-Independence Ceylon

The early years of independence were filled with hope, but also with deep social and political challenges. The country was searching for its identity, and different political groups had different visions for its future. Two major forces began to shape the political landscape in the 1950s:

- **Leftist movements**, which focused on workers' rights, socialism, and equality
- **Sinhala nationalist movements**, which emphasized the dominance of Sinhala language and Buddhist culture

These two forces often clashed, but they also influenced each other in powerful ways.

Rise of Leftist Politics

Lanka Sama Samaja Party (LSSP)

- Founded in **1935**, the LSSP was the first political party in Ceylon and strongly influenced by **Trotskyist Marxism**
- Leaders like **Dr. N.M. Perera** and **Philip Gunawardena** pushed for full independence and workers' rights

During World War II, many LSSP leaders were arrested for opposing the war, which they saw as imperialist.

(Above: Left: Dr. N.M. Perera, Right: Philip Gunawardena)

Communist Party of Sri Lanka (CPSL)

- Formed in **1943** as a Stalinist breakaway from the LSSP
- Supported Soviet-style socialism and focused on gradual reform through cooperation with the government

Bolshevik-Leninist Party

- Created in **1945** by dissidents from the LSSP

- Reunited with the LSSP in **1950**, showing the fluid nature of leftist politics at the time

Hartal of 1953

- A massive strike and protest organized by leftist parties against rising living costs and government policies
- Led to the resignation of Prime Minister **Dudley Senanayake**
- Demonstrated the power of organized labor and leftist activism

Despite their energy and commitment, leftist parties struggled to gain mass support. Their base was mostly urban workers and trade unions, while rural populations remained loyal to more traditional and nationalist parties.

Birth of Sinhala Nationalism and the SLFP

Formation of the Sri Lanka Freedom Party (SLFP)

- In **1951**, **S.W.R.D. Bandaranaike** broke away from the ruling United National Party (UNP) and formed the SLFP

  He had previously founded the **Sinhala Maha Sabha**, a group focused on promoting Sinhala culture and Buddhist values

Sinhala Only Act (1956)

- Bandaranaike's SLFP won a landslide victory in the **1956 general election** by promising to make **Sinhala the sole official language**
- The **Sinhala Only Act (No. 33 of 1956)** was passed, replacing English with Sinhala in government and education

- This move was popular among the Sinhala majority but deeply alienated Tamil-speaking minorities

Impact on Ethnic Relations

- Tamil leaders protested the language policy, leading to rising ethnic tensions
- The **Bandaranaike-Chelvanayakam Pact (1957)** tried to offer concessions to Tamils, but was later torn up under pressure from Sinhala nationalists and Buddhist monks
- These events laid the groundwork for future ethnic conflict and civil unrest

Clash and Convergence

While leftist parties focused on class struggle and equality, Sinhala nationalists emphasized ethnic identity and cultural pride. However, both movements shared some common ground:

- Opposition to Western influence and colonial legacies
- Desire for a more just and independent society
- Use of mass mobilization and grassroots activism

Bandaranaike's SLFP cleverly blended **populist rhetoric**, **socialist policies**, and **Sinhala nationalism**, attracting both rural peasants and disillusioned leftists. This fusion helped the SLFP dominate politics for decades.

Legacy of the 1950s

- **Leftist politics** introduced ideas of social justice, labor rights, and anti-imperialism that still influence Sri Lankan politics today
- **Sinhala nationalism**, born in the 1950s, became a powerful force that shaped language policy, education, and national identity
- The tensions between these two movements—and their impact on ethnic relations—continue to echo in Sri Lanka's political landscape

Dr. Badiuddin Mahmood and the Muslim Factor in SLFP

The name "Buddy" was more than just a nickname—it was whispered in reverence, half awe and half mystery, when I first heard it in my eighth-grade classroom. He was the principal of **Zahira College Gampola**, and under his stewardship, the school didn't just climb the ranks—it soared, becoming one of the finest in Sri Lanka's Central Province.

But what I didn't realize then was that this man, whose influence echoed through assembly halls and report cards, was shaping far more than exam scores. Behind the scenes, Buddy was orchestrating a historic political shift. During the turbulent decades of the 1960s and 1970s, he became a key architect in bridging the Muslim community with the **Sri Lanka Freedom Party (SLFP),** threading their aspirations into the fabric of the party's nationalist and socialist vision. What began as a name in a classroom would grow into a legacy that rewrote political alliances and empowered a people long left on the margins.

Championing Muslim Representation in SLFP

Founder Member of SLFP: Badiuddin Mahmood was among the early architects of the SLFP and maintained a close personal relationship with the Bandaranaike family, which gave him significant influence within the party.

Ministerial Leadership: He served as **Minister of Education** under Sirimavo Bandaranaike from 1960–1965 and again from 1970–1977, using his position to promote educational reforms that benefited Muslim students across the country.

Islamic Socialist Front: Mahmood also led the **Islamic Socialist Front**, a pressure group aligned with SLFP that mobilized Muslim support and countered rival Muslim factions. This group helped consolidate Muslim votes for the SLFP, especially in the Eastern Province.

Educational Reforms and Community Empowerment

- Mahmood's tenure as Education Minister is remembered for a "mini-revolution" in Muslim education. He expanded access to schools, increased the number of Muslim teachers, and introduced **standardization policies** that helped Muslim students enter professional university faculties like medicine and engineering.
- By 1984, there were **671 Muslim schools**, including 125 Maha Vidyalayas, largely due to his efforts.

Political Strategy and National Influence

Mahmood's strategy was to **align Muslim interests with Sinhala nationalism** while promoting social equity. He convinced many Muslims that they were bei ⬚ ng exploited by elite factions and that SLFP's socialist policies offered a better future.

He played a key role in opposing the **District Councils Bill** proposed by the UNP-Federal Party coalition, arguing it threatened national unity and Muslim interests. His campaign helped rally Muslim opposition to Tamil federalist proposals.

Legacy and Limitations

Mahmood's efforts helped transform the Muslim community from a business-focused group into a more educated and professionally diverse population.

However, critics argue that he **neglected religious education reform**, leaving Madrasas untouched and allowing conservative religious ideologies to persist.

In short, Badiuddin Mahmood's leadership within the SLFP was instrumental in **politically empowering Muslims**, expanding their access to education, and positioning them as a vital part of Sri Lanka's post-independence development.

Dr. Badruddin Mahmood, was instrumental in founding the **Islamic Socialist Front**. This party emerged from his belief that the Sri Lanka Freedom Party (SLFP), of which he was also a founding member, could offer more to the Muslim community than the rival United National Party (UNP).

The Islamic Socialist Front was rooted in **progressive socialist ideals** that aligned with Mahmud's faith and vision for uplifting Sri Lankan Muslims through education and employment opportunities. However, over time, the party **did not sustain significant political momentum**. It eventually faded from the national political landscape, likely due to limited electoral success and the dominance of larger parties like the SLFP and UNP.

1956 General Elections in Ceylon: A Political Earthquake and Racial Reckoning

Background: A Nation at a Crossroads

Eight years after gaining independence from Britain in 1948, **Ceylon (now Sri Lanka)** was still governed by the **United National Party (UNP)**, a party dominated by Western-educated elites. The UNP had failed to address growing social inequalities, rising unemployment, and the cultural alienation felt by the Sinhala-speaking majority. The country was ripe for change.

Enter **S.W.R.D. Bandaranaike**, a charismatic leader who broke away from the UNP and formed the **Sri Lanka Freedom Party (SLFP)** in 1951. By 1956, he had built a powerful coalition called the **Mahajana Eksath Peramuna (MEP)**, which included leftist and nationalist parties. Their campaign promised **Sinhala as the sole official language**, cultural revival, and socialist reforms—messages that resonated deeply with the rural Sinhala majority.

The Election Results: A Landslide Victory

Held from **April 5–10, 1956**, the elections were a political earthquake:

- The **MEP coalition won 51 out of 95 seats**, securing a clear majority
- The **UNP was crushed**, dropping from 54 seats to just 8
- Tamil parties like **ITAK** (Federal Party) gained ground in the north, winning 10 seats

This was the **first time in Ceylon's history** that a populist, rural-based coalition defeated the elite-dominated UNP. Bandaranaike became Prime Minister, and the SLFP began reshaping the country's identity.

Political Transformation

The 1956 elections marked the **end of elite dominance** and the **rise of the common man**:

- Parliament was filled with **Sinhala-educated rural leaders**, replacing English-speaking elites
- Political discourse shifted to **vernacular languages**, making politics more accessible
- The SLFP blended **socialist policies** with **Sinhala nationalism**, appealing to both workers and cultural conservatives

This shift democratized politics but also **polarized the nation** along ethnic lines.

Racial Fallout: The Sinhala Only Act and Ethnic Tensions

At a time when the political tides in Sri Lanka were turbulent and unpredictable, few anticipated the role that Dr. Badiuddin Mahmood—a prominent Muslim intellectual and educator—would play in shaping one of the most consequential electoral strategies in the country's history.

Recognizing the growing sentiment for cultural and linguistic identity among the Sinhala majority, Dr. Mahmood is said to have advised S.W.R.D. Bandaranaike to champion the **"Sinhala Only"** policy as a central theme of his campaign. This bold suggestion, though controversial and later deeply divisive, proved electorally powerful. Faced with the formidable dominance of the right-wing United National Party (UNP), Bandaranaike needed a message that resonated with the people's yearning for change.

Promising to establish Sinhala **as the official language within 24 hours** of coming to power, he struck a chord that echoed across the country—and it worked. The election that followed marked a political upheaval, reshaping Sri Lanka's post-independence trajectory and intertwining ethno-linguistic identity with the mechanics of power.

One of the first acts of the new government was the **Sinhala Only Act (Act No. 33 of 1956)**, which made Sinhala the sole official language of Ceylon. This move:

- Marginalized **Tamil-speaking minorities**, especially in government jobs and education
- Ignited **protests by Tamil leaders**, including peaceful sit-ins in Colombo
- Sparked **violent backlash** from Sinhala mobs, leading to riots and looting

The most tragic episode was the **Gal Oya riots in June 1956**, where **over 150 Tamils were killed** by Sinhala mobs. These were the **first major ethnic riots** in post-independence Ceylon and marked the beginning of a long cycle of communal violence.

8

The Gal Oya Riots of June 1956: Sri Lanka's First Ethnic Pogrom

Background: Rising Tensions in Post-Independence Ceylon

By the mid-1950s, political leaders like **S.W.R.D. Bandaranaike** were promoting **Sinhala nationalism**, culminating in the **Sinhala Only Act**, which aimed to make Sinhala the sole official language.

This act sparked outrage among Tamil communities, who feared marginalization. The **Federal Party**, led by **S.J.V. Chelvanayakam**, organized peaceful protests, including a **satyagraha** (nonviolent sit-in) in Colombo on June 5, 1956. The protest was violently attacked by Sinhalese mobs, triggering a wave of ethnic violence across the country.

The Gal Oya Valley: A Powder Keg

The **Gal Oya settlement scheme**, launched in 1949, was a government project to resettle landless peasants in the Eastern Province. It brought together **Sinhalese, Tamils, Muslims, and Veddhas** into newly created villages. However, the **Sinhalese settlers were given prime land**, while Tamils and Muslims were pushed to less fertile areas. This spatial and economic inequality created deep resentment.

By 1956, Gal Oya had become a **symbol of demographic engineering**, with Tamil nationalists viewing it as an attempt to dilute their presence in traditional homelands.

The Riots Erupt: June 11–16, 1956

The violence in Gal Oya was triggered by **rumors** and **retaliatory attacks** following the Colombo riots. Key events included:

False rumors spread that a Sinhalese girl had been raped and paraded naked by Tamil mobs in Batticaloa. Though untrue, this incited rage among Sinhalese settlers.

Sinhalese mobs, including employees of the **Gal Oya Development Board**, seized **government vehicles, dynamite, and weapons** to attack Tamil villages.

Massacres occurred between June 11–16, with estimates of **150+ Tamil civilians killed**, many brutally assaulted, stabbed, or burned.

Tamil refugees fled to police stations and circuit bungalows for protection, while others were forced to abandon their homes.

In retaliation, **Tamil mobs** attacked Sinhalese camps and construction sites on the outskirts of Gal Oya.

The violence was unprecedented in scale and brutality. Police were initially passive, and only after the **army intervened** was order restored.

Consequences

1. **First Major Ethnic Pogrom**

The Gal Oya riots were the **first organized ethnic violence** in independent Sri Lanka. They shattered the illusion of peaceful coexistence and exposed the fragility of communal relations.

2. **Deepening Ethnic Divides**

The riots entrenched **mutual distrust** between Sinhalese and Tamils. Tamil communities began to question their place in a Sinhala-dominated state.

3. **Political Fallout**

The government's **failure to prevent or respond swiftly** to the violence damaged its credibility among minorities. Bandaranaike's Sinhala nationalist policies were seen as enabling the violence.

4. **Precedent for Future Pogroms**

Gal Oya set the stage for **subsequent anti-Tamil riots** in 1958, 1977, and the infamous **Black July of 1983**. It marked the beginning of a cycle of ethnic violence that would eventually lead to civil war.

The Gal Oya riots were not just a spontaneous outbreak of violence—they were the result of **systemic inequalities**, **political manipulation**, and **ethnic polarization**. Understanding this event is crucial to grasping the roots of Sri Lanka's ethnic conflict and the importance of reconciliation.

Positive Outcomes

- **Political empowerment** of rural Sinhala communities
- **Cultural revival** of Sinhala language, arts, and Buddhism
- **Democratization** of governance and public institutions

Negative Consequences

- **Ethnic polarization** between Sinhalese and Tamils
- **Alienation of minorities**, especially in the north and east
- **Seeds of civil conflict**, which would erupt decades later

The 1956 elections changed not just who governed Ceylon, but **how politics was practiced**. It introduced mass mobilization, populist rhetoric, and identity politics—tools that would dominate Sri Lankan politics for generations.

A Turning Point with Mixed Legacy

The 1956 General Elections were a **watershed moment** in Sri Lanka's history. They empowered the majority, challenged colonial legacies, and redefined national identity. But they also **deepened ethnic divisions** and set the stage for future conflict. It was a revolution at the ballot box—one that turned the country upside down, politically and racially.

9

Sinhala Only Policy and the 1958 Racial Riots: Seeds of Division in Sri Lanka

Shadows Over Highlands College: A Student's Memory of the 1958 Tar Campaign

"The Day the Bell Rang Early"

It was a crisp morning in Hatton, unusually cold for May. The mist clung to the tea bushes like a secret, and Highlands College stood quietly against the hills, its classrooms filled with the chatter of Tamil-speaking children. I was in Grade 8, my satchel packed with books and dreams, when the school bell rang—not for recess, but for something far more serious.

The principal, usually calm and composed, summoned us to the assembly hall. His voice trembled as he said, "Children, pack your bags and return home immediately. The country is facing a situation. Schools may be closed for several days."

We didn't understand. To us, it was a surprise holiday. We giggled, whispered, and ran home with the kind of joy only children know. But behind our innocence, the island was beginning to burn.

The Riots We Didn't See

In the days that followed, whispers turned into headlines. Hatton, nestled in the central highlands and surrounded by plantations, was spared the worst of the violence. But elsewhere, the country was unraveling.

The **Sinhala Only Act**, passed in 1956, had sparked deep resentment among Tamil communities. By May 1958, tensions exploded into **Sri Lanka's first island-wide ethnic pogrom**. Tamil homes, shops, and temples were attacked. Mobs roamed the streets of Colombo, Polonnaruwa, and Batticaloa. A Hindu priest was burned alive in Panadura. Babies were thrown into boiling tar.

Though Hatton remained quiet, the fear was palpable. My dad and elder brothers spoke in hushed tones. Radios crackled with news of curfews and killings. We stayed indoors, not out of choice, but out of dread.

The Convoy of Caution

Two weeks later, school reopened—but the world had changed. I remember the school buses lined up like a military convoy. Each bus had **armed policemen** seated near the driver, rifles slung across their shoulders. We were told to travel in groups, escorted like dignitaries, though we were just children.

The roads to Hatton were eerily silent. And then I saw it—the **black tar**.

THE 1958 ANTI-TAMIL POGROMS
– 62 YEARS ON

Photo courtesy of Victor Ivan
A Sinhalese mob beats a Tamil passenger after pulling him out of the car.

The Tar Campaign

Every vehicle, every shop sign, and every license plate that bore Tamil letters and Tamil "Sri" on state-owned buses — had been smeared with black tar. It was a silent protest, a visual scream.

The **Federal Party**, opposing the **Sinhala Only policy**, launched the **Anti-Sri Campaign**, targeting the Sinhala character that had replaced English on license plates in Tamil-majority regions like Jaffna. This campaign was sparked by the government's decision to introduce new vehicle serial numbers marked only with the Sinhala **"Sri" (ශ්‍රී),** without a Tamil equivalent, symbolizing linguistic dominance and exclusion.

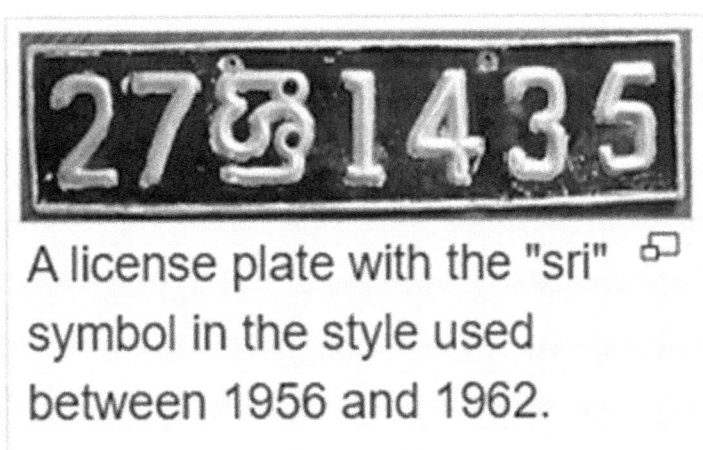

A license plate with the "sri" symbol in the style used between 1956 and 1962.

(Pic: Wikipedia)

In retaliation, **Sinhalese mobs** smeared tar on Tamil-owned properties, offices, and even people. The campaign became a symbol of the **deepening ethnic divide**—a war of symbols that mirrored the violence in the streets.

To me, the tar looked like ink spilled by a giant hand across the country's conscience. It was ugly, eerie, and unforgettable. My parents spoke in hushed tones. Radios crackled with news of curfews and killings. We stayed indoors, not out of choice, but out of dread.

A Child's Awakening

I didn't know politics. I didn't know what "ethnic tension" meant. But I knew fear. I knew silence. I knew that something had broken in the soul of the island.

The **1958 riots** left over **1,000 injured**, **hundreds dead**, and **thousands displaced**. It was the beginning of a long, painful journey toward civil war. And for me, it was the end of innocence.

Remembering the Tar!

*When I think back to Highlands College during those politically explosive days of 1958, the memories come flooding in—laughter in the corridors, lessons that flew over our heads, and the mysterious early bell that sent us scattering like chickens at a hawk's shadow. But lurking in that nostalgia was a darker, stickier symbol of the time: **tar**. Yes, tar. Not the science-lab kind or the one stuck to the roads—this was activist-grade, ideologically-loaded tar, smeared to humiliate and make a point, though the message sometimes missed its mark.*

*They called it the **"Sri Problem,"** but honestly, it was just the world throwing a giant identity crisis party and forgetting to send invites to the minorities. Somewhere amid these fiery debates on language, nationalism, and belonging, there I was—Grade 8, wide-eyed,* *politically illiterate, and blissfully unaware that I'd soon become a reluctant prop in this national drama.*

You see, while the country boiled, my house was being color-washed—because priorities, right? Curfew had me trapped at home like a grounded bird, unable to go outside or escape boredom. That's when I made the fateful error: I leaned against a freshly painted door. Black paint. On a white school shirt. A single blotch, no bigger than a coin, but apparently large enough to spark a two-week comedy special.

When schools reopened, I strutted in, hoping my fashion crime would go unnoticed. But fate had other plans. One of those sharp-eyed classroom comedians spotted the stain and screamed "Tar!"—loud enough to alert the entire classroom. Suddenly, I wasn't just a student, I was an alleged survivor of the infamous Tar Campaign. My stained shirt became legendary, drawing giggles, pointing fingers, and whispered theories. For the whole day I dodged glances, hid behind doorframes, and prayed for invisibility.

Eventually, I gave up and retired the shirt like a fallen soldier—may it rest in unwashed peace.

Historical Background: A Nation in Transition

After gaining independence from British rule in 1948, **Ceylon (now Sri Lanka)** faced the challenge of building a unified national identity. The country was ethnically diverse, with **Sinhalese** making up about 70% of the population and **Tamils**—both Sri Lankan and Indian—comprising around 30%. English had been the language of administration, education, and elite privilege under colonial rule. But as nationalism surged, language became a powerful symbol of sovereignty and cultural pride.

The Sinhala Only Act of 1956

In **1956**, Prime Minister **S.W.R.D. Bandaranaike** and his **Sri Lanka Freedom Party (SLFP)** passed the **Official Language Act No. 33**, commonly known as the **Sinhala Only Act**. This law made **Sinhala the sole official language** of the country, replacing English.

Key Features:

- Sinhala was to be used in government administration, courts, and education.
- Tamil, spoken by nearly a quarter of the population, was excluded from official use.
- The act was passed despite strong opposition from Tamil political leaders and civil society.

Political Motivation:

Bandaranaike's campaign had promised to elevate Sinhala and Buddhism as central to national identity. The act was a fulfillment of that promise, aimed at consolidating support from the Sinhala majority, especially rural voters.

Immediate Consequences

The Sinhala Only Act triggered **widespread discontent among Tamils**, who saw it as a direct attack on their rights and status. Many Tamil civil servants lost their jobs or were forced to learn Sinhala to retain them. University admissions and public services became increasingly inaccessible to Tamil speakers.

In response, the **Federal Party**, led by **S.J.V. Chelvanayakam**, launched peaceful protests and satyagrahas (nonviolent resistance). Tensions escalated rapidly.

The 1958 Racial Riots: A Nation in Flames

The **1958 anti-Tamil pogrom**, also known as the **1958 Racial Riots**, erupted between **May 22 and June 2**. It was the **first island-wide ethnic riot** in independent Sri Lanka.

Causes:

- Tamil protests the Sinhala Only Act
- Rising Sinhala nationalist rhetoric
- Rumors and inflammatory propaganda
- Political manipulation and weak law enforcement

Spread of Violence:

- The violence began in **Polonnaruwa**, where Tamil passengers en route to a Federal Party convention were attacked.
- Mobs targeted Tamil homes, shops, and temples across **Colombo, Batticaloa, Anuradhapura, and Jaffna.**
- A **Hindu priest was burned alive** in Colombo; mobs beat people who couldn't read Sinhala newspapers.
- **Retaliatory attacks** by Tamil mobs occurred in the north and east.

Casualties:

- **Official death toll**: 158
- **Unofficial estimates**: Up to 1,500 killed
- Thousands injured and over **20,000 Tamils displaced**

Government Response

- A **state of emergency** was declared on **May 27**, *five days after the violence began.*
- The **army was deployed** to restore order.
- Tamil refugees were evacuated by ship to safer areas in the north and east.
- The government was criticized for its **slow and inadequate response**, and for **political interference in police operations**.

Why It Happened

The Sinhala Only Act created a **majoritarian state**, where the Sinhala identity was privileged over others. This led to:

- **Alienation of minorities**, especially Tamils
- **Ethnic polarization**, replacing class-based politics
- **Breakdown of trust** between communities
- **Rise of Tamil nationalism**, which later evolved into calls for a separate state

The riots were not spontaneous—they were **planned and politically enabled**, as noted by journalist **Tarzie Vittachi** in his book *Emergency '58*.

Long-Term Impact

Political Shifts

- Tamil parties gained momentum, demanding autonomy and language rights.
- Sinhala nationalism became entrenched in mainstream politics.

Ethnic Conflict

- The 1958 riots were a **precursor to future pogroms** in 1977, 1983 (Black July), and the decades-long **civil war**.
- The events deepened the divide between Sinhalese and Tamils, making reconciliation harder.

The **Sinhala Only Policy** and the **1958 Racial Riots** were turning points that exposed the dangers of **ethnic majoritarianism** and **exclusionary nationalism**. They remind us that building a nation requires **respect for diversity**, **equal rights**, and **inclusive governance**. Sri Lanka's journey since then has been shaped by these lessons—some learned, many still unresolved.

The Forgotten Racial Players: K.M.P. Rajaratne and the JVP in Welimada

K. M. P. Rajaratne

Many of the old timers may remember there was another JVP in the 1950s! Yes, that was the JATHIKA VIMUKTHI PERAMUA, led by a "racist" politician named K.M.P. RAJARATNE.

Konara Mudiyanselage Podiappuhamy Rajaratne was a **fierce Sinhala-Buddhist nationalist**, lawyer, and politician who rose to prominence in the 1950s. Known for his fiery speeches and uncompromising stance on Sinhala supremacy, he was elected to Parliament from **Welimada** in 1956 under the **Mahajana Eksath Peramuna (MEP)** coalition. He was later appointed **Parliamentary Secretary to the Minister of Posts, Broadcasting and Information.**

Rajaratne was a leading figure in the **Sinhala Language Front**, which pushed for Sinhala to be the sole official language of Ceylon. He and fellow nationalist **F.R. Jayasuriya** were dubbed the "*Bhasha Twins*" for their aggressive campaign to remove the **"Reasonable Use of Tamil"** clause from the Sinhala Only Bill.

Birth of the JVP (Jathika Vimukthi Peramuna)

In **1957**, Rajaratne founded the **National Liberation Front (NLF)**, later renamed **Jathika Vimukthi Peramuna (JVP)**—*not to be confused* with the later Marxist JVP of Rohana Wijeweera. This version of the JVP was a **hardline Sinhala nationalist party**, deeply anti-Tamil and opposed to federalism.

The party received **support from local businesses** and was active in rural Sinhala-majority areas like **Welimada**, where it stirred ethnic tensions and mobilized mobs during the **1958 anti-Tamil riots.**

Role in the 1958 Riots and Welimada Violence

During the **1958 racial riots**, Rajaratne played a **provocative and incendiary role**:

- He **incited mobs** in Kurunegala, reportedly saying:

  "There are 10,000 policemen. Kill them all: then we can deal with the federalists (ITAK). They are the only people who are standing in our way."

  In **Welimada**, his stronghold , JVP supporters were involved in **violent attacks on Tamil homes and businesses**, contributing to the region's notoriety during the riots.

- Rajaratne was placed under **house arrest** in Kotte for his role in inciting violence.

Decline and Political Marginalization

After the riots, the **JVP was banned** by the government due to its extremist activities. Rajaratne's political career became erratic:

- He **lost his parliamentary seat** in 1956 due to a prior conviction for failing to declare election expenses.
- He **re-entered Parliament** in 1960 and was re-elected in July 1960 but **forfeited his seat again in 1961**.
- His wife, **Kusuma Rajaratne**, also became an MP and later resigned from government over Tamil language concessions.

By the late 1960s, Rajaratne's influence waned. He was appointed to the **Senate of Ceylon** but eventually **retired from politics** and became an attorney-at-law. He died in **January 2011**, largely forgotten by the mainstream political narrative.

K.M.P. Rajaratne and his JVP represent a **forgotten chapter of Sinhala-Buddhist extremism** that helped shape Sri Lanka's ethnic conflict. His role in the **Welimada riots** and the **1958 pogrom** underscores how **language politics and racial incitement** can destabilize a nation.

While later JVP movements took on Marxist and revolutionary tones, Rajaratne's version was rooted in **ethnic chauvinism**, and its legacy remains a **warning against majoritarian nationalism**.

A comparison of the **two JVPs**—the **Jathika Vimukthi Peramuna** led by **K.M.P. Rajaratne** in the 1950s–60s, and the **Janatha Vimukthi Peramuna** founded by **Rohana Wijeweera** in the late 1960s. Though they shared an acronym, their ideologies, methods, and legacies were vastly different:

Feature	JANATHA VIMUKTHI PERAMUNA (JVP) LED BY K.M.P. RAJARATNE	JATHIKA VIMUKTHI PERAMNUA (JVP) LED BY **ROHANA WIJEWEERA**
Founded	1957	1965-1967
Ideology	Sinhala-Buddhist nationalism, anti-Tamil, anti-federalism	Marxist-Leninist, later Maoist; class struggle and anti-imperialism
Social Base	Rural Sinhala Buddhists, especially in Welimada and Uva	Disillusioned Sinhala youth, rural petty bourgeoisie, unemployed graduates
Key Figures	**K.M.P. Rajaratne, Kusuma Rajaratne**	**Rohana Wijeweera, Upatissa Gamanayake, Somawansa Amarasinghe**
Political Strategy	Parliamentary politics, racial incitement, Sinhala Only advocacy	Armed insurrection (1971, 1987–89), underground activism, later electoral politics
Role in Ethnic Conflict	Incited anti-Tamil sentiment; linked to 1958 Welimada riots	Initially class-based, later adopted Sinhala nationalist rhetoric; opposed Tamil separatism
Major Events	1958 racial riots, house arrest of Rajaratne	1971 insurrection, 1987–89 revolt, banned multiple times
Relationship with State	Briefly part of ruling coalition (MEP); later marginalized	Alternated between rebellion and mainstream politics; re-entered Parliament in 1994
Legacy	Faded from national memory; viewed as a fringe extremist group	Became a major political force; shaped youth activism and leftist discourse

Key Differences

- **Ethnic vs. Class Focus**:

  Rajaratne's JVP was **ethnically driven**, targeting Tamils and opposing federalism. Wijeweera's JVP was **class-driven**, aiming to overthrow capitalist structures and empower the working class.

- **Methods of Struggle**:

  Rajaratne used **parliamentary agitation and racial mobilization**. Wijeweera's JVP used **armed rebellion**, underground cells, and later **electoral participation**.

- **Historical Impact**:

  Rajaratne's JVP contributed to **ethnic polarization** in the 1950s. Wijeweera's JVP led two major **insurrections**, influencing state policy, youth radicalism, and counterinsurgency doctrine.

Though they shared a name, the two JVPs were **ideological opposites**. K.M.P. Rajaratne's JVP was a **racial nationalist movement**, while Rohana Wijeweera's JVP was a **revolutionary leftist force**. One faded into obscurity; the other became a **permanent fixture in Sri Lanka's political landscape**, shaping debates on justice, governance, and national identity.

(References: en.wikipedia.com, universalinstitutions.com)

10

The Assassination of S.W.R.D. Bandaranaike and Its Aftermath

Bandaranaike with Srimavo and E. L. Senanayake on 23 September 1959 in Kandy, two days before his assassination.

(Pic – Wikipedia)

Barely five months after the island-wide racial riots, another shocking piece of news rippled across the country. It reached us while we sat in our classroom, and among the Tamil students, an unexpected reaction unfolded—some clapped, others grinned in subdued elation. Word had spread that Prime Minister S.W.R.D. Bandaranaike had been assassinated. For many Tamil children, the event felt like a moment of poetic justice, though they were far too young to grasp its full gravity.

A belief—rightly or wrongly—had taken root in their minds: that the Prime Minister had played a silent role in the suffering of their communities. His failure to declare a curfew or act during the riots, which had raged for nearly five days unchecked, was seen as complicity in the violence and looting that had devastated Tamil lives.

Solomon West Ridgeway Dias Bandaranaike, elected Prime Minister of Ceylon in 1956, was a transformative figure. He championed **Sinhala nationalism**, **socialist reforms**, and **anti-colonial policies**, which won him mass support but also **created powerful enemies**. His government nationalized key industries, passed the **Sinhala Only Act**, and challenged elite interests—moves that stirred both admiration and resentment.

By 1959, Bandaranaike was leading a **minority government**, weakened by internal divisions and external pressures. His reformist agenda had alienated sections of the Buddhist clergy, business elites, and even members of his own cabinet.

The Assassination: September 25, 1959

S W R D Bandaranaike - Alchetron, The Free Social Encyclopedia

On a quiet morning at his private residence, **Tintagel**, in Colombo, Bandaranaike was meeting citizens as part of his daily routine. Among them was **Talduwe Somarama Thero**, a Buddhist monk and lecturer at the Government College of Ayurveda.

- Somarama approached Bandaranaike under the pretense of discussing educational matters.
- At **9:45 a.m.**, he pulled out a **.45 Webley Mark VI revolver** hidden in his robes and shot the Prime Minister at point-blank range.
- Bandaranaike was rushed to Colombo General Hospital, underwent surgery, and died the next morning from internal injuries.

His final words reportedly included a plea for **clemency** toward his attacker—a gesture that stunned the nation.

Investigation and Trial

The assassination triggered a **state of emergency**, and a massive investigation followed:

Somarama Thero was arrested immediately and later sentenced to death.

- The investigation uncovered a **conspiracy** involving several high-profile individuals:

- **Mapitigama Buddharakkitha Thero**, chief priest of **Kelaniya Temple** and political kingmaker
- **H.P. Jayawardena**, a businessman and Buddharakkitha's associate
- **Newton Perera**, a police inspector who allegedly trained Somarama in firearms
- **Vimala Wijewardene**, Minister of Local Government, though later acquitted

The role of Inspector Newton Perera

Newton Perera: The Policeman Who Supplied the Weapon

Background and Career

- Newton Perera was a **career police officer**, rising through the ranks to become an **Inspector of Police (IP)**.
- He served in various stations including **Maradana** and **Colpetty** and was known for his efficiency and clean record.
- He had **close ties to Kelaniya Temple**, where he became acquainted with **Ven. Mapitigama Buddharakkitha**, the chief monk and later the **mastermind of the assassination plot**.

Role in the Assassination Plot

Newton Perera's involvement was pivotal in **arming the assassin, Talduwe Somarama Thero**:

- At the request of **Buddharakkitha**, Newton procured a **.45 Webley Mark VI revolver** from **Ossie Corea**, a known underworld figure and associate of Stanley de Zoysa (former Finance Minister).
- He also **supplied ammunition**, allegedly obtained through contacts at the **Police Training School** and via **SP B.W. Perera**, who was in charge of police arms and ammunition.
- Newton **delivered the weapon and bullets** to Buddharakkitha at **Wimala Wijewardene's residence**, where the monk frequently stayed.

According to court testimony, Newton even **accompanied the conspirators to Muthurajawela**, where **Somarama practiced firing the revolver**. He later witnessed Somarama firing a test shot into the air.

Trial and Acquittal

Newton was **arrested on ⬚ October 21, 1959**, and charged with **conspiracy to murder**.

- During the **Supreme Court trial in 1961**, he was the **fifth accused**.

38

- Despite his involvement in supplying the weapon, the jury **acquitted him** by a **divided verdict**, citing lack of evidence that he knew the weapon would be used for assassination.
- Justice T.S. Fernando remarked that Newton's conduct was **"unworthy of a police officer"**, though not criminally liable.

Name Resurfacing in the 1962 Coup

- Newton's name reappeared during the **1962 coup investigation** due to his **past association with Ossie Corea**, who had supplied the revolver in 1959.
- Corea was detained preventively during the coup probe, and Newton was questioned again, though **not formally charged**.
- His prior role in the Bandaranaike assassination made him a **person of interest**, but no direct link to the coup was established.

The motive? Not ideology—but **commerce and betrayal**. Buddharakkitha had reportedly grown furious over Bandaranaike's refusal to grant him lucrative contracts for a **shipping company** and a **sugar factory**.

Somarama, described as emotionally unstable and easily manipulated, was convinced he was acting to "save Sinhala Buddhism." He was executed in 1962, after converting to Christianity days before his hanging.

Aftermath and Political Fallout

1. Leadership Vacuum

- Education Minister **W. Dahanayake** was appointed acting Prime Minister.
- Bandaranaike's widow, **Sirimavo Bandaranaike**, later became the **world's first female Prime Minister** in 1960.

2. Rise of Sinhala-Buddhist Nationalism

- The assassination intensified communal politics.
- Sirimavo continued her husband's policies, further embedding Sinhala nationalism into state identity.

3. Disillusionment

- The involvement of Buddhist clergy in the murder shocked the nation.
- Trust in religious institutions and political elites eroded.

4. Judicial and Political Repercussions

- Several ministers resigned or were dismissed.
- The scandal exposed corruption, nepotism, and the misuse of religious influence in politics.

Was There Foreign Involvement?

Despite widespread speculation, **no credible evidence** has emerged to suggest **foreign hands** were behind the assassination:

- **Scotland Yard** assisted in the investigation but found no links to foreign governments.
- Theories about **Western intelligence** or **Tamil separatists** remain **unsubstantiated**.
- The motive was **domestic**—rooted in **business interests**, **political betrayal**, and **personal vendettas**.

Some historians argue that Bandaranaike's **anti-Western stance** and **non-aligned foreign policy** may have made him a target. However, the evidence overwhelmingly points to **internal conspirators**, particularly **Buddharakkitha**, whose ambitions were thwarted by the Prime Minister's refusal to grant favors.

The assassination of S.W.R.D. Bandaranaike was not just a political murder—it was a **national trauma**. It exposed the fragility of post-independence democracy, the dangers of politicized religion, and the cost of reform in a deeply divided society.

While foreign involvement remains a **rumor**, the tragedy was born from **Ceylon's own contradictions**—between idealism and ambition, nationalism and pluralism, reform and resistance.

While writing this chapter, certain questions arose in me, for which I never had any conclusive answers:

Ossie Corea's Role in the Assassination

Ossie Corea, a former excise inspector turned underworld figure, was **not convicted** but was **implicated** in the conspiracy. He was known to associate with Stanley de Zoysa (then Finance Minister) and was allegedly involved in **procuring the murder weapon**—a .45 Webley revolver used by Somarama Thero.

- The revolver was traced back to Corea, and **Newton Perera**, a police inspector, testified that Corea helped supply it to **Buddharakkitha Thero**, the chief conspirator.
- Corea was arrested but later **released** due to lack of direct evidence.
- As for **shaving his head**, there's no confirmed reason in the records. Some speculate it was to **disguise his identity** or **symbolically align with the monks**, but this remains **unverified**.

Why Did Somarama Thero Convert to Christianity?

Just **weeks before his execution**, Talduwe Somarama Thero renounced his robes and was **baptized by an Anglican priest**.

- The conversion was likely a **personal act of repentance** or a **spiritual reckoning** before death.
- He had earlier shown signs of remorse and thanked his defense counsel in court, calling him a "true lion".
- His conversion shocked many, as he had committed the murder in the name of **"country, race, and religion."**

Buddharakkitha's Death in Prison

Mapitigama Buddharakkitha Thero, the mastermind behind the assassination, was sentenced to **life imprisonment** after a legal technicality spared him from the death penalty.

(Pic: colombotelegraph.com)

- He died in **1967** of a **heart attack** after **six years of hard labor** in prison.
- His downfall was dramatic: once a powerful monk with political and business influence, he ended his life in disgrace.

(Pic: dbsjeyaraj.com)

After dissolving Parliament in December 1959, **Wijeyananda Dahanayake** formed the **Lanka Prajathanthravadi Pakshaya (LPP)** and contested **all 101 seats** in the **March 1960 elections**.

- He **lost all but his own seat in Galle**, and the party won only **four seats**.
- There's **no clear record of who funded** this massive campaign. Given Dahanayake's reputation for frugality and populism, it's likely he relied on **grassroots support**, **personal networks**, and **minimal resources**.
- Some speculate that **sympathizers of the SLFP or disillusioned leftists** may have contributed, but no formal funding sources were documented.

Why Was Catholic Action Mentioned?

The term **"Catholic Action"** surfaced during this period due to **political tensions** between **Buddhist nationalist movements** and **Christian institutions**.

- **Bandaranaike's policies**, especially the **nationalization of Christian schools**, had alienated Catholic leaders.
- Some Buddhist nationalists accused **Catholic Action groups** of **undermining Sinhala-Buddhist interests**, though **no direct link** to the assassination was proven.
- The climate was charged with **religious suspicion**, and Catholic Action became a **symbolic scapegoat** in some narratives.

11

Continuing Tamil Problems and the 1960 General Elections

Background: A Nation Still Divided

By 1960, Sri Lanka (then Ceylon) had been independent for over a decade, but the promise of unity remained elusive. The **Sinhala Only Act of 1956**, passed under Prime Minister S.W.R.D. Bandaranaike, had triggered widespread discontent among the **Tamil minority**, who felt increasingly marginalized in a Sinhala-dominated state. The **1958 racial riots**, which left hundreds dead and thousands displaced, deepened ethnic divisions and left a lasting scar on the national psyche.

The **assassination of Bandaranaike in 1959** created a political vacuum, and the country entered 1960 with unresolved ethnic tensions and a fractured political landscape.

The 1960 General Elections: Two in One Year

Sri Lanka held **two parliamentary elections in 1960**—one in **March** and another in **July**—due to political instability and the inability to form a stable government after the first vote.

March 1960 Election

- The **United National Party (UNP)** won **50 seats**, while the **Sri Lanka Freedom Party (SLFP)** secured **46 seats**.
- The **Ilankai Tamil Arasu Kachchi (ITAK)**, also known as the **Federal Party**, won **15 seats**, becoming the dominant Tamil voice in Parliament.
- Both major Sinhala parties—UNP and SLFP—**campaigned on anti-Tamil platforms**, promising to enforce the Sinhala Only policy and repatriate Indian Tamils.

Despite winning the most seats, the UNP failed to form a majority government. Prime Minister **Dudley Senanayake** resigned after a no-confidence motion, triggering a second election.

I was sixteen, too young to vote, but old enough to feel the pulse of a nation on edge. Hatton, the misty heart of Sri Lanka's plantation country, was buzzing with political electricity. It was July 1960, and the Second General Election of the year had turned the island into a battleground of slogans, grief, and fiery rhetoric. I didn't know it then, but I was about to witness history — not from a textbook, but from the front row of a political circus.

*The first meeting I stumbled into was a **United National Party (UNP) rally.** The speaker? None other than **A.C.S. Hameed**, a rising star who would later become Sri Lanka's longest-serving Foreign Minister. He didn't just speak — he performed. With biting sarcasm and theatrical flair, he mocked the rising cost of living. "Gini Petti Polima!" he roared, likening the long queues outside shops to matchbox lines. Then came the punchline: "Mini Petti Polima" — coffin queues. The crowd gasped, laughed, and cheered. It was political theatre at its sharpest, and I was hooked.*

*But the drama didn't end there. Days later, I found myself at a **Sri Lanka Freedom Party (SLFP)** meeting, led by **Mrs. Sirimavo Bandaranaike**, the grieving widow of the assassinated Prime Minister S.W.R.D. Bandaranaike. Her eyes were swollen, her voice trembled, and her sorrow was palpable. She didn't need fiery speeches — her tears did the talking. Cartoons in the papers mocked her, showing her clutching onions to summon tears. But the people weren't laughing. They were moved. Her grief became her campaign, and it worked.*

Then came the moment that jolted me: a group of UNP supporters hurled pamphlets into her vehicle as she departed. The tension was thick. I braced for violence. But the police, alert and firm, held the line. It was my first taste of political rivalry turning raw — and real.

*The SLFP's message didn't resonate much with the Tamil plantation workers in Nuwara Eliya. The speeches were mostly in Sinhala, and the emotional appeal didn't translate across linguistic lines. But nationally, the tide turned. Despite winning fewer votes than the UNP, the SLFP secured a majority of seats, and **Sirimavo Bandaranaike became the world's first female Prime Minister**.*

That election wasn't just a contest of policies — it was a clash of personalities, grief, and wit. And for me, it was the moment politics stopped being abstract and became a living, breathing force.

- The **SLFP**, now led by **Sirimavo Bandaranaike**, widow of the slain prime minister, won **75 seats**, forming a majority government.
- Sirimavo became the **world's first female prime minister**, riding a wave of sympathy and Sinhala nationalist support.
- ITAK increased its strength to **16 seats**, while the **Tamil Congress** retained only one seat.

The **Sri Lanka Freedom Party (SLFP)** pulled off a dramatic victory in the **July 1960 General Elections**, despite receiving **fewer popular votes** than the **United National Party (UNP)**. Here's how it happened—and what it meant for both parties:

How the SLFP Won in July 1960

Sympathy and Legacy

- The SLFP had lost its founder, **S.W.R.D. Bandaranaike**, to assassination in 1959.
- His widow, **Sirimavo Bandaranaike**, was chosen as party leader in May 1960.
- Her candidacy stirred **massive public sympathy**, especially among rural Sinhala voters, who saw her as the torchbearer of her husband's nationalist and socialist vision.

Strategic Alliances

- The SLFP entered **no-contest agreements** with leftist parties like the **Lanka Sama Samaja Party (LSSP)** and the **Communist Party**, allowing it to avoid vote-splitting in key constituencies.
- This tactical move helped the SLFP secure **75 seats**, giving it a **parliamentary majority**, even though it won only **33.2% of the popular vote**.

Populist Platform

- Sirimavo pledged to continue her husband's policies:
    - Full implementation of the **Sinhala Only Act**
    - **Repatriation of Indian Tamils**
    - **Nationalization** of private enterprises and religious schools
- These promises resonated with Sinhala-Buddhist voters and rural communities.

What Happened to the UNP

Popular Vote, But Fewer Seats

- The UNP, led by **Dudley Senanayake**, actually won **37.2% of the vote**—more than the SLFP—but secured only **30 seats**.
- This was due to **inefficient vote distribution** and lack of strategic alliances.

Policy Stance

- The UNP refused to compromise with the **Federal Party**, which represented Tamil interests.
- It opposed nationalization and favored keeping private enterprises and religious schools independent.
- These positions alienated both Tamil voters and left-leaning Sinhala voters.

Leadership Crisis

- After failing to form a stable government in the **March 1960 elections**, Dudley Senanayake's brief tenure ended with a **no-confidence motion**, leading to the July re-election.
- The UNP's image as a party of Westernized elites and its perceived indifference to Sinhala nationalism hurt its appeal.

Aftermath

- **Sirimavo Bandaranaike** became the **world's first female Prime Minister**, a historic milestone.
- The SLFP's win marked a **shift toward Sinhala-Buddhist nationalism and socialist governance**.
- The UNP entered a period of **rebuilding**, eventually returning to power in **1965**, but the 1960 defeat reshaped its strategy and leadership.

12

The Ceylon Workers Congress and S. Thondaman: Kingmaker of Plantation Politics

The Rise of a Kingmaker

In the misty highlands of Sri Lanka, where tea bushes stretch like green carpets over rolling hills, a quiet revolution was brewing—not in parliament, but among the forgotten hands that plucked the leaves.

At a time when estate workers were voiceless, stateless, and stranded—unable to speak Sinhala, navigate bureaucracy, or even find a bed in Colombo—one man stepped in with a plan that was as radical as it was compassionate.

Saumiamoorthy Thondaman, the indomitable leader of the **Ceylon Workers Congress (CWC)**, transformed political outreach into a lifeline. He mobilized his staff to escort plantation workers to government offices, arranged shelter, and ensured their safety in an unfamiliar city. This wasn't just logistics—it was empowerment. Through this grassroots service,

Thondaman didn't just win hearts; he built a political machine. The CWC swelled in numbers, and Thondaman's influence grew so formidable that no government could afford to ignore him. Whether it was the UNP or SLFP, they all knew: if you wanted the estate vote, you needed Thondaman. Thus began his reign as the **Kingmaker of Plantation Politics**, a title earned not through privilege, but through relentless service to the most marginalized.

Origins of the CWC and the Plantation Tamil Struggle

The **Ceylon Workers Congress (CWC)** traces its roots to the **Ceylon Indian Congress (CIC)**, founded in **1939** to represent the interests of **Indian Tamil plantation workers**—a community brought to Ceylon during British rule to work on tea, rubber, and coconut estates. These workers, concentrated in the central highlands, formed the backbone of the island's economy but were socially and politically marginalized.

In **1950**, the CIC was renamed the **Ceylon Workers Congress**, evolving into both a **trade union** and a **political party**. Its mission: to fight for **citizenship rights**, **labor protections**, and **political representation** for the Indian Tamil community.

Saumiyamoorthy Thondaman, born in **1913** in Tamil Nadu, India, migrated to Ceylon and rose from estate management to become the **undisputed patriarch of the Plantation Tamils**. He led the CWC from its inception until his death in **1999**, serving as a **cabinet minister for 21 consecutive years** under **four different presidents**—a testament to his political agility and influence.

Key Achievements

Citizenship for Stateless Tamils: Thondaman was instrumental in reversing the disenfranchisement caused by the **Ceylon Citizenship Act (1948)** and the **Indian and Pakistani Residents Act (1949)**. His persistent lobbying led to the **1986–88 citizenship grants**, restoring rights to thousands.

Labor Rights and Welfare: Under his leadership, the CWC secured better wages, housing, and education for estate workers. He also pushed for **price wage supplements** and **rural industrial development**.

Political Representation: Thondaman ensured that Plantation Tamils had a voice in Parliament, even when they were stateless. He was elected MP for **Nuwara Eliya** in 1947 and later served as a **National List MP** until his death.

Kingmaker Across Party Lines

Thondaman's genius lay in his **pragmatic politics**. He never tied the CWC to a single party but instead **aligned strategically** with whichever party was in power to secure benefits for his people.

With the UNP:

- Joined the **UNP-led government in 1977** under **J.R. Jayewardene**
- Served as **Minister of Rural Industrial Development**
- Supported constitutional reforms and economic liberalization

With the SLFP:

- Initially supported **Sirimavo Bandaranaike** in 1960
- Was appointed to Parliament as a **nominated MP**
- Later helped **topple her government in 1964** by abstaining from a key vote

With the PA and Chandrika Kumaratunga:

- Continued as a cabinet minister under **Chandrika's presidency**
- Played a role in **ethnic reconciliation efforts** and **development programs**

Thondaman's ability to **negotiate across ideological divides** made him a **kingpin of coalition politics**. His support was often decisive in forming governments, especially in closely contested elections.

Thondaman believed in **incremental change**, not confrontation. He rejected **Tamil separatism**, withdrawing from the **Tamil United Liberation Front (TULF)** when it adopted the **Tamil Eelam** agenda in 1975. Instead, he focused on **citizenship, dignity, and economic upliftment** for his people.

His legacy includes:

- **Empowered generations of Plantation Tamils**
- **Institutionalized estate labor rights**
- **Created a political model of minority negotiation within a majoritarian state**

Today, the CWC remains a **powerful voice** in Sri Lankan politics, led by his descendants, and continues to influence national coalitions.

The Architect of Plantation Tamil Empowerment

Thondaman was more than a trade unionist—he was a **statesman**, a **strategist**, and a **symbol of resilience**. Through the CWC, he transformed a disenfranchised labor force into a politically empowered community. His ability to **work with any ruling party**, while never compromising on the core interests of Plantation Tamils, made him one of the most **enduring and effective political figures** in Sri Lanka's post-independence history.

13

Fractures in the Fold: The Splintering of the Ceylon Workers Congress and the Rise of Rival Trade Unions

Introduction

In 1955 I was barely ten when whispers of chaos found their way into playground chatter. A few kids, their eyes wide with the thrill of gossip, spoke of grown-ups clashing at a meeting—angry yelling, chairs flying, and something about a split in "the union." At the time, I didn't quite understand what a trade union was, much less what it meant for it to fracture. But that day marked a schism in the **Ceylon Workers Congress (CWC)** that would reverberate across Sri Lanka's plantation sector like a thunderclap over quiet hills.

In my later years I understood it all.

From Unity to Fragmentation: The Political Journey of CIC and CWC

The political awakening of the Indian-origin plantation workers in Sri Lanka began with the founding of the **Ceylon India Congress (CIC)** on **25 July 1935**, a milestone in collective representation and empowerment. Led by **V. R. M. V. A. Lechumanan Chettiar** as president, and **Abdul Aziz** alongside **H. M. Desai** as joint secretaries, the CIC quickly grew into a vocal advocate for plantation labor rights.

In **1942**, Aziz ascended to the CIC presidency, with **Savumiamoorthy Thondaman** appointed secretary—setting the stage for a rivalry that would define the organization's trajectory. Their leadership tug-of-war intensified over the next decade: **Thondaman defeated Aziz in 1945** to claim the presidency, only for **Aziz to regain it in 1948**, reflecting deep ideological and personal divides.

By **1950**, the CIC underwent a transformative rebranding and became the **Ceylon Workers' Congress (CWC)**, aiming to consolidate its influence in labor politics. But internal tensions were far from resolved. In **November 1955**, a fierce leadership battle reignited, with **Aziz elected president** and **Thondaman's nominee, S. Somasundaram**, installed as secretary. Soon after, Thondaman loyalists staged a dramatic internal coup—**expelling Aziz and his faction on 22 November**. Aziz's response was swift: he founded the **Democratic Workers Congress (DWC)**, officially registered on **1 January 1956**, and aligned it with the **World Federation of Trade Unions**.

The DWC itself struggled to maintain cohesion. By **1962**, key members defected to the **Communist Party's workers' union**, and the party lost veteran **K. G. S. Nair**, who died suddenly of a heart attack. Another split followed in **1968**, when **M. A. Thangavel** and **A. K. Kandasamy** broke away to establish the **Agricultural Plantation Workers Congress**—adding yet another layer of fragmentation.

The passing of Abdul Aziz in **June 1990** sparked further divisions. His son, **Ashraf Aziz**, formed the **Aziz Democratic Workers Congress**, while leadership of the original DWC shifted to **V. P. Ganeshan**. Today, the DWC is helmed by Ganeshan's son, **Mano Ganeshan**, who continues the legacy as a member of parliament representing Colombo.

What began as a unified movement to defend plantation laborers gradually splintered into multiple factions, each bearing the imprint of its founders' ambitions and philosophies. While these divisions complicated the political landscape, they also underscored the enduring urgency for representation, dignity, and leadership within one of Sri Lanka's most vulnerable communities.

Sole Beneficiary of the Splits

The results of union rivalry were anything but civil. Knife fights erupted in lines that once shared tea and conversation. Union meetings became security risks. Blood was spilled in what was supposed to be a fight for worker dignity. The real winner? **Estate management**, who now had a weaponized divide. When one union called for a strike, the rival faction would cross the picket line, keeping the plucking going and profits flowing.

As years passed, the splintering continued like cracks in dry soil. New trade unions mushroomed from the ashes of the old:

National Union of Workers (NUW) led by **V.K. Vellayan** — a former CWC general secretary who sought a more radical approach.

Upcountry People's Front (UPF) founded by **P. Chandrasekaran** — focusing not just on plantation issues but broader Tamil political representation.

Ceylon National Workers Congress (CNWC), helmed by **M.S. Sellasamy** after his dramatic ousting from the CWC.

Agricultural Plantation Workers Congress (APWC) under **M.A. Thangavel** and **A.K. Kandasamy**, breaking away from DWC itself.

Even DWC split again into the **Aziz Democratic Workers Congress (ADWC)** led by **Ashraf Aziz**, continuing the legacy of his father.

While the intentions behind each group varied—from caste grievances to leadership disputes—the impact was the same: confusion and weakened solidarity. Plantation workers were caught between loyalties and left to navigate a political maze with no clear exit.

And all of this—this complex web of rivalry and resistance—started as a murmur in my childhood. A few kids talking about a meeting turned riot. It's surreal how such casual moments mask the undercurrents of history.

Each of these unions claimed to represent the true interests of plantation workers, yet their proliferation often diluted the collective strength of the movement.

The Political Chessboard and the Kingmakers

Despite the fragmentation, the CWC retained its status as a political kingmaker. Successive governments courted its support, offering ministerial posts and policy concessions. However, the internal divisions continued to haunt the union. Leadership disputes—such as the posthumous succession crisis following **Arumugam Thondaman's** death in 2020—led to further infighting and resignations.

Impact on Workers and the Estate Economy

While these unions were born out of genuine grievances and leadership ambitions, their rivalry often came at the cost of worker solidarity. Plantation companies exploited the divisions to suppress wage demands and resist reforms. Strikes were undermined, and workers were left confused about whom to trust. The estate sector, already grappling with economic challenges, became a battleground not just of labor rights but of political survival.

14

Emergence of Tamil Nationalism in Northern Sri Lanka

Origins of Tamil Nationalism

Tamil nationalism in Sri Lanka emerged as a response to **ethnic marginalization**, **language discrimination**, and **political exclusion** following independence in 1948. The **Sri Lankan Tamils**, concentrated in the Northern and Eastern provinces, began to assert their identity in the face of rising **Sinhala-Buddhist nationalism**.

Key early developments:

Communal representation under British rule (1921) led Tamils to view themselves as a distinct minority needing protection.

Arumuga Navalar's Hindu revivalism in the 19th century laid cultural foundations for Tamil identity.

The **All-Ceylon Tamil Congress (ACTC)**, founded in 1944 by **G.G. Ponnambalam**, advocated for the controversial **"50-50" representation** formula in Parliament.

Political Evolution and the Federal Party

In 1949, a faction led by **S.J.V. Chelvanayakam** broke away from the ACTC to form the **Ilankai Tamil Arasu Kachchi (ITAK)**, or **Federal Party**, which became the **main voice of Tamil nationalism** by the mid-1950s.

Key demands of ITAK:

Recognition of **Tamil as an official language**
Federal autonomy for Tamil-majority regions
Protection of **minority rights** under the constitution

The **Sinhala Only Act of 1956** and the **1958 racial riots** intensified Tamil grievances, pushing ITAK to the forefront of Tamil politics.

Fiery Parliamentary Debates and Vocal Tamil Leaders

Throughout the 1950s–70s, Tamil MPs delivered impassioned speeches in Parliament, challenging discriminatory policies and demanding justice for Northern Tamils.

◈ **G.G. Ponnambalam**

- Known for his **oratorical brilliance** and fierce defense of Tamil rights.

- Famously clashed with **Solomon Bandaranaike**, calling himself a "**proud Dravidian**" in response to Sinhala nationalist rhetoric.
- Advocated for **balanced representation**, warning of Sinhala dominance.

S.J.V. Chelvanayakam

- Called the "**Father of Tamil Federalism**."
- Delivered **calm but powerful speeches** advocating nonviolent resistance and federalism.
- Resigned his seat in protest of the 1972 constitution, which removed minority safeguards.

V. Dharmalingam and A. Amirthalingam

(Above: A. Amirthalingam)

Vocal ITAK MPs in the 1970s who later led the **Tamil United Liberation Front (TULF)**.

- In 1977, TULF declared support for **Tamil Eelam**, marking a shift from autonomy to **separatism**.
- Their speeches highlighted **state-sponsored colonization**, **military repression**, and **economic neglect** of the North.
- These debates often grew heated, with **Sinhala MPs accusing Tamil leaders of treason**, while Tamil MPs accused the government of **ethnic cleansing and cultural erasure**.

Impact on Northern Politics

The fiery parliamentary exchanges and growing Tamil nationalism led to:

- **Polarization of national politics**
- **Boycotts of Parliament** by Tamil MPs in protest
- Formation of **militant youth movements** like the **Tamil New Tigers (TNT)** and later the **Liberation Tigers of Tamil Eelam (LTTE)**

Appapillai Amirthalingam, the leading Sri Lankan Tamil politician and former Leader of the Opposition, was **assassinated on 13 July 1989** in Colombo by members of the **Liberation Tigers of Tamil Eelam (LTTE)**.

He had returned from self-exile in India and was living at a residence on Bullers Road with other Tamil United Liberation Front (TULF) leaders. During a meeting arranged by fellow TULF member Vettivelu Yogeswaran with LTTE representatives, two gunmen suddenly opened fire. **Amirthalingam and Yogeswaran were killed**, while another senior politician, M. **Sivasithamparam**, was seriously injured.

The LTTE later admitted responsibility. The killing shocked the nation and marked a turning point in Tamil politics, as Amirthalingam had been a prominent advocate for peaceful resolution and power-sharing within a united Sri Lanka.

By the late 1970s, Tamil nationalism had evolved from **constitutional advocacy** to **armed resistance**, driven by frustration with the **unitary state model** and repeated **broken promises**.

15

The Banda–Chelva Pact: A Broken Promise of Reconciliation

(Pic: Tamil Guardian)

Historical Context

After gaining independence in **1948**, Sri Lanka (then Ceylon) inherited a **plural society** with deep ethnic divisions. The **Sinhalese majority** (about 75%) and the **Tamil minority** (about 15%) had coexisted for centuries, but colonial policies and post-independence nationalism began to fracture this balance.

In **1956**, **S.W.R.D. Bandaranaike**, leader of the **Sri Lanka Freedom Party (SLFP)**, won a landslide election victory by campaigning on a **Sinhala Only** platform. The **Official Language Act**, passed in June 1956, made **Sinhala the sole official language**, marginalizing Tamil speakers in administration, education, and employment.

Tamil opposition, led by **S.J.V. Chelvanayakam** of the **Federal Party (Ilankai Tamil Arasu Kachchi)**, responded with **nonviolent protests**, including a hartal and satyagraha. Ethnic tensions escalated, culminating in **anti-Tamil riots** and widespread violence.

The Pact: A Hope for Compromise

To prevent further unrest, Bandaranaike initiated talks with Chelvanayakam. After several meetings, the **Bandaranaike–Chelvanayakam Pact** was signed on **July 26, 1957**. Key provisions included:

- Creation of **Regional Councils** with administrative powers in Tamil-majority areas
- Recognition of **Tamil as a language of administration** in the North and East
- Local control over **land allocation and colonization schemes**
- A commitment to **decentralization**, though short of full federalism

The pact was seen as a **moderate compromise**: Tamils accepted less than federal autonomy, and Bandaranaike acknowledged Tamil grievances without alienating his Sinhala base—at least initially.

Opposition and Collapse

The pact faced **immediate backlash**:

- **Sinhalese nationalists**, including Buddhist monks, accused Bandaranaike of betraying Sinhala interests
- *J.R. Jayewardene, leader of the **United National Party (UNP)**, organized a **march to Kandy** to protest the pact and invoke Buddhist blessings against it*
- **Tamil hardliners**, like C. Suntheralingham, criticized the pact for not going far enough

On **April 9, 1958**, under pressure from **100 Buddhist monks and 300 protestors** camped outside his residence, Bandaranaike **publicly tore up the pact** and gave a written pledge to abrogate it.

This act shattered Tamil trust in Sinhala leadership. **S. Thondaman**, leader of the **Ceylon Workers Congress**, called it "the saddest day in the history of Ceylon's racial relations."

Aftermath and Consequences

- The **Federal Party launched peaceful protests**, but tensions escalated into the **1958 anti-Tamil pogrom**, with hundreds killed and thousands displaced
- The failure of the pact marked the **beginning of Tamil political radicalization**
- Future attempts at compromise, like the **Dudley–Chelvanayakam Pact (1965)**, also failed under Sinhala nationalist pressure
- The repeated **abrogation of agreements** led many Tamils to abandon faith in parliamentary politics, paving the way for **militant separatism**

Background of Racial Politics in Sri Lanka

Colonial Legacy

- British policies favored **Tamil elites** in education and civil service, creating resentment among Sinhalese
- **Indian Tamils**, brought as plantation laborers, were denied citizenship after independence

Post-Independence Nationalism

- Sinhala leaders promoted **Buddhism and Sinhala language** as pillars of national identity
- Tamil demands for **language parity, federalism, and land rights** were rejected

Ethnic Polarization

- **State-sponsored colonization** of Tamil areas with Sinhalese settlers altered demographics
- **Standardization policies** in education reduced Tamil university admissions
- **Repeated anti-Tamil riots** (1958, 1977, 1983) deepened mistrust

Rise of Tamil Nationalism

- The **Federal Party** evolved into the **Tamil United Liberation Front (TULF)**, which in **1976** called for an independent **Tamil Eelam**
- The **Liberation Tigers of Tamil Eelam (LTTE)** emerged in the 1980s, leading to a **26-year civil war**

Conclusion: A Missed Opportunity

The Banda–Chelva Pact was a **historic chance for reconciliation**, but its collapse symbolized the **failure of Sri Lanka's political system** to accommodate minority rights. It exposed the **fragility of compromise** in the face of populist nationalism and set the stage for decades of **ethnic conflict**.

A Voice That Refused to Be Silenced

Tamil nationalism in Northern Sri Lanka was born from **systemic exclusion** and **political betrayal**. The fiery speeches in Parliament were not just rhetoric—they were **cries for dignity, autonomy, and survival**. Though many of these leaders were later silenced— some assassinated—their legacy continues to shape Tamil political identity and aspirations.

Historical Background of Tamil Issues in Sri Lanka

Ancient and Pre-Colonial Context

- **Early Tamil Settlements**: Tamil-speaking people have lived in northern and eastern Sri Lanka for over two millennia. Historical records show South Indian Tamil kingdoms frequently interacted with the island, through trade, migration, and conquest.
- **Sinhala-Tamil Rivalries**: From the 5th century onward, Sinhalese kingdoms in the south and Tamil kingdoms in the north often clashed. These tensions laid the groundwork for later identity-based divisions.

Colonial Legacy (1796–1948)

- **British Favoritism**: Under British rule, Tamils—especially Sri Lankan Tamils from Jaffna—were disproportionately represented in **civil service and education** due to early access to missionary schools.
- **Indian Tamil Migration**: The British brought **Indian Tamils** from South India to work on tea plantations. These workers were economically and socially marginalized and later became a distinct group from Sri Lankan Tamils.

Divide and Rule:

Colonial policies deepened ethnic divisions by favoring certain communities and creating competition for resources and representation.

Post-Independence Discrimination (1948–1970s)

- **Ceylon Citizenship Act (1948)**: Denied citizenship to most Indian Tamils, rendering them stateless and disenfranchised.
- **Sinhala Only Act (1956)**: Made Sinhala the sole official language, excluding Tamil speakers from government jobs and services.
- **Standardization Policy (1970s)**: Reduced Tamil student admissions to universities, especially in medicine and engineering, sparking resentment.
- **Land Colonization Schemes**: Government-sponsored settlement of Sinhalese in Tamil-majority areas altered demographics and fueled fears of cultural erasure.

Ethnic Riots and Political Marginalization

- **1958, 1977, 1981 Riots**: Tamil communities were targeted in violent pogroms, with little protection from the state.
- **Constitutional Changes**: The 1972 and 1978 constitutions gave Buddhism a privileged status and removed safeguards for minorities.
- **Failed Agreements**: Attempts at reconciliation, like the **Bandaranaike–Chelvanayakam Pact (1957)** and **Dudley–Chelvanayakam Pact (1965)**, were abandoned under Sinhala nationalist pressure.

The Tamil issue in Sri Lanka is not just a post-independence phenomenon—it's the result of centuries of **ethnic, linguistic, and political tensions**, compounded by **colonial manipulation** and **majoritarian governance**. Would you like to explore how these historical patterns compare to other post-colonial conflicts?

16

1961 Schools Take-over in Sri Lanka: Politics, Resistance, and Legacy

The Bell Rang Early

*The smell of chalk and the rustle of morning uniforms still linger in my memory. I was preparing for my **GCE Ordinary Level exams**, focused on textbooks, classwork, and the typical anxieties of a high school student in post-independence Sri Lanka. Then one morning, a quiet announcement shifted everything: **school would begin earlier and end by noon**.*

*At first glance, it seemed trivial—a logistical change meant to accommodate **students from a nearby girls' school during the afternoon hours**. But behind this innocent reshuffling lay a country tangled in the throes of reform and resistance.*

*We soon learned that most privately managed schools had been swept up in a larger national storm: the **Sri Lankan government's decision to take over all assisted private schools**, particularly those run by the **Catholic Church**. The Catholic schools nearby, like hundreds across the country, had become a battleground—not of armed conflict, but of ideology, faith, and fear.*

A School Under Siege

Teachers stopped smiling. Parents stopped whispering. Protest banners emerged at school gates. **Students, parents, and church authorities barricaded themselves inside classrooms**, refusing to hand over control to government-appointed officials. For days, classrooms remained occupied, not by lessons but by prayers and defiance.

Historical Crosscurrents

The confrontation was part of the **Assisted Schools and Training Colleges Act of 1960**, which aimed to nationalize all religiously funded schools to expand **free education**. Elite Catholic institutions, however, feared the loss of autonomy, spiritual values, and teaching staff—especially foreign clergy and nuns.

Church leaders, including **Archbishop T.B. Cooray**, declared their intention to resist with everything they had, even **"by shedding blood."** Occupations spread through **Negombo**, known as "Little Rome," and other Catholic strongholds. The tension escalated until even the **Army was deployed** to handle internal security.

From Resistance to Resolution

What broke the deadlock was not baton or force—it was **compromise**, after **Cardinal Graciano**, a Vatican envoy from India, arrived to mediate.

- Schools like **St. Joseph's College** and **St. Peter's College** were allowed to remain **non-fee-charging private schools**.
- Many religious staff were **absorbed into the state system** as public employees, with limited control over religious instruction.
- **Private religious practices** were permitted under state curricula, allowing schools to preserve aspects of their spiritual identity.

And just like that, our afternoon classrooms were restored, albeit with a new administration and a revised uniformity that felt subtly different.

Long-Term Ripples

Years later, as I look back, I see the broader impact:

- **Poor Catholic children** gained access to once-exclusive schools.
- **Sri Lanka's literacy rate soared**, creating a more educated workforce.
- But schools also lost part of their soul: the personalized faith-based teachings and warmth that came with close-knit communities.

And perhaps most significantly, it marked the moment when **education in Sri Lanka transformed from privilege to public right**, even as the ghosts of its old foundations quietly lingered.

Historical Context: Education and Power

Before independence in 1948, Sri Lanka's education system was heavily shaped by **Christian missionary schools**, especially Catholic institutions. Though Christians made up only about **6.25% of the population**, they received **over 70% of government grants** for denominational schools by 1939. These schools were often elite, fee-charging institutions that catered to urban and affluent communities, while Buddhist, Hindu, and Muslim schools received far less support.

The **Free Education Scheme** introduced by **Dr. C.W.W. Kannangara in 1945** aimed to democratize education, but the **assisted schools**—those run by religious organizations with partial state funding—remained outside full government control.

Political Drivers Behind the Take-over

The **Sri Lanka Freedom Party (SLFP)**, led by **S.W.R.D. Bandaranaike** and later **Sirimavo Bandaranaike**, championed **Sinhala-Buddhist nationalism**. After the SLFP's victory in the **July 1960 elections**, Sirimavo became the world's first female Prime Minister and swiftly moved to **nationalize assisted schools**.

Key motivations included:

- **Equalizing access** to education across ethnic and religious lines
- **Reducing Christian dominance** in elite education
- **Strengthening state control** over curriculum and administration

  Aligning education with nationalist goals, including Sinhala language promotion

The **Schools Take-over Act** was passed in **1961** with a parliamentary majority of 60 votes. Only the **UNP** and **Federal Party** opposed it.

Catholic Resistance and Mobilization

The Catholic Church viewed the take-over as an existential threat. Archbishop **T.B. Cooray** declared in **1959** that Catholics would "fight to the end even by shedding blood" to protect their schools. Resistance included:

- **Occupations of school buildings** by parents and clergy
- **Mass protests**, especially in Catholic strongholds like **Negombo**
- Formation of the **Catholic Education Protection Front**

However, not all Catholics opposed the move. **Leftist Catholic groups**, including members of the **LSSP, MEP**, and **Communist Party**, formed the **National Education Protection Front in Catholic Areas**, which campaigned in favor of the take-over. They argued that poor Catholic children would benefit from free, state-run education.

Eventually, **Cardinal Graciano of India**, sent as a Vatican envoy, advised the Church to **end its resistance**. A compromise allowed elite schools like **St. Joseph's** and **St. Peter's College** to continue as **non-fee-levying private schools**.

Benefits of the Take-over

Expanded Access

- Poor children, including Catholics, gained access to formerly elite schools.

  Education became more **equitable and inclusive**, especially in rural areas.

National Integration

- The curriculum was standardized under state control.
- Sinhala and Tamil languages were promoted over English.

Professional Opportunities

- Many students from marginalized communities entered universities and became professionals, especially in districts like **Puttalam**, which had a large Catholic population.

Problems and Controversies

Loss of Autonomy

- Religious institutions lost control over curriculum and administration.
- Church-run schools were absorbed without compensation.

Quality and Funding Issues

- Some schools suffered from **underfunding**, overcrowding, and lack of resources.
- Illegal "donations" were reportedly collected at admission, despite the non-fee policy.

Cultural Tensions

- The take-over deepened **religious and ethnic divides**, contributing to the **1962 coup attempt**, which was partly motivated by Christian officers' resentment over the school nationalization.

Long-Term Legacy

The Schools Take-over remains one of the most **transformative and controversial reforms** in Sri Lanka's post-independence history. It:

- **Redefined the role of religion in education**
- **Shifted power from elite institutions to the state**
- **Laid the groundwork for mass literacy and social mobility**

Yet, it also exposed the **fragility of pluralism**, as education became a battleground for identity, ideology, and power.

Role of Dr. Badiuddin Mahmud in Schools Take Over

During the school's takeover in Sri Lanka in **1960–1961**, the **Minister of Education** was **Badiuddin Mahmud**. He played a pivotal role in implementing the **Assisted Schools and Training Colleges (Special Provisions) Act No. 5 of 1960**, which enabled the government to nationalize private schools—especially those run by religious organizations like the **Catholic Church** and the **Buddhist Theosophical Society**.

Mahmud is remembered for handling the politically sensitive transition with **tact and firmness**, ensuring that the process did not escalate into violence. His leadership helped navigate the resistance from religious institutions and facilitated compromises that allowed some elite schools to continue as **non-fee-levying private institutions**, such as **St. Joseph's College** and **St. Peter's College**.

The Man Behind the Reform

Dr. Badiuddin Mahmud was no ordinary minister. A product of **Aligarh Muslim University**, a founding member of the **Sri Lanka Freedom Party**, and a visionary educator, he believed that **education was the key to national equity**.

His reforms aimed to:

- **Eliminate elitism** in education
- **Expand access** to rural and marginalized communities
- **Integrate religious schools** into a secular, state-run system

He was also deeply committed to **uplifting the Muslim community**, transforming it from a business-focused group into one rich with teachers, professionals, and university graduates.

Personal Reflection

*As a student, I didn't grasp the full weight of what was happening. I simply packed my books and adjusted to the new timetable. But looking back, I realize I was living through a **quiet revolution**—one that reshaped not just classrooms, but the very soul of Sri Lanka.*

The bell rang early that year, but the lessons it carried echoed far beyond the schoolyard.

17

The 1962 Coup Attempt: A Critical Juncture in Sri Lanka's History

FAILED COUP D'ETAT ATTEMPT OF 1962

Mrs. Sirimavo Bandaranaike   Sir Oliver Goonatillake   Felix R. Dias Bandaranaike

(Pic: thuppahis.com)

A Nation in Transition

By the dawn of 1962, Sri Lanka—then Ceylon—was navigating uneasy terrain. The post-independence years had ushered in a wave of Sinhala-Buddhist nationalism. With the passage of the **Sinhala Only Act (1956)** and the increasing influence of Buddhist clergy in state affairs, **secular and westernized elites**—especially **Christian officers in the military and police**—grew anxious. Their professional authority and cultural identity felt threatened as the state shifted from pluralism toward **ethno-religious majoritarianism**.

The election of **Sirimavo Bandaranaike** as Prime Minister in **July 1960** intensified these concerns. Many feared the erosion of secular governance and the rise of a **Buddhist theocracy** under the ideological influence of civil servants like **N.Q. Dias**, a prominent Buddhist nationalist. (K.M. de Silva & Howard Wriggins, *J.R. Jayewardene of Sri Lanka*)

The Spark: Language and Education Reform

Two major issues became focal points of discontent:

Language Policy: In **January 1961**, the government formally enacted **Sinhala** as the country's **sole official language**, sidelining Tamil and English.

Education Policy: The **takeover of Catholic schools**, which began in **November 1960**, was bitterly opposed by the **Catholic Church and Christian families**. Parents staged occupations, and tensions rose dramatically. The Army was even deployed to manage internal security during the unrest. Cabinet ministers reportedly demanded harsher action against Christian protesters. (Donald Horowitz, *Coup Theories and Officers' Motives*)

The mood among Christian officers soured. Many saw **no future** in the newly restructured system. Historian **Patrick Peebles** noted that although Tamils were often scapegoated, this coup was led by **Sinhalese Christians** who feared marginalization. (*History of Sri Lanka*)

Operation Holdfast: Anatomy of a Conspiracy

The planned coup, code-named **Operation Holdfast**, was scheduled for the night of **Saturday, 27 January 1962**.

Key Conspirators:

- **Colonel F.C. 'Derek' de Saram** and **Colonel Maurice de Mel** (Army)
- **Lt Col Willie Abrahams MBE** (Artillery)
- **DIG C.C. 'Jungle' Dissanayake** (Metropolitan Police)
- **Former DIG Sidney de Zoysa** (Provincial Police)

Name Resurfacing in the 1962 Coup

Newton's name reappeared during the **1962 coup investigation** due to his **past association with Ossie Corea**, who had supplied the revolver in 1959.

Corea was detained preventively during the coup probe, and Newton was questioned again, though **not formally charged**.

His prior role in the Bandaranaike assassination made him a **person of interest**, but no direct link to the coup was established.

Legacy and Reflection

Newton Perera remains a **controversial figure** in Sri Lanka's post-independence history:

He was **never convicted** yet played a **critical logistical role** in one of the nation's most shocking political murders.

His case highlights the **complex web of police, political, and religious alliances** that shaped the era.

In later years, Newton reportedly **reflected on his actions with regret**, claiming he was unaware of the true intent behind the weapon request.

Was Ossie Corea involved in the Coup?

Although Ossie Corea was **not one of the 24 officers indicted** in the 1962 coup trial, his name reappeared due to:

- His **prior detention** during the Bandaranaike assassination investigation
- His **underworld ties** and reputation as a **fixer and arms supplier**
- The **CID's suspicion** that he may have had indirect links to the coup conspirators

According to reports, Corea was **detained for over six months** during the coup investigation but was **never served formal summons**. He was eventually **released from Mahara Prison** on **August 17, 1962**, by order of **Felix Ratnaike**, the Commissioner of Prisons, under instructions from **N.Q. Dias**, the powerful Defence Secretary.

Why He Wasn't Charged

- **Lack of direct evidence** connecting him to the coup plot
- Authorities concluded that he had **no proven ties** to the military officers

The plan was swift and bloodless:

- By **10:00 p.m.**, Colombo's entrances were to be sealed, and a **curfew declared at midnight**.
- **Temple Trees**, the Prime Minister's residence, would be stormed and **Sirimavo Bandaranaike arrested**.
- **Derek de Saram** would then inform **Governor-General Sir Oliver Goonetilleke** that the military had taken control.

The Leak and Collapse

However, unbeknownst to the conspirators, **Stanley Senanayake**, Superintendent of Police in Colombo, had **confided in his father-in-law, Patrick de S Kularatne**, an SLFP MP and trusted ally of the Bandaranaike family. Kularatne immediately alerted the **Inspector General of Police**, interrupting his bridge game at the Orient Club, and informed **Felix Dias Bandaranaike**, Deputy Minister of Defence.

The coup was pre-emptively **aborted**, and its leaders **arrested**. Although eleven of them were convicted, they were later acquitted by the **Privy Council in London** on procedural grounds.

Aftermath and Unintended Consequences

Ironically, the outcome of the failed coup accelerated the very transformations its planners hoped to prevent:

Institutional Purges

N.Q. Dias led a sweeping **restructuring of military and police**, favoring **Sinhala-Buddhist recruitment**.

Multiple regiments were **disbanded**, including:

- The 2nd (Volunteer) Squadron, Ceylon Signal Corps
- The 1st Heavy and 2nd Light Anti-Aircraft Regiments
- The 3rd Field Artillery Regiment

These were merged or reconstituted into units like:

- **Gemunu Watch (1962)** under **Lt. Col John Halangoda**
- **Sinha Regiment**, with cultural symbols like **Kandula the elephant**, reflecting Sinhala royal heritage (Channa Wickremesekera, *A Tough Apprenticeship*)

Changing Composition

According to Horowitz, prior to 1956, **Christians dominated the officer corps**; by 1962, nearly all cadets sent to **Sandhurst** were Sinhala Buddhists. This shift continued under **UNP's Dudley Sennanayake** (1965–70) and **Sirimavo's second government** (1970–77).

Operation Holdfast... and the Holy Photoshop

The 1962 Coup Trial — Sri Lanka's very own political soap opera, minus the commercial breaks. I was just a humble staffer at the Lethenty Plantation Office, minding my ledgers and sipping tea, when my colleague (a walking encyclopedia of courtroom drama) turned our lunch breaks into legal briefings. He followed the trial like it was the World Cup, and I got the highlights — treason, tension, and a cast of characters who could've starred in a Colombo version of Ocean's Eleven.

*Years passed, and the verdict finally dropped: guilty as charged. The SLFP's political newspaper, "ATHTHA", decided to commemorate the occasion with what I can only describe as a **DIY exorcism via photo editing**. There they were — black-and-white mugshots of the convicted coup plotters, each adorned with a **hand-drawn crucifix dangling from their necks**, like a fashion statement from the Vatican's underground resistance.*

*But wait — one photo stole the show. Instead of the tasteful neck-hung cross, this poor soul had a **full-face crucifix**, like someone had mistaken him for a haunted church door. It wasn't just symbolic — it was theatrical. The message? "This one's not just Catholic. He's extra Catholic." Turns out, he had died during the trial, and the editors apparently thought, "Why stop at the neck when you can go full holy mask?"*

It was satire, symbolism, and sacrilege all rolled into one grainy image. And in that moment, I realized Sri Lankan politics didn't need Netflix. It was Netflix — just with more onions, more drama, and a lot more crosses.

18

The Sirima-Shastri Pact: Migration, Citizenship, and the Human Cost of Diplomacy

(Pic: deccanchronicle.com)

The Sirima-Shastri Pact, signed in 1964, was more than just ink on paper—it was an attempt to resolve one of the most complex humanitarian and political dilemmas facing post-independence Sri Lanka and India. At its heart lay the lives of nearly a million Indian Tamil estate workers, whose statelessness reflected the contradictions of nationalism, labor politics, and identity in the wake of colonial rule.

Background: Who Were the Indian Tamils?

- Indian Tamils were brought to Sri Lanka (then Ceylon) during British colonial rule to work in the tea and rubber plantations in the central highlands.
- By independence in 1948, there were approximately one million Indian Tamils in Sri Lanka, mostly living in estate settlements with limited access to education, healthcare, or political power.
- Despite their contributions to the economy, these workers were considered outsiders—caught between two nations but claimed by neither.

The Problem of Statelessness

- In 1948, Sri Lanka passed the **Ceylon Citizenship Act**, which made it nearly impossible for Indian Tamils to qualify for citizenship due to stringent documentation and residency requirements.

- The **Indian and Pakistani Residents (Citizenship) Act** of 1949 only deepened the exclusion.
- As a result, **around 900,000 Indian Tamils were rendered stateless**—stripped of voting rights and national identity.

The Pact of 1964: A Diplomatic Compromise

Prime Minister **Sirimavo Bandaranaike** of Sri Lanka and Indian Prime Minister **Lal Bahadur Shastri** signed the agreement on **October 30, 1964**.

Key terms of the pact:

- Sri Lanka agreed to grant citizenship to **300,000** Indian Tamils.
- India agreed to repatriate **525,000** workers and their families.
- The fate of the remaining **75,000** was to be decided later.

This division of people like cargo containers—by number, not nuance—exemplified the bureaucratic approach to a deeply emotional issue.

Implementation: Bureaucracy vs. Humanity

- Implementation was slow, fraught with logistical nightmares and personal tragedies.
- Repatriation was voluntary in theory, but many were coerced by circumstance or desperation.
- Families were often split across borders—parents sent to India, children remaining in Sri Lanka or vice versa.
- Repatriated workers in India faced hardship adapting, with few support systems and minimal compensation.
- The Sri Lankan government faced criticism for failing to fully honor its commitment to naturalize the 300,000 it promised.

The Pact's Failures and Fallout

- By the mid-1970s, it was clear the pact was faltering—both sides were struggling to meet their quotas.
- Political will waned, and questions arose about the legality and morality of removing long-term residents en masse.
- In 1974, a **second pact** was signed between **Sirimavo Bandaranaike** and **Indian Prime Minister Indira Gandhi**, reaffirming obligations but offering little relief in practice.

Final Resolution: Citizenship and Dignity

In 1986, under **President J.R. Jayewardene**, Sri Lanka passed the **Grant of Citizenship to Stateless Persons Act**.

- This landmark legislation granted citizenship to the remaining Indian Tamils who were stateless—nearly **150,000** people.

- It marked the end of decades of limbo, allowing a generation to finally call Sri Lanka home.

Human Stories Behind the Numbers

The Sirima-Shastri Pact was born of diplomacy, but its consequences were deeply personal:

- Elderly plantation workers, born and raised in Sri Lanka, were forced to spend their final years in unfamiliar Indian towns.
- Children denied education and healthcare due to lack of status.
- Entire communities branded as foreigners despite decades of sweat and toil on Sri Lankan soil.

Reflections

The pact offers powerful lessons:

- Citizenship is not just a legal formality—it is a recognition of belonging.
- Solutions that treat people as numbers risk compounding injustice rather than resolving it.
- And in the tension between national interest and human dignity, it is always the vulnerable who bear the heaviest price.

My Experience During the Sirima-Shastri Repatriation

Between 1964 and 1966, I was a young clerk working at a plantation office in Sri Lanka. As the **Sirima-Shastri Pact** began its slow unraveling across estates, my role unexpectedly took on a new dimension. I became deeply involved in assisting Indian Tamil estate workers with the formalities required to apply for Indian citizenship and Temporary Travel Documents for their repatriation.

Over the course of that period, I helped hundreds of workers navigate the daunting bureaucratic maze. Many of them succeeded in securing their documents, thanks to our collaborative efforts. I took pride in the work—we weren't just processing paper, we were shaping destinies. Yet, despite having their documents in hand, only a handful of families chose to leave.

Most workers hesitated. They wanted to see what lay ahead for those who had already made the journey to India.

Unfortunately, the news that trickled back was sobering.

Some were relocated to tea plantations in the Nilgiris and Coonoor regions, their fates shrouded in uncertainty. One particular case left an indelible mark on me: a respected estate *Thalaivar*—a community leader and a physically imposing figure—returned to his ancestral village in India. Hoping to reclaim long-abandoned property, he was instead met with hostility from locals who had laid informal claim to the land. In a shocking act of violence, his leg was severed—an act meant to silence any further assertion of ownership.

Stories like his traveled estate lines. They sparked fear and grief among the remaining workers, many of whom now questioned whether repatriation promised anything more than displacement and pain. Even those with valid documents began choosing to stay back, seeking stability in the uncertain soil they had long called home.

What stayed with me wasn't just the paperwork—it was the faces behind it. The quiet strength of those who weighed identity, family, fear, and survival all at once. The repatriation process was supposed to offer resolution; instead, for many, it offered a haunting choice between two worlds, neither of which felt entirely safe.

19

1965 General Elections: A Turning Point in Sri Lankan Democracy

The Bus Ride That Changed My Vote — 1965 Elections

*In 1965, I was still working at the Lethenty Plantation Office, surrounded by the hum of typewriters, the scent of tea, and the occasional burst of political debate. The country was gearing up for a pivotal election, and my workplace had become a microcosm of the national divide. One colleague was a dyed-in-the-wool supporter of the **Sri Lanka Freedom Party (SLFP)**, while another swore allegiance to the **United National Party (UNP)**. Their banter was relentless, their loyalty unwavering, and their enthusiasm contagious.*

*The political climate was already simmering. The SLFP government, led by **Sirimavo Bandaranaike**, had suffered a dramatic blow when **30 MPs defected** over the controversial **Lake House nationalization issue**, which many saw as an attack on press freedom and a tilt toward authoritarianism. Rumors swirled—was this a foreign-instigated coup? A capitalist backlash? A Marxist maneuver? No one knew for sure, but the government was dissolved, and fresh elections were announced.*

My SLFP friend threw himself into party activities, attending youth meetings and rubbing shoulders with local leaders. Meanwhile, the UNP loyalist spent sleepless nights strategizing with his mentor, a prominent businessman from Maskeliya who treated politics like chess and voters like pawns. I, at first, leaned toward the SLFP—perhaps out of habit, perhaps out of sympathy for Mrs. Bandaranaike's widowhood campaign.

But then came the bus ride.

*It was late evening, and I was returning from Hatton. The bus was packed with SLFP supporters fresh from a rally, their voices loud and their spirits high. That's when I heard it: "**Anna Cheenek Innawa!**" — "There's a Chinese!" The chant was mocking the UNP's fear-mongering that a vote for SLFP would invite a communist invasion. The SLFP crowd turned the tables, ridiculing the UNP's paranoia with theatrical sarcasm. It was funny, yes, but also unsettling. The tone was aggressive, the insults sharp, and the atmosphere thick with tribalism.*

That bus ride shook me. I began to wonder: if this was the face of SLFP's grassroots, what kind of governance would follow? Would dissent be tolerated? Would moderation survive?

On election day, standing in the booth with my ballot in hand, I made a snap decision. I voted for the UNP. It felt like a betrayal of my earlier convictions, but also like a safeguard against extremism. Ironically, I regretted it later—not because the UNP failed, but because I realized I had let fear, not reason, guide my choice.

The 1965 election was more than a contest of parties. It was a referendum on identity, ideology, and the future of democracy. And for me, it was a lesson in how even a bus ride can tip the scales of history.

The Lake House Controversy: Influence, and Political Fallout

LAKE HOUSE - Pic: Daily News Archives

In the early 1960s, Sri Lanka's political landscape was already tense, but the storm truly broke in **1964** when Prime Minister **Sirimavo Bandaranaike's SLFP government** attempted to **nationalize Lake House**, the country's most influential media empire. Known formally as the **Associated Newspapers of Ceylon Limited (ANCL)**, Lake House had been founded by **D.R. Wijewardene**, a Cambridge-educated media magnate whose newspapers had become the voice of the island's elite and a powerful tool in shaping public opinion.

The SLFP's move to take over Lake House was part of a broader socialist agenda aimed at nationalizing key industries and institutions. But this particular decision struck a nerve. Lake House wasn't just a business—it was the **nerve center of political discourse**, and its editorial stance had long favored the **right-leaning UNP**, especially under the influence of **Esmond Wickremesinghe**, D.R.'s son-in-law.

The takeover was seen by many as an attempt to **silence dissent and control the press**, triggering outrage among opposition parties, business leaders, and even members within the SLFP itself. The tipping point came when **C.P. de Silva**, the Leader of the House and Minister of Land, Irrigation and Power, **crossed the floor of Parliament**—a dramatic act of defiance that led to the collapse of the government on **December 3, 1964**.

This political earthquake set the stage for the **March 1965 general election**, where the UNP, led by **Dudley Senanayake**, capitalized on the backlash. The party promised to restore democratic norms and press freedom, forming a **seven-party coalition government** known as the *Hath Havula* (Group of Seven). The Lake House controversy had not only toppled a government—it had reshaped the electoral battlefield and redefined the role of media in Sri Lankan politics.

Election Overview

Held on **March 22, 1965**, the sixth parliamentary election in Sri Lanka (then Ceylon) was a **high-stakes contest** between the **United National Party (UNP)** and the **Sri Lanka Freedom Party (SLFP)**. The SLFP government under **Sirimavo Bandaranaike** had lost its majority in **December 1964**, prompting fresh elections.

The Hath Haula Coalition

The **1965 General Elections**, held on **March 22**, resulted in a **hung Parliament**:

PARTY	SEATS WON	VOTE SHARE
UNP	66	39.31%
SLFP	41	30.18%
Federal Party (ITAK)	14	5.38%
LSSP	10	7.47%
Communist Party	4	2.71%
SLFSP (C.P. de Silva)	5	3.22%
Tamil Congress	3	2.44%
MEP	1	2.39%
JVP (K.M.P. Rajaratne)	1	0.46%
Independents	6	-

With **76 seats needed for a majority**, the UNP fell short. However, **Dudley Senanayake** formed a **seven-party coalition**, famously called the **Hath Haula (Seven-Headed)** National Government. The coalition included:

- **UNP**
- **Federal Party (ITAK)**
- **Sri Lanka Freedom Socialist Party (SLFSP)**
- **All Ceylon Tamil Congress (ACTC)**

    ⬚ **Mahajana Eksath Peramuna (MEP)**

- **Jathika Vimukthi Peramuna (JVP)** – not to be confused with the later Marxist JVP
- **Ceylon Workers Congress (CWC)**

This coalition was sealed by the **Dudley–Chelvanayakam Pact**, which promised concessions to Tamil demands, including district councils and administrative use of Tamil in Tamil-speaking regions.

Political Developments (1965–1969)

Ethnic Reconciliation

- **Murugesan Tiruchelvam**, representing the Federal Party, was appointed **Minister of Local Government**, marking the **first Tamil cabinet minister in a decade**.

- The pact with the Federal Party was seen as a **symbol of ethnic cooperation**, though it faced backlash from Sinhala nationalists.

Language and Religion

- In **1966**, the government introduced **Tamil Language Regulations**, making Tamil officially "parallel" to Sinhala in Tamil-speaking areas.
- Sinhala hardliners protested, and a **state of emergency** was declared to quell unrest.
- The **Christian Sabbath (Sunday)** was replaced by the **Buddhist Poya full moon day** as the national holiday, appeasing Buddhist activists but alienating Catholics.

Foreign Policy and Diplomacy

- Relations with the **United States improved**, reversing the diplomatic chill caused by the previous SLFP government's nationalization of foreign oil companies.
- Sri Lanka signed **tea trade agreements** with **Middle Eastern and East European countries**, including a notable pact at the **1969 Mauritius Tea Conference**.

Political Stability

- Dudley Senanayake became the **first Prime Minister to complete a full five-year term** in Sri Lanka's history.
- The coalition held together despite ideological differences, largely due to Senanayake's moderate leadership and strategic concessions.

Economic Conditions (1965–1969)

Mixed Economic Model

- The UNP pursued a **mixed economy**, emphasizing **private sector growth** while maintaining **state welfare programs**.
- **Private investment doubled** compared to the public sector, reversing the socialist trend of the previous SLFP government.

Economic Challenges

- A **global rice shortage in 1965** led to a **50% increase in import costs**, straining the budget.

  Export commodity prices (tea, rubber, coconut) **declined sharply**, reducing foreign exchange earnings.

- In **1966**, the government declared a **state of emergency** due to **food riots**, and **cut the subsidized rice ration by half**, a deeply unpopular move.

GDP and Growth

- GDP in 1965 was approximately **$1.7 billion**, with a **growth rate of 2.5%**, reflecting modest expansion.
- The economy remained **fragile**, with inflationary pressures and limited industrial diversification.

A Balancing Act

The **1965–1969 period** was marked by:

- **Political pragmatism**, with the UNP forging a broad coalition to govern
- **Ethnic outreach**, though limited and contested
- **Economic moderation**, with mixed results

While the **Hath Haula coalition** preserved democratic governance and avoided major scandals, its **economic struggles** and **ethnic tensions** foreshadowed deeper challenges that would erupt in the 1970s.

Was the Election Free and Fair?

The **1965 elections were widely regarded as free and fair**, with:

- **81.13% voter turnout**, indicating strong public engagement
- **No major allegations of vote rigging or violence**
- Peaceful transfer of power from SLFP to UNP

However, the political climate was **tense and polarized**:

- The SLFP had alienated minorities through aggressive **Sinhala-only policies** and **school nationalization**
- The UNP capitalized on economic stagnation and promised **moderation and coalition-building**

While the election itself was clean, the **underlying ethnic and ideological divisions** foreshadowed deeper national challenges.

20

Dudley–Chelvanayakam Pact (1965)

A Missed Opportunity for Ethnic Reconciliation

By the mid-1960s, Sri Lanka (then Ceylon) was grappling with deepening ethnic tensions. The **Sinhala Only Act of 1956**, the **abrogation of the Bandaranaike–Chelvanayakam Pact in 1958**, and repeated **anti-Tamil riots** had alienated the Tamil minority. The **Federal Party (Ilankai Tamil Arasu Kachchi or ITAK)**, led by **S.J.V. Chelvanayakam**, had emerged as the principal Tamil political voice, advocating for **regional autonomy**, **language parity**, and **minority rights**.

In the **March 1965 general elections**, no party won an outright majority. The **United National Party (UNP)**, led by **Dudley Senanayake**, secured **66 seats**, while the **Federal Party** held **14 seats**, making it the **kingmaker** in a hung Parliament.

On **March 24, 1965**, **Dudley Senanayake** and **S.J.V. Chelvanayakam** met and signed a formal agreement to secure Tamil support for a UNP-led coalition government. The pact promised several key reforms:

Language Rights

- **Tamil Language Special Provisions Act** would be implemented to allow Tamil as a language of **administration and record** in the **Northern and Eastern Provinces**.
- Tamil speakers would be able to **transact official business in Tamil** throughout the island.

Legal Proceedings

- The **Language of Courts Act** would be amended to allow **legal proceedings in Tamil** in the Northern and Eastern Provinces.

District Councils

- **District Councils** would be established with powers over subjects to be mutually agreed upon.

  The central government would retain authority to issue directions in the **national interest**.

Land and Colonization

Amendments to the **Land Development Ordinance** would prioritize land grants in the North and East as follows:

1. **Landless persons in the district**
2. **Tamil-speaking residents of the province**
3. **Other citizens**, with preference to Tamil speakers from elsewhere.

The pact was seen as a **moderate compromise**, short of federalism but aimed at **decentralization and ethnic accommodation**.

The pact enabled the formation of a **seven-party National Government**, dubbed the **Hath Haula (Seven-Headed)** coalition. It included:

- UNP
- Federal Party (ITAK)
- All Ceylon Tamil Congress (ACTC)
- Sri Lanka Freedom Socialist Party (SLFSP)
- Mahajana Eksath Peramuna (MEP)
- Jathika Vimukthi Peramuna (JVP of K.M.P. Rajaratne)
- Ceylon Workers Congress (CWC)

For the first time in a decade, a **Tamil leader—Murugeysen Tiruchelvam**—was appointed as **Minister of Local Government**, symbolizing ethnic inclusion.

Despite its promise, the pact faced **intense backlash**:

Sinhala Nationalist Resistance

- The **SLFP**, now in opposition, accused the UNP of **dividing the country**.
- **Leftist allies** like the **LSSP** and **Communist Party** joined protests.
- Public rallies denounced the pact as a threat to **Sinhala-Buddhist supremacy**.

Implementation Failure

- The promised **District Councils** were never established.
- **Tamil language regulations** were delayed and diluted.
- **Land allocation priorities** were ignored in practice.

Breakdown of Trust

- Chelvanayakam grew disillusioned with the UNP's **lack of commitment**.

- In **1972**, he resigned from Parliament in protest against the new **Republican Constitution**, which entrenched Sinhala dominance and Buddhism's privileged status.

Legacy and Historical Assessment

The **Dudley–Chelvanayakam Pact** was the **last serious attempt** at constitutional compromise before Tamil politics shifted toward **separatism**. Its failure reinforced Tamil perceptions that **Sinhalese-led governments could not be trusted** to honor agreements.

Key Takeaways:

- The pact was a **missed opportunity** for peaceful ethnic accommodation.
- It showed that **moderation and negotiation** were possible—but fragile.
- Its collapse contributed to the **radicalization of Tamil youth**, leading to the rise of the **LTTE** and decades of civil war.

Conclusion: A Fragile Bridge That Never Held

The Dudley–Chelvanayakam Pact remains a poignant reminder of what Sri Lanka could have been—a **multi-ethnic democracy built on compromise and mutual respect**. Instead, the pact's failure deepened the ethnic divide and set the stage for **conflict, mistrust, and militarization**.

21

Emergence of JVP Movement

The **Janatha Vimukthi Peramuna (JVP)** was founded on **May 14, 1965**, by **Rohana Wijeweera**, a Marxist activist disillusioned with the **old left**—namely the **LSSP** and **Communist Party**, which had joined bourgeois coalitions.

Rohana Wijeweera, educated in **Moscow**, broke away from the **Ceylon Communist Party (Peking Wing)** and launched the JVP as a **revolutionary alternative**, focused on:

Marxist–Leninist ideology
Youth mobilization
Anti-imperialism and anti-elitism

Early Activities

- Conducted **political education camps** across the country
- Built a **semi-clandestine network** among students, workers, and farmers
- Published newspapers like *Janatha Vimukthi* and *Rathu Balaya*

The JVP rejected parliamentary politics and aimed to **build a grassroots revolutionary movement**. By 1970, it had become a formidable force, especially among **rural Sinhala youth**.

Political Climate and Repression

The **UNP government (1965–1970)** viewed the JVP with suspicion but did not immediately suppress it. However, the **SLFP-led coalition** that returned to power in

1970 began cracking down on JVP activities, culminating in the **1971 insurrection**, where the JVP attempted to overthrow the state.

Two Currents, One Crossroads

The **1965 elections** marked a **return to democratic stability** but also exposed the **limits of electoral politics** in addressing deep-rooted social and ethnic grievances. While the UNP formed a broad coalition, the **JVP emerged outside the system**, channeling the frustrations of a generation that felt **betrayed by both left and right**.

Together, these developments set the stage for **Sri Lanka's political volatility in the 1970s**, where **democracy and revolution** would collide.

Revolution in the Shadows: The Early Years of the JVP (1965–1971)

The mid-1960s in Sri Lanka marked a period of political disillusionment and ideological fragmentation. The traditional left, once a beacon of working-class hope, had begun to lose credibility after aligning with capitalist coalitions. Into this vacuum stepped a group of radical youth led by **Rohana Wijeweera**, whose vision would birth the **Janatha Vimukthi Peramuna (JVP)**—a revolutionary movement that would shake the foundations of the Sri Lankan state.

Founding Sparks: Akmeemana, 1965

On **14 May 1965**, a group of seven young men gathered at a modest home in **Akmeemana**, Galle, for what would become a historic meeting. Led by **Rohana Wijeweera**, a former medical student at the **Patrice Lumumba University** in Moscow, the group sought to create a new revolutionary force. Disillusioned by the **Ceylon Communist Party (Peking Wing)** and its perceived ideological compromises, Wijeweera and his comrades envisioned a movement rooted in **Marxist–Leninist principles**, tailored to Sri Lanka's unique socio-political landscape.

Whispers in the Jungle: JVP's Early Classes

In the aftermath of the 1971 Janatha Vimukthi Peramuna (JVP) Insurrection, I spoke to several young men of my age who confessed they'd attended the initial "classes" organized by the movement. Most described them as intriguing at first—political crash courses offered with a mix of passion and mystery. But after a few sessions, many quietly backed away, sensing that what they'd stepped into was far more intense than they had imagined.

*I remember one particularly surreal account from Hatton, where a group of curious 15-year-old schoolboys ventured to **Duke Nose Mountain**, drawn by whispers of a new political awakening. There, nestled in a clearing carved out of the jungle, they found rudimentary seats laid out in the undergrowth. At the center stood a familiar face—an old boy from their school—delivering fiery lectures on revolution, ideology, and the supposed failures of the system.*

Some students were hooked, attending every session like disciples at the altar of change. But most grew uneasy. The rhetoric became darker, the ideas more radical, and the path ahead increasingly uncertain. Without drama or confrontation, many simply stopped showing up.

The movement, after all, was not offering mere political education—it was crafting a blueprint for rebellion.

What happened in Hatton was no exception. Similar stories emerged from villages and towns across the country. The JVP's strategy of quietly cultivating rural youth through informal sessions—often held in secluded temples, graveyards, or jungle patches—created a network of partially indoctrinated individuals, some of whom would later play roles in the insurrection, while others faded back into normal life, shaken but unchanged.

The Five Lectures: Political Education as Mobilization

One of Wijeweera's earliest innovations was the creation of the **"Five Classes"**—a series of lectures designed to politically educate the masses. These covered:

1. The economic crisis in Sri Lanka
2. Neo-colonialism and imperialism
3. Indian expansionism
4. The failure of traditional leftist parties
5. The need for armed revolution

These lectures were delivered in cemeteries, temples, and remote villages, often lasting up to 18 hours a day. They became the ideological backbone of the movement, transforming passive listeners into committed revolutionaries.

Ideological Roots and Global Influences

The JVP's ideology was a hybrid of **Maoist**, **Trotskyist**, and **Castroist** thought. Wijeweera rejected both the Soviet and Chinese lines, instead crafting a uniquely Sri Lankan revolutionary strategy. Influenced by the **Zanzibar Revolution of 1964**, he proposed a **"scattered and instantaneous struggle"**—a nationwide uprising targeting police stations and military installations simultaneously.

Organizational Structure and Recruitment

By **1969**, the JVP had formalized its structure with a **Central Committee**, **District Secretaries**, and **five-member cells** operating in secrecy. Recruitment focused on **Sinhala-educated rural youth**, many from marginalized castes such as **Wahumpura** and **Batgama**. The movement gained traction in universities, particularly **Vidyalankara**, **Peradeniya**, and **Vidyodaya**, where it took control of student unions.

Militarization and Preparations for Insurrection

Between **1969 and 1970**, the JVP began stockpiling weapons, manufacturing crude bombs, and training cadres in basic combat. Secret camps were established in **Kurunegala**, **Tissamaharama**, and **Anuradhapura**. Uniforms were stitched in university dorms, and hideouts were built in temples and farms. The goal was clear: a **24-hour revolution** that would cripple the state before it could respond.

Government Surveillance and Arrests

The growing visibility of the JVP alarmed the authorities. In **May 1970**, Wijeweera was arrested in **Hambantota**, just days before the general election. Though released in **July**, the movement was now under intense surveillance. Explosions at hideouts in **Nelundeniya** and **Peradeniya** further exposed their preparations, prompting mass arrests and a crackdown on JVP activities.

The 1971 Insurrection

On **5 April 1971**, the JVP launched its first armed uprising. Attacks were carried out on **74 police stations**, primarily in the **Southern** and **Sabaragamuwa** provinces. Though poorly armed and inadequately trained, the insurgents briefly seized control of several towns. The government, aided by foreign military support from **India**, **Pakistan**, and the **Soviet Union**, swiftly crushed the rebellion. Thousands were killed, and over **5,700** surrendered.

22

1970 General Elections:

A Leftward Shift in Sri Lanka's Political Landscape

Election Overview

Held on **May 27, 1970**, the **8th parliamentary election** in Sri Lanka (then Ceylon) marked a **watershed moment** in the country's post-independence history. It was the **last election held under the Soulbury Constitution**, and it ushered in a **Leftist Coalition government** that would redefine Sri Lanka's political, economic, and constitutional trajectory.

PARTY/ALLIANCE	LEADER	SEATS WON	VOTE SHARE
Sri Lanka Freedom Party (SLFP)	Sirimavo Bandaranaike	91	36.86%
Lanka Sama Samaja Party (LSSP)	Dr. N.M. Perera	19	8.68%
Communist Party of Ceylon (CPC)	Pieter Keuneman	6	3.39%
United National Party (UNP)	Dudley Senanayake	17	37.91%
Federal Party (ITAK)	S.J.V. Chelvanayakam	13	4.92%
All Ceylon Tamil Congress (ACTC)	G.G. Ponnambalam	3	2.32%

The **United Front (UF)** coalition—comprising the **SLFP**, **LSSP**, and **CPC**—won a **commanding majority** of **116 seats**, enabling them to form a government without needing support from minority parties.

Sirimavo Bandaranaike (SLFP)

- First female Prime Minister in the world
- Championed **socialist policies**, **nationalization**, and **Buddhist cultural revival**
- Led the **United Front coalition** to victory

Dr. N.M. Perera (LSSP)

- Veteran Trotskyist and economist
- Advocated for **workers' rights**, **state planning**, and **industrial democracy**
- Became **Minister of Finance** in the UF government

Pieter Keuneman (CPC)

- Marxist intellectual and urban planner
- Appointed **Minister of Housing and Construction**
- Pushed for **low-cost housing** and **urban reform**

Dudley Senanayake (UNP)

- Incumbent Prime Minister before the election
- Represented **conservative and pro-Western interests**
- His government was criticized for **economic stagnation** and **elitism**

The **United Front's Common Programme** was a radical departure from previous centrist policies. It included:

- **Extensive nationalization** of plantations, banks, and foreign-owned enterprises
- **Land reform**, redistributing estates to landless peasants
- **Industrial democracy**, with worker participation in management
- **Non-aligned foreign policy**, distancing from Western influence
- **Drafting a new Republican Constitution**, severing ties with the British monarchy

In **1972**, the UF government declared Sri Lanka a **republic**, renamed the country, and promulgated a new constitution that gave **Buddhism the "foremost place"** and centralized power in the **National State Assembly**.

Disgruntled Elements and Rising Tensions

Despite its sweeping mandate, the UF government faced growing opposition from various quarters:

Economic Discontent

- **Inflation and unemployment** worsened due to global commodity price drops
- **Shortages of essential goods** and rationing led to public frustration
- The government's **import substitution policies** failed to stimulate growth

Ethnic Alienation

- Tamil parties like the **Federal Party** felt betrayed by the lack of meaningful devolution
- The **1972 Constitution** removed safeguards for minorities, intensifying Tamil nationalism

Youth Radicalization

- Disillusioned Sinhala youth, especially unemployed graduates, turned to **revolutionary politics**
- The **Janatha Vimukthi Peramuna (JVP)**, led by **Rohana Wijeweera**, emerged as a **Marxist-Leninist insurgent group**
- In **April 1971**, the JVP launched an armed **insurrection**, attacking police stations and attempting to overthrow the government

Intellectual and Religious Dissent

- Christian elites and secular intellectuals criticized the **Buddhist nationalist tilt**
- *The **purge of Christian officers** from the military and police after the 1962 coup attempt continued under the UF Legacy and Historical Significance*

The 1970 elections marked:

- The **peak of leftist influence** in Sri Lankan politics
- The **beginning of constitutional nationalism**, with Buddhism and Sinhala language enshrined
- The **radicalization of youth movements**, leading to decades of insurgency
- The **decline of liberal democratic pluralism**, replaced by centralized governance

While the UF government made strides in **social welfare**, **education**, and **healthcare**, its failure to manage the economy and accommodate ethnic diversity sowed seeds of **long-term instability**.

Dr. N.M. Perera's Tenure as Finance Minister: A Radical Balancing Act

Dr. **Nanayakkarapathirage Martin Perera**, better known as **N.M. Perera**, was a towering figure in Sri Lankan politics and economics. A founding member of the **Lanka Sama Samaja Party (LSSP)** and a disciple of Harold Laski at the London School of Economics, he brought a rare blend of academic rigor and socialist idealism to the Ministry of Finance during his two terms: briefly in **1964**, and more prominently from **1970 to 1975**.

Balancing the Budget — A Rare Feat

Despite the economic headwinds, Perera achieved what few finance ministers have: **a balanced budget**. His strategy included:

Higher taxation on wealth and luxury goods:

- **Price controls** and **rationing** of essentials
- **Forced and voluntary savings schemes**
- **Demonetization** of large currency notes to catch tax evaders
- Creation of the **National Savings Bank** in 1972 to mobilize domestic savings

He also prioritized **non-inflationary financing**, emphasizing austerity and long-term planning over short-term popularity.

One of Perera's most successful initiatives was the formation of the **State Gem Corporation**, which formalized the gem trade and curbed smuggling. Gem exports skyrocketed from **Rs. 3.4 million in 1971** to **Rs. 234 million in 1974**, making gems the third-largest export earner.

During the **1973 oil crisis**, Perera banned the import of subsidiary food items to reduce the trade deficit. He championed **self-reliance**, pushing for local production and import substitution—even at the cost of public approval.

Dr. N.M. Perera remains the **only Sri Lankan Finance Minister to have balanced the national budget** while navigating a socialist transformation. His tenure was marked by intellectual courage, fiscal discipline, and a commitment to economic justice. Though controversial, his policies laid the groundwork for a more self-sufficient Sri Lankan economy.

The 1970 Demonetization in Sri Lanka: A Bold Attempt to Flush Out Black Money

The First Devaluation of the Rupee

When the term *"devaluation of the rupee"* was first mentioned, I—like millions of others—was utterly confused. Rumors circulated, especially among supporters of the UNP, that the government was planning to confiscate people's savings. The public was instructed to surrender their Rs. 50 & 100 currency notes to banks, where they would be credited to individual accounts. However, many hoarders of undeclared cash chose not to comply. As a result, millions of rupees in black money went unreturned, and those notes were automatically invalidated—thereby partially resolving the monetary imbalance.

When Perera assumed office in **1970**, Sri Lanka was grappling with a severe **foreign exchange crisis** and a **domestic financial imbalance**. Rather than accept the stringent conditions of the **International Monetary Fund (IMF)**, Perera chose a bold path: **devaluation of the Sri Lankan rupee**?

This was the first such move in the country's history, aimed at boosting exports and curbing imports to stabilize the economy.

What many mistook for a devaluation was actually a **demonetization**—a targeted move to invalidate high-value currency notes, specifically the **Rs. 50 and Rs. 100 denominations**, in an effort to expose **undeclared wealth** and **black money**.

What Actually Happened

On **October 26, 1970**, under the **Prevention of the Avoidance of Income Tax Act**, the government declared all Rs. 50 and Rs. 100 notes printed before that date **illegal tender**.

Citizens were required to **surrender these notes to banks** by **November 3, 1970**, or risk losing their value entirely.

The surrendered notes were credited to bank accounts, and the **details of the depositors were shared with the Inland Revenue Department** to assess tax liabilities.

Targeting Black Money

The move was designed to **flush out hoarded cash** that had evaded taxation. Many **wealthy individuals**, especially those aligned with the **United National Party (UNP)**, feared exposure and **chose not to surrender their notes**, resulting in **millions of rupees being automatically cancelled.**

According to economist **W.D. Lakshman**, the operation brought a **substantial amount of money back into the banking system** and helped maintain a **healthy tax-to-GDP ratio.**

Public Reaction

Contrary to fears, **ordinary citizens were largely unaffected**. The strong banking infrastructure ensured smooth processing for those who complied.

The demonetization was **secretly executed**—even the **Governor of the Central Bank, William Tennekoon**, was unaware until the new notes arrived.

Replacement notes were printed by **Thomas De La Rue**, and controversially featured the **raised hand symbol** of the ruling party, which later led to their discontinuation due to election law violations.

Was It Successful?

While the move **did not significantly boost tax revenue**, it **did eliminate a portion of black money** and **symbolized a strong stance against tax evasion.**

The Central Bank had to absorb the **cost of the operation**, and some critics viewed it as **politically motivated.**

This episode remains one of the most **audacious and controversial monetary interventions** in Sri Lanka's history.

Global Demonetization: Comparing Sri Lanka's 1970 Move with Other Nations

Demonetization has been used by governments worldwide to combat black money, corruption, inflation, and counterfeit currency. Sri Lanka's 1970 demonetization under Dr. N.M. Perera shares similarities with other bold monetary interventions—but also stands out in its execution and impact.

Sri Lanka (1970)

- **Targeted Notes**: Rs. 50 and Rs. 100 notes printed before October 26, 1970
- **Objective**: Flush out black money and tax evaders
- **Method**: Citizens had to surrender notes to banks; details were shared with tax authorities
- **Outcome**: Millions in black money were never surrendered, effectively canceled; ordinary citizens were largely unaffected

India (2016)

- **Targeted Notes**: ₹500 and ₹1,000 notes (86% of cash in circulation)
- **Objective**: Curb black money, counterfeit currency, and promote digital payments
- **Method**: Sudden announcement; citizens given limited time to deposit or exchange notes
- **Outcome**:
- 99.3% of demonetized currency returned to banks
- Minimal impact on black money, which was mostly held in assets, not cash
- Boosted digital transactions and financial inclusion

Other Notable Examples

COUNTRY	YEAR	TARGETED NOTED/POLICY	OUTCOME/IMPACT
USA	1969	Bills above $100	Curbed black money circulation; banking system strengthened
Ghana	1982	50 cedi note	Public turned to foreign currency; trust in banks eroded
Nigeria	1984	New colored notes	Confusion and black-market growth; policy failed
Myanmar	1987	80% of currency invalidated	Triggered mass protests; economic instability
Soviet Union	1991	50- and 100- ruble notes	Economic disruption; contributed to USSR collapse
Zimbabwe	2015	Replaced local currency	Hyperinflation persisted; economy destabilized
Venezuela	2016	100 bolivar notes	Violent protests; deadline extended; inflation worsened
European Union	2002	National currencies replaced by Euro	Smooth transition due to long preparation

Key Takeaways

Sri Lanka's 1970 move was **surgical and secretive**, targeting specific denominations and linking deposits to tax enforcement.

India's 2016 demonetization was **sweeping and disruptive**, with mixed results on black money but long-term gains in digitization.

Global patterns show that **success depends on preparation, communication, and infrastructure**. Sudden moves often lead to chaos, while well-planned transitions (like the Euro) tend to succeed.

23

From Coup to Constitution: The Road to the Republic of Sri Lanka

Prelude: The 1962 Coup and Its Undercurrents

The **1962 coup attempt**, led by senior **Christian officers** in the military and police, was a reaction to the rising tide of **Sinhala-Buddhist nationalism**. These officers feared the erosion of secular governance and the marginalization of minorities—especially Christians—under the **Sri Lanka Freedom Party (SLFP)** government.

The failed coup exposed deep fractures in Sri Lanka's post-independence identity. It accelerated the **purging of Christian officers**, the **restructuring of the military**, and the **recruitment of Sinhala-Buddhist personnel**, laying the groundwork for a more ideologically aligned state apparatus.

But the most profound shift was yet to come.

The Push for a Republican Constitution

Following the SLFP's landslide victory in the **1970 general elections**, Prime Minister **Sirimavo Bandaranaike**—widow of the slain S.W.R.D. Bandaranaike—formed a **United Front coalition** with the **LSSP** and **Communist Party**. Their manifesto promised a **new constitution** that would:

- Declare Sri Lanka a **free, sovereign, and independent republic**
- Sever all remaining ties with the **British Crown**
- Enshrine **socialist democracy** and **fundamental rights**

On **July 21, 1970**, Parliament was converted into a **Constituent Assembly**, tasked with drafting this new constitution. The process was led by **Dr. Colvin R. de Silva**, Minister of Constitutional Affairs and a prominent Marxist intellectual.

May 22, 1972: Birth of the Republic

After **22 months of deliberation**, the **Republican Constitution** was adopted on **May 22, 1972**. Key changes included:

TRANSFORMATION	DETALS
Name Change	Ceylon officially became Sri Lanka
Head of State	The **Governor-General** (British Crown's representative) was replaced by a **President**
Legislature	The **bicameral Parliament** (Senate + House) was replaced by a **unicameral National State Assembly**
Religion	**Buddhism** was given the **"foremost place"** in the state

Language	**Sinhala** was reaffirmed as the sole official language
Legal Sovereignty	All references to the **British monarchy** were removed; **Section 29** of the Soulbury Constitution, which protected minority rights, was abolished

The constitution was hailed as a **"home-grown product"**, crafted entirely by Sri Lankan lawmakers without British oversight.

Political and Cultural Impact

Achievements

- **Full sovereignty**: Sri Lanka was no longer a dominion of Britain
- **Symbolic independence**: The British Crown ceased to be the source of legal authority
- **National pride**: The move was celebrated as a culmination of the independence struggle

Controversies

- **Minority alienation**: The removal of Section 29 and the elevation of Buddhism deepened ethnic tensions
- **Tamil boycott**: The **Federal Party** withdrew from the Constituent Assembly after its proposal for **language parity** was rejected
- **Opposition dissent**: The **UNP** voted against the constitution, citing lack of public consultation and excessive centralization of power

Legacy and Connection to the 1962 Coup

The **1962 coup** was a symptom of elite anxiety over the changing identity of the state. The **1972 Republican Constitution** was the formalization of that change—a decisive shift from **colonial pluralism** to **majoritarian nationalism**.

It marked the end of:

- **British legal influence**
- **Christian elite dominance**
- **Secular governance as a default**

And the beginning of:

- **Sinhala-Buddhist state ideology**
- **Centralized executive power**
- **Ethnic polarization**, which would later fuel civil conflict

Dr. Colvin R. de Silva - The Architect of Sri Lanka's 1972 Republican Constitution

(References: en.wikipedia.org, www.colombotelegraph.com, island.lk, factum.lk)

(Pic – Daily Mirror)

The principal architect of Sri Lanka's **1972 Republican Constitution** was **Dr. Colvin R. de Silva**, who served as the **Minister of Constitutional Affairs** in the United Front government led by **Prime Minister Sirimavo Bandaranaike**.

Dr. de Silva, a prominent Marxist intellectual and senior figure in the **Lanka Sama Samaja Party (LSSP)**, chaired the **drafting committee** responsible for shaping the new constitution. His legal expertise and ideological convictions played a central role in crafting a document that:

- Declared Sri Lanka a **sovereign republic**, severing ties with the British Crown
- Elevated **Buddhism** to the "foremost place" in the state
- Reaffirmed **Sinhala** as the sole official language
- Replaced the bicameral legislature with a **unicameral National State Assembly**
- Removed **Section 29** of the Soulbury Constitution, which had protected minority rights

The constitution was adopted on **May 22, 1972**, and marked a decisive shift toward **majoritarian nationalism and centralized governance**.

24

April 1971 Shadows: The Day the Country Stilled

It was an afternoon bathed in the golden stillness of the hill country—a typical day in the highlands of Norwood (Dickoya District), where the hum of the tea factory and rustle of leaves offered a rhythm as predictable as the sun's descent behind the hills. As a member of the office staff at one of the estate's most reputable plantations, I was absorbed in routine ledgers and reports, expecting nothing beyond the ordinary.

But as I returned to my quarters, the familiar clink of boots on gravel signaled an unexpected visit. The security guard from the adjoining factory stood at my doorstep, his face taut with urgency. What he said next would unravel the illusion of peace that hung over the nation like morning mist. "They've stormed a police station down south," he muttered—"killed the officers... taken the weapons." The radio confirmed the fragments with scratchy dispatches, and as I sat glued to the broadcast, the news took on the shape of something chilling and unreal.

Sri Lanka, long thought of as serene and slow-moving, was convulsing. What began as an isolated act of violence would soon swell into a nation-wide rebellion—led by disillusioned youth, carried out with militant precision, and answered with a crackdown so fierce it would leave thousands of bodies and untold grief buried in silence.

The April 1971 JVP Insurrection: Sri Lanka's First Armed Rebellion

The Spark: What Happened on 5th April 1971?

In the early hours of **Monday, 5 April 1971**, Sri Lanka (then Ceylon) was jolted by a **coordinated armed uprising** led by the **Janatha Vimukthi Peramuna (JVP)**, a Marxist-Leninist youth movement founded by **Rohana Wijeweera**. The insurrection began with **simultaneous attacks on over 74 police stations** across the country, targeting government infrastructure and attempting to seize weapons.

The first attack occurred prematurely on **4 April** at **Wellawaya Police Station**, where **five policemen were killed**, inadvertently alerting the government to the impending rebellion. By dawn on 5 April, the JVP launched its full-scale offensive, aiming to **cripple the state's security apparatus** and ignite a nationwide revolution.

Pic: Colombo Telegraph

The Obituary That Sparked a Revolution: A Misfire in the JVP's 1971 Insurrection

The JVP's Strategy for a Coordinated Uprising

The **Janatha Vimukthi Peramuna (JVP)**, led by **Rohana Wijeweera**, had meticulously planned a **nationwide armed rebellion** to begin at **11:30 p.m. on 5 April 1971**. Their strategy hinged on **simultaneous attacks** on police stations across the island, aiming to overwhelm the state's security apparatus and seize weapons.

To communicate the exact date and time of the uprising to its decentralized cells—many operating in remote rural areas—the JVP devised a **coded message system**. One of the most ingenious methods involved placing a **paid obituary notice** on **Radio Ceylon**, the state-owned broadcaster.

The Obituary Code: A Cryptic Signal

The JVP's leadership inserted a **seemingly innocent obituary announcement** into Radio Ceylon's daily broadcast. The message was **coded**, containing **pre-arranged phrases and timing cues** that signaled the go-ahead for the insurrection.

However, the **cadres at Wellawaya misinterpreted the message**, believing the attack was to begin **on the night of 4 April**, not 5 April. Acting prematurely, they **stormed the Wellawaya Police Station**, killing several officers and seizing weapons.

The Fallout: Alerting the Entire Nation

This **early attack** had unintended consequences:

- It **alerted the government** and **police stations islandwide** to the impending rebellion.
- Security forces were placed on **high alert**, and emergency protocols were activated.
- The element of **surprise**, crucial to the JVP's strategy, was lost.

As a result, many police stations were able to **fortify their defenses**, and the government began **mobilizing the military** even before the full-scale insurrection began on 5 April.

Historical Significance

This mix-up is now considered one of the **most consequential miscommunications** in Sri Lanka's modern history. A single **radio obituary**, meant to be a covert signal, inadvertently **derailed a revolution** and allowed the government to **pre-emptively respond**, ultimately crushing the uprising within weeks.

Reconstructed Obituary Broadcast — Radio Ceylon, April 1971

"We regret to announce the passing of Mr. N.M. Perera, beloved leader and father of the oppressed masses. His funeral will be held on Monday at 11:30 p.m., at the residence of Mr. D.S. Senanayake in Welikanda. Friends and comrades are kindly requested to gather without delay. May his revolutionary spirit live forever. Jai Janatha!"

Decoding the Message

Though it may sound like a sincere death notice, the broadcast was in fact **coded language**—designed to instruct JVP operatives to **launch the uprising at 11:30 p.m. on Monday, 5 April**:

- **"N.M. Perera"** was a reference to the death of bourgeois leftism, symbolizing the **rise of militant revolution**
- **"Monday at 11:30 p.m."** was the **exact time for coordinated attacks**
- **"D.S. Senanayake in Welikanda"** was likely a symbolic or deliberately incorrect location intended to mask true logistics
- **"Jai Janatha!"** ("Victory to the People") was a known revolutionary slogan used by the JVP

This cryptic broadcast was meant to **unify timing across the island**, where rebel cells lacked direct communication channels.

The Misfire in Wellawaya

Unfortunately for the JVP, rebels in **Wellawaya misread the message** and launched their attack **a full day early**, on the night of **4 April 1971**, killing five policemen and stealing weapons. This premature strike **alerted police stations nationwide**, allowing authorities to fortify defenses and **pre-emptively respond to the broader insurrection**.

Had the obituary been understood correctly, the coordinated assault on **more than 74 police stations** might have been far more devastating.

Historical Footnote

The use of **Radio Ceylon**—then the most powerful radio station in South Asia—for covert messaging highlights the **audacity and ingenuity** of the JVP. But it also underscores the **fragility of underground operations**, where a single misstep can collapse an entire movement.

The fake obituary is now etched into the annals of Sri Lankan political folklore—a moment when coded language, broadcast live to a nation, inadvertently **set fire to a revolution before its matchstick was ready**.

The Strategy and Spread

The JVP's plan was based on **"scattered and instantaneous struggle"**, inspired by revolutionary models like the **Zanzibar Revolution**. Cadres—mostly **rural Sinhala youth aged 16–25**—were trained in secret camps and indoctrinated through the **Five Lectures**, which emphasized anti-imperialism, economic crisis, and the failure of traditional leftist parties.

Key districts under temporary rebel control included:

- **Matara**, **Ambalangoda**, and parts of **Deniyaya**
- **Sabaragamuwa Province** and **Southern Province**
- Remote jungle areas in **Kurunegala**, **Anuradhapura**, and **Tissamaharama**

The rebels used **homemade bombs**, **shotguns**, and **Molotov cocktails**, and blocked roads with felled trees. Despite their fervor, they lacked military discipline and adequate firepower.

Government Response and Suppression

(Above: Suspected JVP members at a Detention Camp)

Prime Minister **Sirimavo Bandaranaike**, leading the **United Front coalition**, declared a **state of emergency on 16 March**, anticipating unrest after Wijeweera's arrest. Following the 5 April attacks, the government launched a **massive counter-offensive**:

- **Army and police** units were deployed nationwide
- **India**, **Pakistan**, and the **Soviet Union** provided military assistance
- **North Korean supply vessels** were intercepted, allegedly carrying arms for the JVP

The insurrection was **largely quelled within three weeks**, though mop-up operations continued until **June 1971**. The government regained control of all rebel-held areas, and **thousands of youth were arrested**.

In the chaotic aftermath of the **1971 JVP insurrection**, Sri Lanka entered a period of intense surveillance, suspicion, and sweeping arrests. Thousands of young people—many barely out of school—were detained, often on the flimsiest of grounds. Simply attending one or two of the JVP's infamous "Five Classes" or being seen near a suspected training camp was enough to be branded a threat. Students were rounded up en masse and transported to hastily established detention centers scattered across the island—from repurposed farms to military barracks, and even remote jungle camps. These makeshift facilities became holding pens for a generation caught between ideology and innocence.

For parents, it was a time of unbearable anxiety. Rumors swirled about torture, disappearances, and secret executions. Some families spent weeks traveling from camp to camp, clutching photographs and pleading with guards for news of their children. Others, especially from affluent backgrounds, acted swiftly—sending their sons and daughters abroad to escape the tightening grip of the state. Universities in India, the UK, and the Soviet bloc saw a sudden influx of Sri Lankan students, many of whom would never return.

A relative of the author managed to send his two sons to a European country, leveraging personal connections and diplomatic channels. In a stroke of fortune and strategy, the young men escaped the turmoil that had enveloped their homeland. They went on to complete their education abroad, assimilate into their new environment, and eventually gain citizenship—building new lives far removed from the fear and repression that gripped Sri Lanka.

Such stories of exodus were not uncommon. For many affluent families, exile was the only safeguard against arbitrary arrest or worse. The decision to send children overseas was often made in haste, fueled by whispers of mass detentions and disappearances. Yet for those who succeeded, it was a lifeline—a path that led not only to survival, but to flourishing in foreign lands.

But these escapes also left scars. The children who stayed behind, whose families lacked connections or financial power, were often thrust into a brutal reality. For every student who boarded a plane to safety, countless others were left behind, navigating a world where one's political affiliations—or mere perceptions of them—could decide one's fate.

The legacy of 1971 is etched in stories like this—of survival, separation, and silent sorrow. And for those who found refuge elsewhere, Sri Lanka remained in the rearview mirror: distant, complicated, and forever part of their origin story.

Meanwhile, the insurrection had galvanized a wave of civilian involvement in national defense. Teachers, clerks, and retired servicemen volunteered for duty, some even rising to command local security divisions. The lines between military and civilian blurred as fear and patriotism fused into a collective response to the perceived threat.

The arrests continued for months. Some detainees were eventually released after interrogation; others were quietly transferred to long-term detention. And then there were those who simply vanished. No trial, no record, no goodbye. Their names faded from official memory, but not from the hearts of those who waited in vain. The insurrection may have lasted only weeks, but its shadow lingered for years—etched into the lives of families, communities, and a nation still reckoning with the cost of rebellion.

Death Tolls and Human Cost

The insurrection's human toll remains contested:

SOURCE	ESTIMATED DEATHS
Official Government	1,200 – 12,000
Neutral Estimates	15,000–20,000+
Activist Claims	Up to 50,000
Police Casualties	37 killed, 195 wounded
Military Casualties	26 killed, 310 wounded

Many deaths occurred in **remote jungles**, where **suspected rebels were executed without trial**. The **mass arrests**—over **16,000 detain detainees**—included students, farmers, and even schoolchildren.

Fate of Politicians and Legal Aftermath

Sirimavo Bandaranaike remained in power and oversaw the drafting of the **1972 Republican Constitution**, which declared Sri Lanka a **sovereign republic** and gave Buddhism the "foremost place".

Felix Dias Bandaranaike, Minister of Public Administration, led the crackdown and was instrumental in forming **Criminal Justice Commissions (CJCs)** to try insurgents

JVP Leadership

- **Rohana Wijeweera** was arrested before the insurrection but later tried under the **CJC Act** and sentenced to **imprisonment**
- Other leaders like **Victor Ivan**, **Sanath**, and **Loku Athula** were also captured and tried
- Trials began in **June 1972** and concluded in **December 1974**, with mixed verdicts: some were imprisoned, others received suspended sentences or were acquitted

Opposition Politicians

J.R. Jayewardene, leader of the **UNP**, criticized the government's handling but gained *political capital*, eventually becoming **President in 1978**

Leftist allies like the **LSSP** and **Communist Pa ⬚ arty** supported the crackdown, despite ideological discomfort

The 1971 insurrection was a **turning point** in Sri Lanka's political history:

- It **shattered the myth of rural passivity**
- Introduced a **culture of organized political violence**
- Inspired future insurgencies, including the **LTTE's separatist movement**
- Led to **standardization in university admissions**, which alienated Tamil youth and fueled ethnic tensions

The JVP itself re-emerged in the **late 1970s** as a legal political party, only to launch a **second, more brutal insurrection in 1987–1989**.

25

North Korea and 1971 JVP Insurrection: A Diplomatic Intrusion

Background: A Leftward Tilt in Foreign Policy

In **July 1970**, shortly after the **United Front government** came to power under **Prime Minister Sirimavo Bandaranaike**, Sri Lanka established diplomatic relations with **North Korea (DPRK)**. The embassy in Colombo was opened as part of a broader foreign policy shift toward **non-alignment and socialist solidarity**, which also included ties with **East Germany** and **China**.

However, within months, suspicions began to mount that the **North Korean mission** was engaged in **subversive activities**, particularly in support of the **Janatha Vimukthi Peramuna (JVP)**—a radical Marxist youth movement preparing for armed rebellion.

In the months leading up to the **April 1971 JVP insurrection**, Sri Lanka's newspapers—particularly the *Times of Ceylon*—began publishing unusually large articles featuring **North Korea** and its then-supreme leader, **Kim Il Sung**. These pieces were often accompanied by striking black-and-white photographs and dense blocks of text extolling revolutionary ideals, self-reliance, and anti-imperialist struggle. At the time, many readers—including me were puzzled by the sudden flood of foreign propaganda in local media. The articles seemed disconnected from Sri Lanka's immediate concerns, and few had the time or inclination to wade through their ideological fervor.

Only after the insurrection erupted did the puzzle pieces begin to fall into place. The **Janatha Vimukthi Peramuna (JVP)**, a radical leftist youth movement, had launched a coordinated armed uprising against the government. In the aftermath, the Sri Lankan authorities uncovered disturbing signs of **foreign ideological influence**, and suspicion quickly turned toward **North Korea**. Though no direct evidence of arms or training was publicly confirmed, the government cited the **overzealous propaganda activities** of the North Korean embassy—including the distribution of revolutionary literature and guerrilla warfare manuals—as justification for **expelling the entire diplomatic mission** in April 1971.

The full-page articles I saw were part of a broader campaign by the **Ceylon–North Korea Friendship Societies**, which had been actively promoting Kim Il Sung's revolutionary philosophy. These materials were later found in **JVP hideouts**, further fueling suspicions of ideological collusion. Prime Minister **Sirimavo Bandaranaike** herself hinted at foreign embassies aiding "terrorists" in a radio address, though she stopped short of naming North Korea directly.

In hindsight, those unread articles weren't just filler—they were ideological breadcrumbs leading to one of the most dramatic diplomatic ruptures in Sri Lanka's history.

The North Korean Embassy was accused of:

- **Distributing revolutionary literature** through local "Ceylon–North Korea Friendship Societies"
- Promoting **Juche ideology** (North Korea's self-reliance doctrine), which was found in JVP hideouts and training camps
- Running **propaganda articles** in local newspapers glorifying **Kim Il-sung** and guerrilla warfare
- Allegedly **funding JVP cells** by exchanging foreign currency on the black market

Though **no direct evidence of arms transfers** was confirmed, the **Sri Lankan government** believed the embassy was **ideologically and logistically supporting the insurgents**.

The Expulsion: April 1971

On **April 17, 1971**, just days after the JVP launched its insurrection, the government issued a dramatic statement:

"The Government has decided in its own interest that all Korean staff and their families in the Embassy of the Democratic People's Republic of Korea in Ceylon should leave immediately."

This marked the **expulsion of the entire North Korean diplomatic mission**, though formal diplomatic ties were not severed. The move was unprecedented and signaled the government's belief that **foreign ideological interference** had played a role in the uprising.

Evidence and Controversy

While the **Criminal Justice Commission** trials of JVP leaders did not produce conclusive evidence of North Korean involvement, several indicators persisted:

- **18 North Koreans** affiliated with the JVP were reportedly **arrested on May 15, 1971**
- **North Korean supply vessels** were intercepted by the **Sri Lankan and Indian navies**, allegedly carrying materials for the rebels

    Prime Minister Bandaranaike hinted in a **radio address on April 25, 1971,** that one embassy had "given strength and support to the terrorists," without naming North Korea directly

Aftermath and Legacy

- The embassy closure did **not end diplomatic relations**, but **North Korea's presence in Sri Lanka remained dormant** for years.
- The incident became a **case study in Cold War diplomacy**, illustrating how **ideological alliances** could backfire.

Influence of Juche Ideology on the JVP

Juche, meaning "self-reliance," is the political and philosophical doctrine developed by **Kim Il-sung** in North Korea. It emphasizes national independence, centralized leadership, anti-imperialism, and revolutionary struggle.

How Juche Echoed in the JVP's Ideology:

- **Leadership Cult**: Rohana Wijeweera was revered much like a revolutionary icon, mirroring the personalized ideology around Kim Il-sung.
- **Anti-Imperialist Rhetoric**: The JVP denounced foreign influence, capitalism, and colonial legacies, akin to Juche principles.
- **Guerrilla Discipline**: The movement adopted decentralized cells, strict ideological training, and loyalty culture drawn from Asian revolutionary models.
- **Self-Sufficiency Doctrine**: The JVP rejected foreign political support and sought to create a "homegrown revolution."

Pamphlets glorifying Kim Il-sung and North Korea's revolutionary struggle were reportedly found in JVP hideouts, underscoring the ideological connection.

JVP Ideology

Rohana Wijeweera's **real intention** was to ignite a revolutionary transformation in Sri Lanka by dismantling what he saw as a corrupt, neo-colonial state and replacing it with a **Socialist Republic** led by the working class and rural youth. His vision was deeply rooted in **Marxist–Leninist ideology**, but he adapted it to Sri Lanka's unique conditions.

A Closer look:

Wijeweera believed that Sri Lanka's independence was a façade, with power still concentrated among elite families and capitalist interests.

He saw traditional leftist parties as compromised and ineffective, especially after they joined coalition governments.

His goal was to **empower disenfranchised youth**, particularly from rural and lower-caste backgrounds, through revolutionary education and armed struggle.

Strategic Vision

As early as **1965**, Wijeweera was already planning for an armed rebellion. He even selected remote farm locations with smuggling potential for weapons.

He rejected Maoist and Cuban revolutionary models, arguing they didn't suit Sri Lanka's geography or political climate.

Instead, he developed the **"Scattered and Instantaneous Struggle"** strategy—an all-at-once nationwide attack ⬜ police stations to paralyze the state.

Political Education as a Weapon

He created the **Five Classes**, a series of lectures that indoctrinated youth in revolutionary theory and justified armed insurrection.

These classes were not just ideological—they were tactical, laying out the rationale for violent revolution and the rejection of parliamentary politics.

Execution vs. Intention

While his intention was to spark a swift revolution, the 1971 uprising was poorly coordinated and under-resourced. Despite its failure, it revealed deep social fractures and positioned the JVP as a persistent force in Sri Lankan politics.

Wijeweera's ultimate aim wasn't just regime change—it was a **complete societal overhaul**, replacing elite dominance with grassroots socialist governance.

Timeline & Foreign Involvement in the 1971 JVP Insurrection

DATE	COUNTRY	ROLE/ALLEGED INVOLVEMENT
July 1970	North Korea	Embassy opened in Colombo as part of SLFP's leftist diplomatic outreach.
Early 1971	North Korea	Accused of spreading pro-Juche literature; suspected of ideological support to JVP.
March 1971	India	Provided military assistance and logistic support to Colombo after early signs of uprising.
April 5, 1971	JVP	Launched armed rebellion; attacked 74+ police stations.
April 17, 1971	Sri Lankan Govt.	Expelled North Korean diplomats for alleged links to JVP
Mid-April 1971	Pakistan, USSR, India	Sent troops, arms, and technical support to suppress rebellion.
May 15, 1971	Sri Lankan Police	Allegedly arrested 18 North Koreans linked to underground operations.
June 1971	Regional Intelligence	Began monitoring revolutionary activity and cut certain diplomatic channels.

Reflection

The JVP's insurgency wasn't only a Sri Lankan phenomenon—it was shaped by **global revolutionary currents**, particularly East Asian models. While **no definitive proof of material aid from North Korea** emerged, their embassy's ideological role was enough to trigger diplomatic fallout and symbolic rupture.

Revolutionary Image

- The JVP, under **Rohana Wijeweera**, adopted a **guerrilla-style revolutionary framework**, much like Che Guevara's campaigns in Cuba and Bolivia.
- Wijeweera's charisma, underground organizing, and emphasis on **armed struggle against capitalist and imperialist structures** drew comparisons to Guevara's tactics.

Youth Mobilization

- The JVP was composed largely of **rural Sinhala youth**, many of whom were unemployed or disillusioned with traditional leftist parties.
- Their **militant training camps**, ideological lectures, and rejection of parliamentary politics mirrored Guevara's emphasis on **direct action and revolutionary consciousness**.

Government Labeling

- The **Sri Lankan government and media** began referring to the JVP as the "**Che Guevara clique**" or "**Che Guevara movement**" during the **1970–71 crackdown**, especially after Wijeweera's arrest in **May 1970**.
- This label was not officially adopted by the JVP but became a **popular shorthand** for their radical leftist identity.

Cultural and Political Symbolism

- **Che Guevara's image**—beret, beard, and rifle—became a global symbol of rebellion. The JVP's **anti-imperialist rhetoric**, **rejection of Soviet revisionism**, and **grassroots mobilization** resonated with this iconography.
- The movement's **Five Lectures**, which served as ideological training manuals, emphasized **self-reliance, anti-capitalism, and revolutionary discipline**, all hallmarks of Guevara's philosophy.

While the "Che Guevara movement" label was initially used to **discredit and exoticize** the JVP, it inadvertently **amplified their appeal** among radical youth. It also placed the JVP within a **global context of 1960s–70s revolutionary movements**, from Latin America to Southeast Asia.

Today, the nickname remains a **historical footnote**, reflecting the **romanticized and feared image** of the JVP's early years.

26

The 1971 American Embassy Attack: A Forgotten Chapter of the JVP Insurrection

While most of the JVP's attacks focused on **police stations and military posts**, one unusual and controversial incident occurred in **Colombo**: an **attack on the American Embassy**.

Why Target the U.S. Embassy?

The JVP viewed **American imperialism** as a threat to Sri Lanka's independence and socialist future. The U.S. was seen as a supporter of capitalist governments and a symbol of foreign influence. Although the **main JVP leadership did not officially sanction the attack**, a **splinter group**—possibly acting on its own radical interpretation of anti-imperialist ideology—targeted the embassy to make a political statement.

The Attack and Its Aftermath

- The attack was **not large-scale**, but it caused alarm.
- The **U.S. government quickly clarified** that it did not believe the **main JVP** was behind the incident.
- The Sri Lankan government, already under pressure from the insurrection, **tightened security** around diplomatic missions.
- The incident added to the **international concern** about the uprising, prompting **military aid** from countries like **India, Pakistan, and the Soviet Union**.

The Splinter Group

While the JVP was a tightly organized movement, it had **internal divisions**. Some members broke away due to ideological differences or frustration with leadership. These

splinter groups sometimes acted independently, and the embassy attack is believed to be one such case.

- The **main JVP leadership distanced itself** from the attack.
- The group responsible may have included **radical youth** who wanted to escalate the revolution beyond local targets.

The attack on the American Embassy in Colombo is a **lesser-known episode** of the 1971 insurrection, but it reflects the **volatile mix of ideology, youth rebellion, and anti-imperialist sentiment** that defined the era. It also shows how **splinter actions** can complicate a movement's image and strategy.

Dharmasekera Group

The **Dharmasekera Group** played a controversial and disruptive role in the political landscape surrounding the **1971 JVP insurrection** in Sri Lanka. Here's a simplified breakdown of their origins, actions, and impact:

Origins and Split from the JVP

- The group was led by **G.I.D. "Castro" Dharmasekera**, a former student leader at Vidyalankara University.
- Initially part of the **Janatha Vimukthi Peramuna (JVP)**, Dharmasekera and his followers were **expelled in 1969** due to ideological differences and internal disputes.
- After the split, they formed **two new organizations**:

- **Maoist Youth Front (Maovadee Tharuna Peramuna)**
- **Front to Protect the Motherland (Mathrubhumee Arakshaka Sangamaya)**

Role in the 1971 Insurrection

- The Dharmasekera Group became **hostile toward the JVP** and allegedly **collaborated with the government** to expose and suppress the movement.
- They were accused of **provoking conflict** and creating conditions that allowed the **United Front (UF) government** to crack down on the JVP.
- On **March 6, 1971**, during a protest outside the **American Embassy in Colombo**, a **police officer was killed**. The demonstration was organized by the Dharmasekera Group—not the JVP—but the government used the incident to declare a **State of Emergency** and begin mass arrests.

Alleged Collaboration with Authorities

- Dharmasekera reportedly **informed Minister J.R. Jayewardene** about the JVP's activities before the 1970 elections, triggering media attention and police investigations.
- This led to the formation of a **special CID unit** and the branding of JVP members as "Che Guevarists".

Legacy and Controversy

- The Dharmasekera Group is remembered as a **splinter faction** that played a **counter-revolutionary role** during a critical moment in Sri Lanka's history.
- Their actions are seen by some as having **undermined the JVP's uprising**, while others view them as **ideologically purist Maoists** who rejected the JVP's direction.
- Their actions are seen by some as having **undermined the JVP's uprising**, while others view them as **ideologically purist Maoists** who rejected the JVP's direction.

27

Closure of the Israeli Embassy in Colombo (1972) and the Backlash

Sri Lanka had established diplomatic ties with Israel in **1949**, and by the 1960s, Israel was providing **technical assistance** in agriculture and water management. However, the **foreign policy of Prime Minister Sirimavo Bandaranaike** shifted dramatically in the early 1970s.

Reasons for Closure

- **Non-Aligned Movement (NAM)**: Sri Lanka, under Bandaranaike, aligned strongly with NAM principles, which leaned toward **supporting the Palestinian cause**.
- **Pressure from Arab Nations**: Several **PLO representatives visited Colombo**, urging the government to sever ties with Israel.
- **Domestic Muslim Sentiment**: Sri Lanka's **Muslim minority**, politically influential and sympathetic to Palestine, opposed Israeli presence.
- **Condemnation by Israeli Envoy**: In 1972, Israeli Ambassador **Yitzhak Navon** criticized Sri Lanka's engagement with Arab groups. Within two months, Bandaranaike **closed the Israeli Embassy**, citing Israel's violation of **UN Resolution 242**.

Aftermath

- Sri Lanka strengthened ties with the **Palestinian Liberation Organization (PLO)**.
- The closure was praised by **Arab leaders** as a bold pro-Palestinian gesture.

Israel's diplomatic presence remained dormant until **reopening in 1984** under J.R. Jayewardene.

The Food Crisis (1972–1975)

The perception that Sri Lanka's **Food Crisis (1972–1975)** was directly caused by antagonizing the United States—particularly through the closure of the Israeli Embassy—is a compelling narrative, but it oversimplifies a complex web of geopolitical, economic, and environmental factors. Let's unpack this idea and explore the broader context:

Geopolitical Tensions and Diplomatic Fallout

In **1970**, Prime Minister **Sirimavo Bandaranaike** led a **leftist coalition** that pursued **non-alignment** but leaned toward **socialist and anti-imperialist policies**.

In **1971–72**, her government **closed the Israeli Embassy** and aligned more closely with the **Palestine Liberation Organization (PLO)**.

This move was seen as part of a broader **anti-Western posture**, which included nationalizing industries and distancing from Western allies like the **USA** and **Israel**.

While the U.S. did not officially impose sanctions, **Sri Lanka's access to Western aid and trade** may have been informally restricted or deprioritized.

Economic Vulnerabilities and Agricultural Decline

Sri Lanka was heavily dependent on **food imports**, especially **rice and wheat**, much of which came from the **United States** under **PL-480 aid programs**.

The **termination or reduction** of such aid—whether due to diplomatic tensions or shifting U.S. priorities—exacerbated food shortages.

The government's push for **self-sufficiency** in agriculture was **poorly planned**, with inadequate investment in irrigation, fertilizer, and rural infrastructure.

Global Food Crisis and Climate Shocks

The **1972–75 global food crisis** was triggered by a **severe drought**, a **strong El Niño**, and **Western agricultural policies** that reduced grain production to drive up prices.

Countries like Sri Lanka, already vulnerable, were hit hard by **rising global grain prices** and **limited foreign exchange reserves**.

The **UN's response** was slow and focused on long-term solutions rather than emergency relief, leaving many nations to fend for themselves.

Foreign Exchange and Debt Pressures

Sri Lanka's **foreign debt** and **trade deficits** worsened during this period, limiting its ability to import food and fuel.

The government's ideological stance made it reluctant to seek help from institutions like the **IMF** or **World Bank**, which were viewed as tools of Western imperialism.

A Confluence of Factors

While the **closure of the Israeli Embassy** and **antagonism toward the U.S.** may have contributed to diplomatic isolation, the **food crisis was not solely a political backlash**. It was the result of:

- Poor domestic planning
- Global climate and market disruptions
- Ideological rigidity in foreign policy
- Structural economic weaknesses

Food Which Saved Mass Sri Lanka from Mass Starvation.

Government Response

- **Rationing**: Rice rations were cut from **2 lbs to 1 lb per person per week**.
- **Subsidy Reductions**: Food subsidies were slashed, triggering **public unrest**.
- **Import Controls**: Severe restrictions on food imports led to **black markets** and hoarding.

Social Impact

Malnutrition rose, especially among children and rural communities.
Urban protests and **student agitation** intensified.
The crisis eroded public confidence in the **United Front government**, setting the stage for political change.

J.R. Jayewardene's Political Exploitation of the Crisis

As **Leader of the Opposition**, J.R. Jayewardene capitalized on the government's failures:

- **Criticized rationing and inflation**, positioning the UNP as a pro-market alternative.
- Promoted **economic liberalization**, contrasting with the SLFP's socialist policies.
- Advocated for **foreign investment**, including ties with Israel and the West.

Political Maneuvering

- **Mass Mobilization**: The UNP organized **civil disobedience campaigns** and **Satyagrahas** demanding early elections.

- **Media Use**: Leveraged: Leveraged newspapers and radio to highlight government mismanagement.

- **International Outreach**: Engaged with Western diplomats and **Israeli contacts** to prepare for future alliances.

Outcome

- By **1977**, Jayewardene led the UNP to a **landslide victory**, securing **141 out of 168 seats**.
- He became **Sri Lanka's first Executive President in 1978**, ushering in a new era of **economic liberalization** and **foreign policy realignment**, including **restoring ties with Israel**.

Between 1972 and 1975, Sri Lanka faced:

- **Diplomatic realignment**, severing ties with Israel under NAM pressure.
- A **crippling food crisis**, exposing the fragility of socialist economic planning.
- The **rise of J.R. Jayewardene**, who used the crisis to reshape the country's political and economic future.

Of Breadlines and "Bathalawathis": Surviving the Sri Lankan Food Crisis 1972-75

*In the early 1970s, my family—like most others across the island—found itself playing a daily game of survival bingo. The prize? A few cups of rice or a loaf of bread. Essential food items had become mythical creatures: talked about, rarely seen. Wheat flour had virtually disappeared from shelves, and getting hold of bread required the patience of a monk and the stamina of a marathon runner. **People queued outside bakeries before sunrise, armed with ration cards and a desperation.***

Hotels slashed their menus and guest lists alike; lavish banquets became budget buffets, with celebrations forcibly downsized to a hundred guests—assuming those guests were okay with tapioca curry and Kurakkan Rotti. The government imposed strict limits on transporting rice: individuals could carry only a few kilos unless they were smuggling it in their socks. Citizens were urged to convert their backyards into emergency farms growing cassava, sweet potato, and Bathala—a root vegetable whose popularity skyrocketed as rice faded into folklore.

But the real victims of this gastronomic downfall were the **plantation workers.** *Their lives revolved around hard labor and heavy meals. With rice and flour missing in action, they turned to wild yams like culinary Indiana Joneses and unpurified Atta Flour. I personally saw mothers mixing flour with water to feed their children as a poor man's milk substitute—a breakfast that tasted of compromise and irony.* **The roadsides became public health warnings, with diarrhoea and dysentery setting up permanent residence.**

One of the most harrowing consequences of that period was the deepening poverty among already destitute plantation workers, whose hardships compounded day by day. In a desperate bid to feed their families, they were forced to part with their few remaining valuables. Gold jewelry—often kept as heirlooms or savings—was the first to go, sold or pawned for meager sums. And as their situation worsened, they turned to the only other possessions of worth they had left: silver and brass household utensils. I remember witnessing firsthand the grim scenes in towns across plantation regions—pawn shops overflowing with these metal wares, each one representing a story of sacrifice. These items, second only to gold in value within their homes, were surrendered for just a few rupees— barely enough to buy a day's worth of food. The sheer volume of such exchanges was a haunting testament to their suffering

And then came the politics.

At one memorable "Political Exploitation Meeting," UNP supporters greeted J.R. Jayewardene not with garlands of jasmine, but **with a necklace of bread loaves strung on a rope**—*like some rebel version of a bakery festival.*

JRJ, never one to miss a theatrical beat, promised he would import all that surplus Western wheat allegedly tossed into the ocean—flour so abundant it apparently had its own passport.
Meanwhile, opposition leaders served up satire with side dishes of sass. The Prime Minister, **Mrs. Sirimavo Bandaranaike,** *was lovingly nicknamed* **"Mrs. Bathalawathi"—Lady Tapioca**—*because in those days, she might as well have been the national crop ambassador.*

A Harvest of Lessons: When Scarcity Sprouted Resilience

If there's one unexpected virtue that bloomed during the grim food crisis of the early 1970s, it was the rediscovery of **home gardening.** *Faced with ration lines and missing meals, families turned desperation into innovation.*

Every inch of usable soil—be it a backyard patch, roadside verge, or crevice between water channels—was claimed for cultivation. **Bathala (sweet potato)** *and* **Manioc** *became survival staples, transforming idle land into green lifelines.*

Paddy farmers, once reliant on state subsidies and market cycles, suddenly became frontline providers—not just for commerce, but for their own kin. Driven by urgency and pride, they **amplified their yields,** *adopting seasonal rhythms with newfound purpose.*

Yet, as scarcity waned and politics waxed, the spirit of agrarian self-sufficiency quietly wilted. **Subsequent governments**, *eager to placate voters, threw open the gates to* **cheap imports**—*rice, flour, lentils—everything that had once been a reason to cultivate now became a reason to stop. Markets overflowed; gardens emptied. The culture of growing to eat slipped beneath layers of convenience and policy.*

Ironically, what began as a **grassroots revolution born of crisis** *ended as a* **forgotten footnote** *in Sri Lanka's economic story—a reminder that sometimes, the seeds of resilience are most fertile when planted by necessity.*

28

Land Reforms in Sri Lanka: A Turning Point for Plantations

In 1972, the government of Sri Lanka made an important decision to change how land was owned and used. This decision came in the form of **Land Reform Law No. 1**, which tried to make land distribution more fair. At the time, a small number of rich individuals and companies controlled large areas of farmland and tea estates, while many people, including workers, had no land of their own.

Goals of the Law

The government wanted to:

- Stop people from owning too much land.
- Give extra land to the **Land Reform Commission (LRC)**, a new government organization.
- Help poor farmers get land to grow food.
- Reduce inequality between rich landowners and poor workers.

Under the law:

- A person could own **only up to 25 acres of rice land** or **50 acres of other farmland**.
- Any land beyond that was taken by the government and managed by the LRC.

Effects on Plantation Lands

Many of Sri Lanka's biggest tea, rubber, and coconut estates were affected by this new law. These plantations we e often owned by companies, including foreign businesses, and covered hundreds of acres. After the law passed:

- A large portion of estate land was **taken over by the government**.
- In **1975**, another law made it possible to take land from **public companies** too.

To manage this land, the government set up two state agencies:

- **Janatha Estates Development Board (JEDB)**
- **Sri Lanka State Plantation Corporation (SLSPC)**

These agencies were supposed to run the plantations, take care of the land, and help workers have better lives.

Challenges and Consequences

Even though the idea was good, many problems happened:

- The estates became **less efficient** because large plantations were split up.
- There were **fewer profits** from tea exports, which hurt the country's economy.
- The new government agencies didn't always manage the land well.
- Plantation workers hoped for better conditions, but many still lived in poverty and faced job uncertainty.

Long-Term Impact

Over time, people saw both good and bad sides to the land reforms:

- The rich landowners lost land, but sometimes they **weren't paid fairly** for it.
- Poor farmers and some plantation workers got access to land, but **not always enough to change their lives**.
- Political issues and lack of expert knowledge made it hard to reach the law's goals.

The **Land Reform Law of 1972** was a bold effort to change a system that had favored wealthy landowners for generations. While it helped raise awareness of inequality and brought some changes, many of its promises were not fully kept—especially for the workers who had hoped it would transform their lives.

The key architect behind Sri Lanka's Land Reform Law No. 1 of 1972 was **Hector Kobbekaduwa,** who served as the **Minister of Agriculture and Lands** under Prime Minister Sirimavo Bandaranaike's government. Kobbekaduwa was a strong advocate for socialist policies and played a central role in designing and implementing the land reform program.

His vision was to reduce inequality in land ownership, empower rural farmers, and dismantle the dominance of large estate owners—many of whom were foreign or corporate entities. The reforms he championed led to the creation of the **Land Reform Commission**, which oversaw the acquisition and redistribution of land.

29

Land Reform 2 in Sri Lanka: Extending the Revolution

After the first land reform law in 1972, which limited how much land individuals could own, the Sri Lankan government realized that more action was needed. Many large estates were still owned by **public companies**, especially in the plantation sector. So, in **1975**, the government passed a second law—**Land Reform (Amendment) Law No. 39**—to continue the transformation of land ownership.

Purpose of Land Reform 2

The second phase of land reform aimed to:

- **Take over estate lands** owned by **public companies**, not just individuals.
- **Strengthen government control** over plantation lands.
- **Improve productivity** and **worker welfare** through state management.
- Continue the goal of **reducing inequality** in land ownership.

This law was a bold step toward nationalizing the plantation economy, which had long been dominated by corporate and foreign interests.

What Changed in Land Reform 2

Legal Expansion

- The 1975 law **expanded the powers** of the **Land Reform Commission (LRC)**.
- It allowed the government to **vest lands owned by public companies**, including **agency houses** and **estate management firms**.

  These lands were then managed by **state-run plantation boards**.

Scope of Acquisition

- Over **400,000 acres** of plantation land were taken over.
- This included **tea, rubber, and coconut estates**, many of which were profitable and well-managed before nationalization.

New Management Structures

The government created or expanded agencies like:

- **Janatha Estates Development Board (JEDB)**
- **Sri Lanka State Plantation Corporation (SLSPC)**

- These bodies were responsible for running the estates and improving conditions for workers.

Impact and Challenges

Economic Effects

- **Productivity declined** in many estates due to poor management and lack of investment.
- The **tea industry**, a major source of export income, suffered setbacks.
- Bureaucratic delays and political interference made it hard to run the estates efficiently.

Social Outcomes

- Some workers gained **better housing and services**, but many still faced **low wages** and **job insecurity**.
- The reforms did not fully solve the problems of **poverty** and **marginalization**, especially for **Indian Tamil estate workers**.

Compensation Issues

- Former owners were promised **compensation**, but payments were often delayed or insufficient.
- This led to legal disputes and dissatisfaction among dispossessed companies.

Legacy of Land Reform 2

Land Reform 2 was a major turning point in Sri Lanka's agrarian history. It showed the government's commitment to **socialist ideals** and **economic restructuring** but also revealed the **limits of state control** in complex industries like plantations.

Mixed Results

The reforms **changed ownership**, but not always **out** ⬚ **outcomes**.

- Many estates became **less profitable**, and workers continued to struggle.
- Over time, some of the nationalized lands were **privatized again** or **leased to private companies**.

Land Reform 2 was a bold continuation of Sri Lanka's effort to make land ownership fairer and more productive. While it succeeded in breaking up large corporate holdings, it faced serious challenges in delivering long-term benefits to workers and the economy.

30

A Summit of Sovereignty — Sri Lanka and the 1976 Non-Aligned Movement

(Pic: ft.lk)

Introduction: A Small Island on the Global Stage

In August 1976, Sri Lanka stepped into the spotlight of international diplomacy by hosting the **5th Summit of the Non-Aligned Movement (NAM)** in **Colombo**. For a country still navigating its post-independence identity, this was more than a conference—it was a declaration of relevance, a moment of pride, and a bold assertion of its commitment to global equity. With **86 member nations**, **30 observers**, and **over 60 heads of state or government** in attendance, the summit became the **largest international gathering ever held in Sri Lanka**, transforming Colombo into a hub of geopolitical discourse.

Key Leaders and Delegations

The summit was chaired by **Prime Minister Sirimavo Bandaranaike**, the world's first female head of government, whose leadership gave the event both gravitas and grace. Among the notable attendees:

- **Indira Gandhi** – Prime Minister of India
- **Field Marshal Josip Broz Tito** – President of Yugoslavia
- **Fidel Castro** – President of Cuba
- **Muammar Gaddafi** – President of ⬜ Libya
- **Zulfikar Ali Bhutto** – Prime Minister of Pakistan
- **Archbishop Makarios** – President of Cyprus

These leaders, representing diverse ideologies and continents, converged in Colombo to reaffirm their commitment to **non-alignment**, **sovereignty**, and **economic justice**.

Core Themes and Outcomes

The summit focused on reshaping global power dynamics and advocating for a **New International Economic Order (NIEO)**. Key resolutions included:

- **Economic Sovereignty**: A call for restructuring global trade and monetary systems to favor developing nations

  Disarmament: Condemnation of the arms race and ⬚ push for nuclear and conventional weapons bans

- **Anti-Colonialism and Anti-Imperialism**: Strong support for liberation movements in Palestine, Panama, and Africa

- **Zionism as Racism**: A controversial resolution defining Zionism as a form of racism, echoing sentiments from previous NAM summits
- **Solidarity and Collective Action**: Reinforcement of mutual assistance among member states against external pressures

The summit also formalized the structure of the **NAM Coordination Bureau**, establishing a 25-member body to meet regularly at the UN Headquarters in New York.

Sri Lanka's Diplomatic Triumph

Hosting the summit was a **diplomatic masterstroke** for Sri Lanka. The **Bandaranaike Memorial International Conference Hall (BMICH)**, purpose-built for the event, became a symbol of national pride. The government declared public holidays, issued commemorative coins and stamps, and welcomed foreign dignitaries with elaborate ceremonies. The summit flats built to house delegates still stand as architectural reminders of this historic moment.

Prime Minister Bandaranaike's role was pivotal—not only in organizing the event but in steering discussions toward **moderation**, **economic reform**, and **peaceful coexistence**, resisting more radical proposals from newer member states.

- The 1976 Colombo Summit marked a **high point in Sri Lanka's foreign policy**. It showcased the country's ability to convene global leaders, influence international discourse, and advocate for the rights of the Global South. Though the momentum of NAM would later wane amid shifting geopolitical tides, the summit remains a testament to Sri Lanka's commitment to **sovereignty**, **solidarity**, and **global justice**.

From Diplomacy to Opportunity — Arab Delegates and Sri Lanka's Labour Migration Boom

Arab Engagement at the 1976 Non-Aligned Summit

The **5th Non-Aligned Movement (NAM) Summit**, held in **Colombo from August 16–19, 1976**, was a landmark event in Sri Lanka's diplomatic history. Among the 86 participating nations were **key Arab states**, including **Egypt**, **Libya**, **Saudi Arabia**, and **Kuwait**, represented by influential leaders such as **Anwar Sadat** and **Muammar Gaddafi**. Their presence signaled not only solidarity with the Global South but also a growing interest in **economic cooperation and labour exchange** with developing nations like Sri Lanka.

Prime Minister **Sirimavo Bandaranaike**, who chaired the summit, emphasized economic justice and development, aligning Sri Lanka's foreign policy with the aspirations of Arab nations seeking skilled and semi-skilled labour for their booming oil economies.

Opening the Gateway to Arab Job Markets

The summit served as a **catalyst for bilateral discussions** that laid the groundwork for **labour migration agreements**. Arab delegates expressed interest in recruiting workers from Sri Lanka, particularly in sectors such as:

- **Construction and infrastructure**
- **Domestic services**
- **Healthcare and nursing**
- **Hospitality and retail**

These discussions were informal but pivotal. They helped **normalize the idea of Sri Lankan labour migration to the Middle East**, which had previously been limited and unstructured.

UNP Government and the Labour Migration Boom

When the **United National Party (UNP)** returned to power in **1977** under **J.R. Jayewardene**, the groundwork laid during the summit was swiftly capitalized upon. The UNP government:

- **Established formal diplomatic channels** with Arab nations to facilitate worker recruitment
- Created the **Sri Lanka Bureau of Foreign Employment (SLBFE)** to regulate and promote overseas employment
- Encouraged **labour migration as a national economic strategy**, recognizing its potential to generate foreign remittances

By the early 1980s, **thousands of Sri Lankans**—especially women from rural areas— were employed in **Saudi Arabia, Kuwait, UAE, and Qatar**, sending back remittances that **bolstered the national economy** and supported countless families.

Economic Impact and Social Transformation

The Arab job market became a **lifeline for Sri Lanka's working class**, and remittances soon rivaled traditional exports like tea and garments. This migration wave:

- **Reduced unemployment** during a period of economic liberalization
- **Empowered rural households**, especially women
- **Shifted social dynamics**, with migrant families gaining upward mobility

The UNP's ability to harness this opportunity was seen as a **strategic success**, linking foreign policy with domestic economic reform.

A Summit That Changed Lives

The 1976 NAM Summit was more than a diplomatic gathering—it was a **launchpad for Sri Lanka's integration into the global labour economy**. The presence of Arab delegates and the relationships forged during those days in Colombo opened doors that would transform the lives of **millions of Sri Lankans** in the decades to follow.

Colonel Muammar Gaddafi of Libya – The Hero of the Summit

Muammar Gaddafi's rise to near-celebrity status during the **1976 Non-Aligned Movement (NAM) Summit in Colombo** was a fascinating blend of **charisma, political symbolism, and cultural resonance**—especially among Sri Lanka's Muslim community. Here's why he became the "Hero of the Summit":

When Gaddafi stole the show

Charismatic Presence and Media Sensation

Gaddafi arrived in Colombo with **striking looks**, dressed in flowing Bedouin robes and exuding a movie-star aura. He **signed glossy photographs** of himself and handed them out wherever he went, creating a buzz that felt more like a rock concert than a diplomatic summit. His **green eyes, confident demeanor**, and flamboyant style captivated the public, especially women, who flocked to catch a glimpse of him.

Connection with Sri Lanka's Muslim Community

Gaddafi made a point to **visit a mosque in Colombo** and addressed the local Muslim community directly. His pan-Islamic rhetoric and support for Muslim causes resonated deeply, especially during a time when **Muslim identity politics** were gaining traction globally. Many Muslim households displayed his image as a symbol of **solidarity, pride, and admiration** for a leader who stood up to Western powers.

Symbol of Anti-Imperialism and Revolutionary Spirit

As a prominent figure in the **Non-Aligned Movement**, Gaddafi represented resistance to Western hegemony and support for **Third World liberation movements**. He was known for **funding revolutionary groups**, advocating for **Palestinian rights**, and challenging colonial legacies—messages that struck a chord with many Sri Lankans.

His avoidance of Egyptian President Anwar Sadat during the summit, due to political tensions, added to his mystique and rebellious image.

Unforgettable Antics and Maverick Behavior

Gaddafi's **arrival was dramatic**—his advance team of 87 security personnel landed without visas, causing a diplomatic stir.

He **ignored protocol**, skipped ceremonial guards, and demanded midnight meetings with other leaders, including Algeria's Houari Boumédiène.

His entourage distributed **parrots and posters** across Colombo, turning the summit into a surreal spectacle.

The summit was Sri Lanka's **largest international event** at the time, and Gaddafi's flamboyance made him its most memorable guest. For many Sri Lankans—especially Muslims—he embodied **defiance, dignity, and global recognition**.

His popularity was not just political—it was **emotional and symbolic**, offering a sense of pride and representation on the world stage.

31

Stirring the Pot: Land Promises and Plantation Tensions Before the 1977 Elections

In the months leading up to Sri Lanka's **1977 general elections**, political tensions were rising across the country. The ruling **Sri Lanka Freedom Party (SLFP)**, led by **Prime Minister Sirimavo Bandaranaike**, was facing growing criticism over economic hardship, ethnic unrest, and unpopular policies. Amid this backdrop, **Anura Bandaranaike**, the son of Sirimavo and a rising figure in the SLFP, made a bold move that stirred emotions in the **upcountry plantation regions**.

The Promise That Sparked Hope—and Conflict

Anura Bandaranaike, campaigning in the central highlands, made a **public promise to allocate land to the indigenous Sinhalese population** living in and around plantation areas. These lands were part of the **state-owned estates** that had been nationalized during the earlier **land reform programs** of the 1970s. His proposal was framed as a way to empower the **Kandyan Sinhalese**, many of whom had long felt neglected and marginalized in the plantation economy dominated by **Indian Tamil laborers**.

This promise quickly gained attention—and **created confusion and tension**.

Tamil Workers Respond

The **Tamil plantation workers**, many of whom had lived and worked on these estates for generations, saw the promise as a threat to their **livelihoods and housing security**. In response, **some Tamil families began applying for land themselves**, hoping to secure a piece of the estates they had helped cultivate. This unexpected reaction **deepened ethnic tensions** in the region.

- **Sinhalese villagers** felt they were being denied rightful access to ancestral lands.
- **Tamil workers** feared displacement and further marginalization.
- **Estate managers and local officials** were caught in the middle, unsure how to respond to competing claims.

A Plan Nipped in the Bud

As tensions escalated, the SLFP leadership realized that Anura's land promise was **politically risky**. The party was already losing support due to economic struggles and rising ethnic unrest. The **United National Party (UNP)**, led by **J.R. Jayewardene**, was gaining momentum with promises of economic liberalization and ethnic reconciliation.

To avoid further controversy, the SLFP **quietly shelved the land distribution plan**. No formal policy was enacted, and the applications submitted by Tamil workers were **left unanswered**. The issue faded from public discourse as the election campaign intensified.

A Dark Day in Talawakelle: Land, Protest, and Tragedy

In the years leading up to Sri Lanka's 1977 general elections, tensions were running high in the country's plantation regions. Workers were growing increasingly frustrated with poor wages, lack of land rights, and broken promises from politicians. The situation reached a boiling point during a **General Strike** in the plantations—one that I was a participant.

Measuring Land, Igniting Anger

During this time, **land authorities arrived in Talawakelle** to begin measuring estate lands. Their goal was to assess plots for possible redistribution—a move that had been hinted at in political speeches, especially promises made to the **indigenous Sinhalese population**. However, many **Tamil plantation workers**, who had lived and worked on these lands for generations, feared they would be excluded or displaced.

When the officials began their work, **a group of workers stormed the site**, demanding that the process be stopped. They saw the land measurement as a threat to their homes, their jobs, and their dignity. The protest quickly escalated.

Police Open Fire

In the chaos that followed, **police opened fire on the crowd**. One worker was tragically killed—a devastating moment that sent shockwaves through the community. The incident occurred during the height of the general strike, when emotions were already raw and trust between workers and authorities was at its lowest.

This death became a symbol of the **deep injustice** faced by plantation workers. It exposed the **fragility of their rights** and the **violence they endured** when they tried to defend them.

The Aftermath

The land measurement plan was **quietly abandoned**.
The strike continued, but the mood had changed—grief and fear replaced hope.
No major investigation or public apology followed, and the incident was **largely erased from official records**.

Yet for those who were there, like me, the memory remains vivid. It is a reminder of how **land, identity, and survival** are deeply connected in Sri Lanka's plantation history.

The **1977 elections** resulted in a **landslide victory for the UNP**, which won **140 out of 168 seats** in Parliament. The SLFP suffered its worst defeat in history, and Anura Bandaranaike lost his seat. The tensions in the plantations were overshadowed by **larger national issues**, including the rise of Tamil separatism and the beginning of a new political era.

Anura Bandaranaike's land promise in the upcountry plantations was a **short-lived but impactful moment** in Sri Lanka's political history. It revealed the **deep divisions** between ethnic communities and the **fragility of land ownership** in post-reform Sri Lanka. Though the plan was abandoned, it left behind **memories of mistrust and fear—** a reminder of how political promises can stir hope but also ignite conflict.

32

1977 Elections: A Political Earthquake

It was a reckoning long in the making. The 1971 JVP insurrection had already shaken the nation to its core—thousands of Sinhalese youth lost their lives in a violent, failed revolution. What followed were years of hardship: the devastating Food Crisis of 1972 to 1975, a deepening economic downturn, and growing discontent across all sectors of society. Even the pride of hosting a successful Non-Aligned Movement Summit in Colombo in 1976 couldn't mask the growing frustration of the public. By the time the

1977 general election arrived, the tide had clearly turned. The party led by **Prime Minister Sirimavo Bandaranaike**, once seen as a symbol of resilience, was handed a **historic and resounding defeat**, marking one of the most significant shifts in Sri Lanka's post-independence political landscape.

On **21 July 1977**, Sri Lanka held one of the most important elections in its history. The ruling **Sri Lanka Freedom Party (SLFP)**, led by **Prime Minister Sirimavo Bandaranaike**, had become deeply unpopular due to economic hardship, strict government controls, and rising ethnic tensions. People were frustrated with shortages, unemployment, and the lack of personal freedoms.

The opposition party, the **United National Party (UNP)**, led by **J.R. Jayewardene**, promised a new direction. They spoke of **economic liberalization**, **free trade**, and **modernization**. Their campaign also included popular promises like **extra food rations** and **constitutional reform**.

The Result

- The UNP won **140 out of 168 seats**—a **landslide victory** never seen before in Sri Lanka.
- The SLFP was reduced to just **8 seats**, its worst defeat ever.

- The **Tamil United Liberation Front (TULF)** won **18 seats**, becoming the **official opposition**—a first for a Tamil party.

This election marked the **end of the socialist era** and the **beginning of a new political and economic chapter**.

The Dawn of the Open Economy

After the victory, **J.R. Jayewardene** became Prime Minister and later the **first Executive President** under a new **constitution in 1978**. He introduced sweeping changes to Sri Lanka's economy.

Key Reforms

- **Trade liberalization**: Import restrictions were removed, and tariffs were lowered.
- **Foreign investment**: Tax incentives were offered, and new laws protected investors.
- **Privatization**: State-owned businesses were sold or leased to private companies.
- **Free Trade Zones**: Areas like **Katunayake** were developed to attract export-oriented industries.
- **Accelerated Mahaweli Project**: A massive irrigation and hydroelectric scheme was launched.

These reforms were inspired by global trends in **neoliberal economics**, similar to what was happening in **Thatcher's UK** and **Reagan's USA**.

The Rise of Political Corruption

While the open economy brought **growth and modernization**, it also opened the door to **widespread corruption**.

How It Started

- **MPs and ministers** were allowed to do business with the government—something previously banned.
- **Land Reform Commission lands** were sold at low prices to political allies.
- **Licenses and contracts** were handed out based on political loyalty, not merit.
- **Development projects** were chosen not for national benefit, but for personal gain.

Even though **J.R. Jayewardene** himself was not known for personal greed, his policies created a system where **political patronage and personal enrichment** became normalized.

Long-Term Effects

- Many development projects failed to deliver promised benefits.
- Public debt increased due to mismanaged investments.

- The gap between rich and poor widened.
- Corruption became deeply embedded in Sri Lanka's political culture.

Ethnic Tensions and Violence

The 1977 elections also intensified **ethnic divisions**. The **TULF's call for Tamil Eelam** alarmed the Sinhalese majority. In **August 1977**, anti-Tamil riots broke out, leading to deaths and destruction. This marked the beginning of a **cycle of violence** that would later explode into **civil war**.

A Mixed Legacy

The **1977 elections** were a turning point. They brought:

- **Economic freedom**, modernization, and global integration.
- But also, **political corruption**, inequality, and ethnic unrest.

J.R. Jayewardene's era reshaped Sri Lanka—but not always for the better. The open economy gave new opportunities, but the lack of accountability and fairness planted seeds of **mistrust and instability** that would haunt the country for decades.

Even though **J.R. Jayewardene** himself was not known for personal greed, his policies created a system where **political patronage and personal enrichment** became normalized.

33

The Mahaweli Project: Development, Disparity, and Debate

The **Mahaweli Development Project** is the **largest multipurpose development program** ever undertaken in Sri Lanka. Launched in the 1960s and accelerated in **1977** under President **J.R. Jayewardene**, it aimed to transform the country's economy by using the waters of the **Mahaweli River** for **irrigation, hydropower, and settlement**.

Goals of the Project

- Provide **irrigation** to dry zones for farming.
- Generate **hydroelectric power**.
- Resettle **landless families**.
- Reduce **poverty and unemployment**.
- Boost **agricultural production** and **food security**.

Benefits to Farmers and Corporates

The project brought major changes to Sri Lanka's rural landscape:

For Farmers

- Over **140,000 families** were resettled in newly irrigated lands.
- Farmers received **2.5 acres of irrigated land** and **home gardens**.
- Access to water allowed **double cropping** and **higher yields**.

For Corporates and Individuals

- Construction contracts and land deals made **some individuals and companies very wealthy**.
- **Foreign aid** and **government spending** created opportunities for **political allies and business elites**.
- Allegations of **land grabbing** and **preferential treatment** surfaced, especially in later phases.

The Water Distribution Controversy

While the project was meant to benefit the **entire country**, concerns grew over **unequal water distribution**, especially in **Tamil-majority areas** in the **North and East**.

Where Did the Water Go?

- Most irrigation systems (Systems A to H) were developed in **North Central**, **Central**, and **North-western Provinces**.
- These areas were largely **Sinhalese-majority** regions.
- **Eastern Province**, which includes many **Tamil farming communities**, received **limited water access** despite being part of the dry zone.

Why Was This a Problem?

- Tamil farmers in areas like **Batticaloa** and **Trincomalee** continued to face **water scarcity**.
- Promised **canal extensions** and **reservoirs** were delayed or never built.
- Some critics argued that the project was **ethnically biased**, favoring Sinhalese settlers over Tamil communities.

Evidence and Studies

- The **Mahaweli Master Plan** included **13 irrigation systems**, but only a few reached Tamil-majority districts.
- The **Mahaweli Water Security Investment Program**, launched decades later, aimed to correct this by transferring water to the **North and East**, but progress has been slow.
- Studies have warned that **failure to equitably distribute water** could lead to **social unrest** and **regional inequality**.

Political and Social Impact

The uneven distribution of Mahaweli waters became a **symbol of marginalization** for Tamil communities:

- It added to **ethnic grievances** during a time of rising tensions.
- Tamil politicians and civil society groups demanded **fair access** to irrigation and development.
- The issue was often **ignored or downplayed** by central authorities.

The Mahaweli Project was a **landmark achievement** in Sri Lanka's development history. It brought **electricity**, **food security**, and **economic growth**. But it also left behind **questions of fairness**, especially in how its benefits were shared.

While **Sinhalese farmers and urban elites** gained much, **Tamil communities** in the dry zones of the North and East were **left behind**. The promise of national development was not fully realized for all.

The **Mahaweli Development Project** was the brainchild of **C.P. de Silva**, a visionary civil servant and later a prominent politician in Sri Lanka. As **Minister of Agriculture, Lands, Irrigation and Power**, he played a central role in conceptualizing and initiating the project during the 1960s.

C.P. de Silva envisioned using the waters of the **Mahaweli River**—Sri Lanka's longest river—to transform the dry zone into fertile farmland, generate hydroelectric power, and resettle landless families. He commissioned feasibility studies with international agencies like the **United Nations Development Programme (UNDP)** and the **Food and Agriculture Organization (FAO)**, which led to the creation of the **Mahaweli Master Plan**.

Although the project was later accelerated under **President J.R. Jayewardene** in 1977, it was C.P. de Silva who laid the foundation and pushed for its approval in Parliament. His deep commitment to agricultural development and rural upliftment earned him the nickname **"Minneriya Deviyo"** among the people of the North Central Province.

Role of Gamini Dissanayake

Gamini Dissanayake played a **transformational role** in Sri Lanka's development history, especially as the **Minister of Mahaweli Development** from 1977 to 1990. His leadership was central to turning the **Mahaweli Development Project**—the largest infrastructure initiative in post-independence Sri Lanka—into a reality.

Architect of the Accelerated Mahaweli Program

Originally designed to span **30 years**, the Mahaweli Project was fast-tracked under Dissanayake's stewardship and **completed in just 6 years**. This ambitious move required:

- Coordinating **foreign aid and technical expertise** from countries like the UK, Germany, and Sweden.
- Overseeing the construction of **five major dams**: Kotmale, Victoria, Randenigala, Rantambe, and Maduru Oya.
- Developing **irrigation systems** that transformed arid regions into fertile farmland.
- Resettling **over 140,000 families**, providing them with land, housing, and access to water.

Economic and Social Impact

Under his leadership, the project:

- Generated **hydroelectric power** that still supplies a significant portion of Sri Lanka's electricity.
- Boosted **rice production** and **food security**.
- Created **new townships** and improved rural infrastructure.
- Elevated Sri Lanka's reputation for executing large-scale development with limited **resources.**

Broader Political Influence

Beyond Mahaweli:

- Dissanayake was a **senior figure in the United National Party (UNP)** and served as **Leader of the Opposition** in 1994.
- He was the **UNP's presidential candidate** in 1994 but was tragically **assassinated by the LTTE** during the campaign.
- He also played a key role in **Sri Lanka gaining Test status in cricket**, showcasing his influence beyond politics.

Gamini Dissanayake is remembered as a **visionary leader** who combined charisma, technical understanding, and political will to reshape Sri Lanka's landscape.

34

The 1978 Constitution: A Turning Point in Sri Lanka's Governance

In **1978**, Sri Lanka adopted a new constitution that changed the way the country was governed. This constitution was introduced by **President J.R. Jayewardene**, who had won a massive victory in the **1977 general elections**. With a **five-sixths majority** in Parliament, JRJ had the power to reshape the political system—and he did.

The most important change was the creation of an **Executive Presidency**, replacing the earlier **Westminster-style parliamentary system**. This move was meant to bring **stability**, **strong leadership**, and **economic reform**. But over time, it also led to **concentration of power**, **political corruption**, and **erosion of democratic checks and balances**.

The Good: Strengths and Achievements

Economic Reform

JRJ used the new constitution to launch **Sri Lanka's open economy**, ending decades of state control. Foreign investment increased, and **Free Trade Zones** were created.

The **Mahaweli Development Project** was accelerated, bringing irrigation, electricity, and new settlements.

Strong Leadership

The Executive President had a **fixed term** and was **directly elected by the people**, giving the role democratic legitimacy.

The system allowed for **decisive action** without constant interference from Parliament.

Judicial Independence (on paper)

The constitution promised **separation of powers** between the Executive, Legislature, and Judiciary.

It created a **Supreme Court** and **Court of Appeal** with powers to review laws and protect rights.

The Bad: Flaws and Weaknesses

Concentration of Power

- The President could **appoint and dismiss ministers**, **control the police**, and **influence the judiciary**.

- Parliament became **weaker**, especially since many MPs were also ministers, blurring the lines of accountability.

Undermining Democracy

- JRJ extended Parliament's term through a **controversial referendum in 1982**, avoiding fresh elections.
- The **proportional representation system** delayed elections and made it harder for voters to hold MPs accountable.

Rise of Political Corruption

- The constitution allowed MPs and ministers to **engage in business**, leading to **conflicts of interest**.
- **State contracts and land deals** were often awarded based on political loyalty, not merit.

The Ugly: Path to Presidential Dictatorship?

Many critics argue that the 1978 Constitution laid the foundation for **authoritarian rule**:

Abuse of Emergency Powers

The President could declare **states of emergency** and **bypass normal legal procedures**. These powers were used during **ethnic riots**, **civil unrest**, and **political crackdowns**.

Weak Checks and Balances

The **Attorney General** and **Inspector General of Police** were appointed by the President, limiting independent investigations. The **Judiciary** was vulnerable to political pressure, especially in high-profile cases.

Ethnic Tensions and Civil War

The constitution failed to address **Tamil grievances**, and the **Tamil United Liberation Front (TULF)** became the opposition.

The lack of meaningful devolution and rising Sinhala nationalism contributed to the **1983 Black July riots** and the start of the **civil war**.

The 1978 Constitution was a bold attempt to modernize Sri Lanka's governance and economy. It brought **development**, **foreign investment**, and **strong leadership**. But it also **centralized power**, weakened democratic institutions, and opened the door to **corruption and authoritarianism**.

Over the years, many amendments were made to fix its flaws—especially the **19th Amendment** in 2015, which tried to reduce presidential powers. Yet the debate continues:

Was JRJ's constitution a visionary step forward, or a dangerous path to dictatorship?

Many critics argue that the 1978 Constitution laid the foundation for **authoritarian rule**:

Abuse of Emergency Powers

The President could declare **states of emergency** and **bypass normal legal procedures**. These powers were used during **ethnic riots**, **civil unrest**, and **political crackdowns**.

Weak Checks and Balances

The **Attorney General** and **Inspector General of Police** were appointed by the President, limiting independent investigations.

The **Judiciary** was vulnerable to political pressure, especially in high-profile cases.

Ethnic Tensions and Civil War

The constitution failed to address **Tamil grievances**, and the **Tamil United Liberation Front (TULF)** became the opposition.

The lack of meaningful devolution and rising Sinhala nationalism contributed to the **1983 Black July riots** and the start of the **civil war**.

The 1978 Constitution was a bold attempt to modernize Sri Lanka's governance and economy. It brought **development**, **foreign investment**, and **strong leadership**. But it also **centralized power**, weakened democratic institutions, and opened the door to **corruption and authoritarianism**.

Over the years, many amendments were made to fix its flaws—especially the **19th Amendment** in 2015, which tried to reduce presidential powers. Yet the debate continues: Was JRJ's constitution a visionary step forward, or a dangerous path to dictatorship?

35

JULY 1983 - Prophecy of Fire: A Personal Journey Through Black July

(Pic: sangam.org)

*In early July 1983, I was working in the **Kingdom of Saudi Arabia**, preparing eagerly for my departure home on the **8th of July**. The days leading up to that flight felt unusual, particularly one restless night when I experienced a disturbing dream—**Colombo city engulfed in flames**. It was vivid, chaotic, and left me shaken. I shared the strange vision with a close friend, then brushed it aside as one of those dreams best forgotten.*

*Three weeks later, while **holidaying in Colombo**, that dream returned—not in sleep, but in life.*

*On the **morning of 25th July**, I made my way to the **bus stop at Maligawatte**, intending to travel to **Ratmalana**, where I had recently purchased a house. It needed repairs before I could move my family in. The crowd at the stop felt unusually tense, but I thought little of it. Once aboard the bus, nearing **Maradana Junction**, I noticed **shops in flames**. Strangely, some people were dragging boxes and goods out into the street—at first glance, it seemed they were trying to save merchandise from a fire.*

*It was not until I reached Ratmalana that the pieces fell into place. I stopped to buy a newspaper and saw the headline: **"13 Policemen Killed in Jaffna."** I couldn't read further. Sharing what I'd seen in Maradana with the shopkeeper, he replied sharply, "Don't you know* *the bodies of the policemen were brought to Borella Cemetery, and the riots started from there?" In that instant, clarity hit me like a lightning bolt. **My dream had come to life.***

The Spark That Ignited the Inferno

On **23 July 1983**, the **Liberation Tigers of Tamil Eelam (LTTE)** ambushed an army patrol in **Thirunelveli, Jaffna**, killing **13 Sinhalese soldiers**. Their bodies were flown to Colombo, and the government held a **military funeral** at **Kanatte Cemetery** on **24 July**. Thousands of mourners gathered, emotions boiling over into rage. That night, **anti-Tamil riots erupted**, beginning in Borella and spreading like wildfire across Colombo.

The First Days of Riots

From **24–26 July**, Colombo descended into chaos:

- **Tamil shops and homes** were looted and torched.
- **Electoral lists** were allegedly used to identify Tamil properties.
- Some mobs operated with apparent **state backing or passive police presence**.
- Tamil civilians were **dragged from vehicles**, beaten, hacked—and in some cases—**burned alive**.

Worse still was the **Welikada Prison massacre**, where Tamil inmates were attacked and murdered by fellow prisoners with **guard complicity**—first on **25 July**, then again on **27**

Beyond Colombo: A Nation in Flames

The violence spread fast:

- In **Kandy, Galle, Kurunegala**, Tamil homes and businesses were attacked.
- In **Trincomalee and Batticaloa**, Tamil communities suffered reprisals.

- Army operations in **Jaffna** resulted in **civilian deaths**, destruction of property, and mass arrests.

The Welikada Prison Massacre

Background: Ethnic Tensions and Political Turmoil

Post-independence Sri Lanka saw rising Sinhalese nationalism, marginalizing the Tamil minority through policies like the *Sinhala Only Act* (1956) and university standardization.

Tamil grievances culminated in the formation of militant groups like **TELO** and **LTTE**, demanding an independent Tamil Eelam.

In July 1983, the killing of 13 Sinhalese soldiers by LTTE militants in Jaffna triggered **Black July**—a week of anti-Tamil pogroms across the country, with thousands killed and displaced.

The Welikada Prison Massacre: A Chilling Sequence

It was just past sunset on July 25, 1983, when the walls of **Welikada Prison**—meant to guard the guilty from the innocent—became the stage for a blood-soaked betrayal. Outside, Colombo burned. The streets convulsed with rage following the deaths of 13 Sinhala soldiers in the North. The government's grip had loosened. But what happened within those stone walls was something far darker—a madness unleashed not in the chaos of war, but in the cold corners of supposed order.

Inside, **Tamil political prisoners** sat in fearful silence. Men like **Sellarasa "Kuttimani" Yogachandiran** and **Ganeshanathan Jeganathan**, poets of revolution, sat with folded hands, clinging to thoughts of freedom, of justice. Kuttimani had once pledged his **eyes to a future Tamil child**, so that the child might one day behold a liberated homeland. He didn't know those very eyes would become trophies of hate.

The door burst open.

What followed was not a riot—it was ritualistic slaughter.

The attackers were fellow inmates, emboldened by whispered encouragements, armed with crude weapons and bloodlust. With no guards in sight, they descended like a plague. Kuttimani was dragged out first. They gouged out his eyes—mocking his promise of vision. They severed his tongue, silencing the voice that had dared to dream. One of the men drank from his spilling blood and screamed, "I've tasted the blood of a Tiger!"

The carnage was intimate. No shots fired, no warning. Just fists, iron rods, and screams thick with despair. **Dr. S. Rajasunderam**, a gentle Gandhian, begged for mercy. In return, he was bludgeoned—his body flung like a ragdoll. The floor of the prison, soaked in blood, seemed to weep.

Two days passed.

The survivors—half mad, starved, caged like animals—pleaded for protection. **They were locked in a room**, huddled together like frightened children. Then it happened again.

On July 27, another group of inmates **broke into the padlocked chamber**, unleashed by negligence or something far more sinister. **Eighteen more Tamil prisoners were butchered**, some while clutching rosaries, others while reciting final prayers.

No sirens. No rescue.

Only the quiet whimper of history being carved into flesh.

Memory as Resistance

No one was charged. No guards reprimanded. The state paid compensation but **never admitted guilt**. The massacre turned blood into ink for the Tamil cause. It radicalized moderates, shattered faith in reconciliation, and widened the chasm between communities.

Even now, decades later, **the Welikada massacre remains unspoken in textbooks**, unmarked by plaques, unnamed in the annals of justice. But memory survives—in stories like this, in the silence of mothers who lost their sons, and in the trembling hands that still light candles in defiance.

The Aftermath of Black July

Tamil youth turned to armed resistance, and recruitment into the **LTTE and other militant groups** surged.

The Toll and Trauma

IMPACT AREA	ESTIMATE
Deaths	400–3,000 Tamils
Injured	Over 2,000
Displaced	150,000+
Homes/Businesses Destroyed	Thousands
Economic Loss	$300 million
Refugees to India	Tens of Thousands

Many Sri Lankan refugees—especially during the height of the civil war—reached **European countries** through a mix of legal and irregular pathways, often driven by desperation and lack of safe alternatives.

How Did They Travel Without Visas?

Irregular Migration Routes

- Many refugees used **human smuggling networks** to travel via **sea or land routes**, often through **South Asia, the Middle East, and Eastern Europe**.

- Some traveled on **fraudulent documents** or overstayed **tourist or transit visas** in intermediary countries before reaching Europe.
- Others entered **Schengen countries** through **porous borders**, especially before stricter EU border controls were implemented.

Asylum on Arrival

- Upon arrival in Europe, many **applied for asylum at airports or border checkpoints**, invoking international protection under the **1951 Refugee Convention**.
- European countries are obligated to process asylum claims, even if the individual entered **without a valid visa**, as long as they can demonstrate a **credible fear of persecution**.

Where Did They Go?

Between **1990 and 1995**, nearly **98,000 Sri Lankan nationals** applied for asylum in Europe, with **24,000 applications in 1991 alone**. Popular destinations included:

- **France**
- **Germany**
- **United Kingdom**
- **Italy**
- **Switzerland**
- **Netherlands**

Acceptance rates varied widely. For example, **Ireland and Spain** had relatively high success rates, while **Japan and Germany** rejected most applications.

Why Was This Possible?

- **Humanitarian policies** in Europe allowed asylum seekers to enter and apply for protection, even without visas.
- Many Sri Lankans were fleeing **ethnic violence**, **forced recruitment**, or **state persecution**, especially Tamils suspected of LTTE links.
- Some European countries had **family reunification programs** or **community sponsorships**, easing entry for relatives of earlier migrants.

The riots were **not spontaneous**. Scholars and survivors argue that they amounted to a **state-sponsored pogrom**—designed or allowed to unfold as vengeance against the Tamil population.

The Long Road to War

Black July marked a turning point in Sri Lanka's history. Trust between ethnic communities shattered. The **Tamil diaspora grew**, forming advocacy networks abroad. The LTTE's cause gained sympathy and support, and by the mid-1980s, Sri Lanka was in the grip of a **full-fledged civil war**—one that would last **nearly 30 years**, claiming **over 100,000 lives**.

The Political Leadership Behind the 1983 Sri Lankan Racial Riots: Motives and Legacy

The 1983 racial riots in Sri Lanka—commonly referred to as **Black July**—marked a turning point in the island's post-independence history. What began as a reaction to the killing of 13 Sinhalese soldiers by the Liberation Tigers of Tamil Eelam (LTTE) in Jaffna spiraled into a week-long pogrom against Tamil civilians. The violence left thousands dead, tens of thousands displaced, and catalyzed a civil war that would last nearly three decades. While the riots were carried out by mobs, **political leadership played a pivotal role** in both enabling and exacerbating the violence.

Key Political Figures Involved

President J.R. Jayewardene (UNP)

Role: President of Sri Lanka during the riots.

Actions:

- Gave an infamous interview to *The Daily Telegraph* on July 11, 1983, stating: *"I am not worried about the opinion of the Jaffna people... really, if I starve the Tamils out, the Sinhala people will be happy."*
- Delayed imposing curfews and failed to condemn the violence promptly.
- Overruled Prime Minister Premadasa's objections and insisted on holding the soldiers' funeral in Colombo, which became a flashpoint for mob violence.

Motives:

- Appeasement of Sinhala nationalist sentiment.
- Suppression of Tamil separatism through intimidation and state-backed violence.
- Consolidation of power by marginalizing Tamil political representation.

Prime Minister Ranasinghe Premadasa

- **Role**: Prime Minister under Jayewardene.

- **Actions**:

- Opposed the decision to hold the soldiers' funeral in Colombo, fearing violence.
- Had limited influence over the unfolding events due to Jayewardene's dominance.

His gangs led by a notorious underworld thug led the riots and looting where I was staying. I didn't believe the official statement.

There's compelling evidence that **Ranasinghe Premadasa's role in the 1983 riots was far more complex** than simply being sidelined by President Jayewardene.

Allegations of Premadasa's Involvement

While official accounts often portray Premadasa as opposing the funeral in Colombo, **multiple sources suggest that elements loyal to him may have played a role in orchestrating violence**.

The **Jatika Sevaka Sangamaya (JSS)**, a trade union affiliated with the UNP and reportedly under Premadasa's influence, was **accused of organizing mobs** that looted and attacked Tamil properties.

Eyewitness accounts and investigative reports, including those by the *International Commission of Jurists*, described the violence as **systematic and premeditated**, with **electoral rolls used to identify Tamil households**.

Conflicting Narratives

- Some reports claim Premadasa **warned against the funeral**, fearing it would incite violence.
- Others argue that **his political machinery was deeply embedded in the urban working class**, and that **his supporters were among the most active during the riots**, especially in Colombo.
- The *Sri Lanka Guardian* and other retrospectives have noted that **Premadasa's political ambitions and populist base may have motivated indirect involvement**, even if he wasn't publicly leading the charge.

No Accountability

Despite widespread allegations, **no formal investigation ever held Premadasa or other top leaders accountable** for the violence.

The lack of judicial inquiry has left much of this history in the realm of speculation, contested

Motives:

- Attempted to prevent escalation but was politically sidelined.

Cyril Mathew (UNP Cabinet Minister)

Role: Minister of Industries and a known Sinhala nationalist.

Actions:

Allegedly organized mobs and provided voter lists to identify Tamil households. Maintained armed squads and operated above the law.

Motives:

- Ethno-nationalist agenda aimed at eradicating Tamil economic and cultural presence.
- Strengthening Sinhala Buddhist dominance in urban centers.

Tissa Weeratunga (Army Commander)

Role: Commander of the Sri Lankan Army.

Actions:

Oversaw military operations in Jaffna prior to the riots. Allegedly responsible for retaliatory massacres of Tamil civilians following the ambush.

Motives:

- Military suppression of Tamil militancy.
- Retaliation for the deaths of soldiers.

The Nature of the Violence

Systematic and Organized: Mobs were transported in government vehicles, armed with voter lists, and targeted Tamil homes and businesses.

State Complicity: Security forces were either passive or actively participated in the violence. The Welikada Prison massacre, where 53 Tamil prisoners were killed, was carried out with the alleged involvement of prison officials.

Economic Destruction: Tamil-owned shops and establishments were looted and burned, aiming to dismantle the Tamil economic base.

Underlying Motives

- **Sinhala Nationalism**: The ruling elite used ethnic tensions to galvanize support among the Sinhalese majority.
- **Political Expediency**: The UNP government sought to weaken Tamil political influence, especially after the Tamil United Liberation Front (TULF) gained traction advocating for Tamil Eelam.
- **Distraction from Economic Crisis**: The riots diverted attention from growing economic discontent and rising authoritarianism.
- **Suppressing Tamil Militancy**: The government viewed Tamil militancy not as a political issue but as terrorism to be crushed militarily.

Accountability

- **No Justice**: To date, no political or military leader has been held accountable for the atrocities of Black July.
- **Civil War**: The riots fueled Tamil militancy, swelling the ranks of the LTTE and plunging the country into a 26-year war.
- **Diaspora and Memory**: Thousands of Tamils fled abroad, and July remains a month of mourning and remembrance for the diaspora.

July 25, 1983. A day etched into my memory with unbearable clarity. That morning, as I traveled from Ratmalana, the world outside the bus windows appeared undisturbed—familiar shops stood untouched, the city moved with its usual rhythm. But within moments, everything changed. Flames leapt from storefronts like angry spirits unleashed. Vehicles burned in rows like pyres of despair. The air, once still, turned frantic. People ran with terror etched into their faces. Inside the bus, women screamed as armed rioters—wielding swords, crowbars, and sticks—forced their way in. It felt like the gates of hell had opened along Galle Road.

At Wellawatte and Bambalapitiya, I saw mobs shatter windows, loot businesses, and torch homes. Even children joined the violence, throwing stones with a chilling sense of duty, targeting any building believed to belong to Tamils. The cruelty blurred all logic. Tear gas hissed in the air, but strangely, it wasn't directed at the rioters—it drifted outward, as if avoiding confrontation.

The next morning, from the safety of a second-floor apartment where my family and I had taken refuge, I watched men parade through the streets with looted possessions. One scene still haunts me. A crowd confronted a Muslim man trying to protect a parked car which was owned by a Tamil couple —he claimed it was his, hoping to shield it from destruction. But the mob wouldn't listen. With ruthless efficiency, they smashed the car, doused it in petrol, and lit it ablaze. The fire devoured more than metal—it scorched the bonds of community.

Then they turned to the Tamil couple's apartment on the third floor. I stood frozen as their modest belongings—a steel cupboard, faded furniture, and books—were thrown out onto the road. Things of little monetary value, but full of meaning, savings, and love. As these fragments of a life scattered on the pavement, women and children below clapped and cheered, celebrating ruin as if it were some glorious conquest. The young couple had already fled. They never saw their home fall apart. But I did. I wanted to document it—to raise a lens against the madness. But fear silenced my instincts. I too belonged to a minority. I too felt exposed.

On August 6, I boarded my flight back to Saudi Arabia. At the airport, Tamil families were gathered in silent grief, clutching children and bags. Many were headed to Madras, from where I heard they would seek asylum in distant lands. In that crowd, I saw my old schoolteacher—once a beacon of knowledge at Highlands. He told me his house had been damaged, and he was leaving Sri Lanka—not knowing if he would ever return.

That night in Saudi, I recalled a dream I saw the day I left on 8th July. Strange, vivid, almost prophetic. It felt like a warning. And in its shadow, I understood—this was not simply the burning of homes. It was the collapse of empathy. The day when the flames of vengeance scorched every fragile thread that held us together. It wasn't just Colombo that burned. It was Sri Lanka's soul.

Ashes and Echoes

They cheered as cupboards fell like flags of conquest,
Books torn from shelves, dreams flung like dust.
The clatter of chairs became a battle hymn,
As silence whispered, "This was once home."

Behind curtains, hearts dared not beat too loud,
A camera slept in fear's trembling hands.
Even fire seemed confused—why burn memories so small?
But in that smoke, a nation's soul unraveled.

And as the sky turned the color of forgetting,
We boarded planes carrying fragments of ourselves—
Looking back at soil that could no longer shelter,
Praying one day it might still forgive.

36

From Black July to a Nation at War: Sri Lanka's Turbulent Years (1983–2006)

The racial riots of **Black July 1983** did not just leave a trail of destruction—they marked the **beginning of a bloody civil war** that would haunt Sri Lanka for the next three decades. Between **1983 and 2000**, the country witnessed **assassinations, bombings, military offensives**, and **shifting political landscapes**, all shaped by the conflict between the Sri Lankan state and the **Liberation Tigers of Tamil Eelam (LTTE)**.

1983: The Flashpoint of War

The killing of 13 Sinhalese soldiers by the LTTE in Jaffna sparked riots that left **thousands of Tamils dead**, homes destroyed, and families displaced. The government's delayed response and the public perception of state complicity **galvanized Tamil militancy**. The LTTE gained sympathy and recruits, as trust between ethnic communities shattered.

By the end of 1983:

- Tamil political parties like the **TULF** were weakened.
- The LTTE and other militant groups took control of the Tamil nationalist cause.
- A **Tamil armed struggle** had formally begun.

How These Attacks Were Carried Out

Guerrilla Ambushes: Early attacks like the 1983 Jaffna ambush used small, mobile units targeting military patrols.

Massacres: LTTE often used automatic weapons and grenades to attack civilians in villages, buses, and religious sites.

Suicide Bombings: Introduced in the late 1980s, notably by the elite **Black Tigers** unit. These were used against military, political, and economic targets.

Conventional Warfare: By the mid-1990s, LTTE had evolved into a semi-conventional force with artillery, naval units (Sea Tigers), and even rudimentary air capability.

Ethnic Cleansing: Systematic expulsion of Muslims from Northern Province in 1990, including forced displacement and confiscation of property.

Triggers Behind the Violence

Ethnic Marginalization: Tamil grievances over language, education, and land policies post-independence.

Failed Peace Talks: Repeated breakdowns in negotiations (1985, 1990, 1995, 2002) often led to renewed violence.

Military Offensives: Government operations in Tamil areas provoked retaliatory strikes.

Demographic Engineering: State-sponsored Sinhalese settlements in Tamil-majority regions were seen as threats to Tamil identity.

Religious and Cultural Tensions: Attacks on Buddhist monks and Muslim civilians reflected deeper communal rifts.

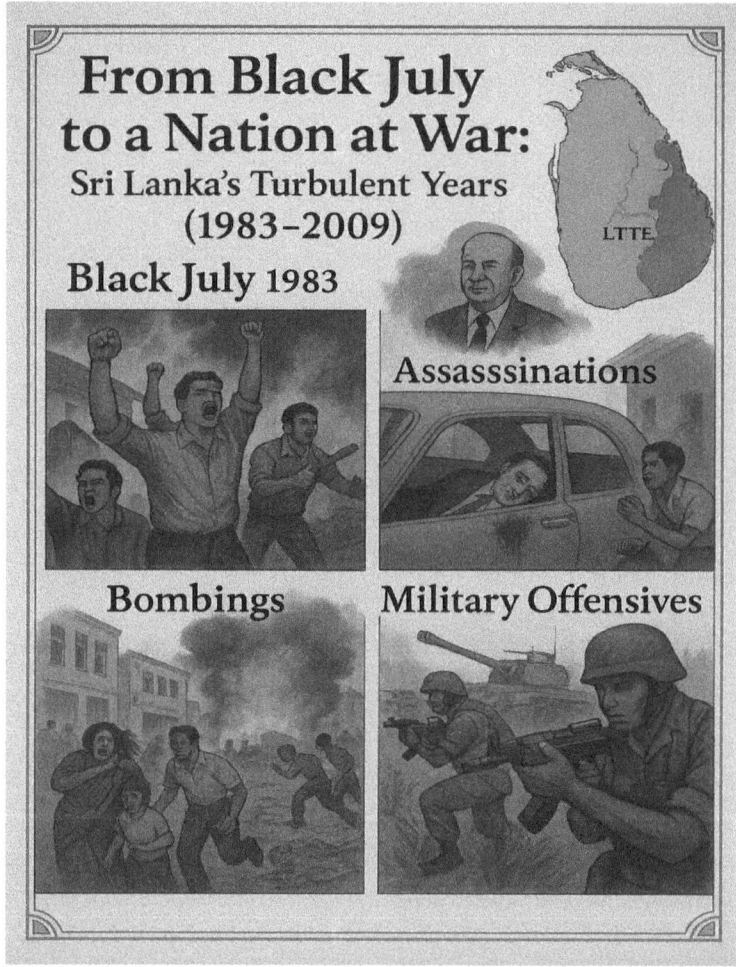

Here's a detailed timeline of major **LTTE attacks in Sri Lanka's North and East**, along with how they were executed and what triggered them. These events span the **Sri Lankan Civil War (1983–2009)**, which was rooted in ethnic tensions between the Sinhalese-majority government and Tamil separatists seeking an independent state called **Tamil Eelam**.

Timeline of Key LTTE Attacks in the North and East

DATE	LOCATION	ATTACK DETAILS	TRIGGER/CONTEXT

July 23, 1983	Jaffna	Ambush on army patrol killing 13 soldiers	Sparked anti-Tamil riots (Black July), marking the start of civil war
Nov 30, 1984	Kent & Dollar Farms, Mullaitivu	Massacre of 62 Sinhalese settlers	Retaliation for state-sponsored colonization of Tamil areas
May 14, 1985	Anuradhapura	Mass shooting at sacred Buddhist site; 146 killed	Revenge for military operations in Tamil regions
Apr 17, 1987	Habarana	Bus bombing killing 127 civilians	Escalation of guerrilla tactics amid failed peace talks
July 2, 1987	Aranthalawa, Ampara	Massacre of 35 Buddhist monks	LTTE targeting religious symbols of Sinhalese identity
June 11, 1990	Eastern Province	Massacre of 600+ surrendered police officers	Breakdown of peace talks with Premadasa government
Aug 3, 1990	Kattankudy, Batticaloa	Massacre of 147 Muslims in mosques	Rising Tamil-Muslim tensions; LTTE viewed Muslims as government collaborators
Aug 11, 1990	Eravur, Batticaloa	Massacre of 116–173 Muslims	Ethnic cleansing campaign in Eastern Province
May 25, 1995	Kallarawa, Trincomalee	Killing of 42 Sinhalese fishermen	LTTE targeting economic assets and Sinhalese settlers
July 18, 1996	Mullaitivu	Overrun army base; 1,498 troops killed or missing	LTTE's largest conventional military victory
Sept 18, 1999	Gonagala, Ampara	Massacre of 54 civilians, including women and children	Retaliation for military offensives in Eastern Province
June 15, 2006	Kebithigollewa, Anuradhapura	Claymore mine attack on civilian bus; 66 killed	LTTE accused of targeting civilians to provoke ethnic backlash

37

The Food Drop: A Show of Force

On **4 June 1987**, India launched **Operation Poomalai** (meaning "Garland of Flowers" in Tamil):

- **Five Indian Air Force An-32 transport planes**, escorted by **Mirage 2000 fighter jets**, flew over **Sri Lankan airspace** without permission.
- They dropped **25 tons of food and medicine** over **Jaffna**, claiming it was a **humanitarian mission**.
- The escorting fighter jets were armed, making it clear that India was prepared to defend the mission if challenged.

This was seen by many as a **brief invasion of Sri Lankan sovereignty**. The Sri Lankan government, led by **President J.R. Jayewardene (JRJ)**, was stunned.

JRJ's Address to the Nation

President Jayewardene addressed the nation shortly after the incident:

- He expressed **shock and disappointment** over India's unilateral action.
- He emphasized that Sri Lanka was a **sovereign nation**, and its airspace had been violated.
- He tried to **calm public anger**, especially in **Colombo**, where **tensions were rising** and **anti-Indian sentiment** was growing.

JRJ was in a difficult position. He had to balance **national pride** with **diplomatic caution**, knowing that India was a powerful neighbor.

Rising Tensions in Colombo and Beyond

The Indian food drop caused **widespread unrest**:

- In **Colombo**, people protested against India's actions.
- **Sinhalese nationalists** accused JRJ of being weak and demanded a stronger response.
- The **Sri Lankan military** was frustrated, as their operation in Jaffna was halted under Indian pressure.
- The **LTTE**, emboldened by India's support, refused to negotiate and continued their fight.

The Indo-Lanka Accord

The Indo-Lanka Accord and the Sri Lankan Tamils
| Daily FT

To ease tensions, India and Sri Lanka signed the **Indo-Lanka Peace Accord** on **29 July 1987**:

- It called for a **ceasefire, devolution of power**, and the **merging of the Northern and Eastern provinces**.

- India sent the **Indian Peace Keeping Force (IPKF)** to enforce the agreement.
- However, the LTTE rejected the accord and began fighting the IPKF, leading to **new conflict**.

A Turning Point in Sri Lanka's History

- The 1987 food drop was more than a humanitarian gesture—it was a **political and military statement**. It marked the beginning of **India's direct involvement** in Sri Lanka's civil war and changed the dynamics of regional diplomacy. For Sri Lanka, it was a moment of **humiliation**, **tension**, and **uncertainty**—but also the start of a new phase in its long and painful conflict.

1987: Indo-Lanka Accord and Arrival of the IPKF

In an attempt to resolve the conflict, **India brokered the Indo-Lanka Accord** in **July 1987**. The deal included:

- **Devolution of powers** to Tamil-majority provinces.
- **Disarmament of the LTTE**.
- Deployment of the **Indian Peace Keeping Force (IPKF)** in Sri Lanka.

But the LTTE **refused to disarm**, and tensions with the IPKF exploded into full-scale conflict. Between 1987 and 1990:

- Over **1,000 LTTE cadres** were killed fighting the IPKF.
- Civilians bore the brunt of violence from **both sides**.
- The LTTE gained popularity for standing up to Indian forces.

The Guard of Honour That Turned Violent

Rajiv Gandhi had arrived in Colombo to sign the **Indo-Sri Lanka Peace Accord** with President **J.R. Jayewardene**, a controversial agreement aimed at resolving the ethnic conflict and deploying the **Indian Peace Keeping Force (IPKF)** in Sri Lanka's north and east. The accord was met with **hostility from Sinhalese nationalists**, who viewed it as foreign interference.

On the morning of **30 July 1987**, Gandhi was inspecting a **Guard of Honour** presented by the **Sri Lankan Navy** at the **Presidential Palace**, not the airport as often misremembered. As he walked past the naval contingent, a sailor named **Vijitha Rohana Wijemuni**, enraged by India's role in Sri Lanka's internal affairs, suddenly **swung his ceremonial Lee-Enfield rifle** at Gandhi's head.

A Narrow Escape

Gandhi's reflexes saved him. He **ducked just in time**, and the rifle struck his **left shoulder below the ear**, causing a bruise but sparing his life. Security personnel, including Gandhi's bodyguards and Sri Lankan officers, **immediately restrained the attacker**, who was then taken into custody. Despite the incident, Gandhi **continued with the ceremony**, showing composure and refusing to let the attack derail the diplomatic moment.

He later told reporters, *"I saw a reverse gun coming up. I sort of ducked down a little bit in a reflex action... the brunt of the blow came on my shoulder."*

Aftermath and Court Martial

Vijitha Rohana was **court-martialed** and charged with **attempted culpable homicide not amounting to murder** and **insulting a state leader**. He was sentenced to **six years in prison** but was **pardoned after two and a half years** by President **Ranasinghe Premadasa**.

Rohana later became a **political candidate** and an **astrologer**, remaining a controversial figure in Sri Lankan public life.

Political and Symbolic Impact

The attack symbolized the **deep resentment** among segments of the Sinhalese population toward India's involvement in Sri Lanka's conflict. It also highlighted the **fragility of diplomatic relations** during a time of intense internal strife. Gandhi's calm response helped maintain the momentum of the peace accord, but the incident remained a **stark reminder of the tensions simmering beneath the surface**.

President **Ranasinghe Premadasa** boycotted the signing ceremony of the **Indo-Sri Lanka Peace Accord** in July 1987 due to his **strong opposition to the agreement and India's involvement** in Sri Lanka's internal affairs.

At the time, Premadasa was serving as **Prime Minister under President J.R. Jayewardene**, and although both belonged to the **United National Party (UNP)**, their views on the accord diverged sharply. Premadasa believed the accord:

- **Compromised Sri Lanka's sovereignty**, especially by allowing the **Indian Peace Keeping Force (IPKF)** to be deployed in the North and East.
- Was **imposed under pressure** from India, particularly after the **Operation Poomalai** food drop, which violated Sri Lankan airspace.
- Would **inflame tensions** among Sinhalese nationalists and further destabilize the South, where the **JVP** was already gaining momentum.

His absence from the ceremony was a **symbolic protest**, signaling his discomfort with the accord and its long-term implications. Later, as **President in 1989**, Premadasa would go on to **demand the withdrawal of the IPKF**, aligning with the LTTE briefly to achieve that goal.

Indian Peace Keeping Force (IPKF) in Sri Lanka & Civil War in North and East (Period: 1987 to 1990)

Between 1987 and 2005, Sri Lanka's Northern and Eastern provinces were engulfed in a protracted and evolving civil war. This period began with **India's military intervention** under the Indo-Sri Lanka Accord and transitioned into a decade of fierce battles, failed peace efforts, and shifting political dynamics. The conflict pitted the **Sri Lankan government** against the **Liberation Tigers of Tamil Eelam (LTTE)**, who sought an independent Tamil homeland.

1987–1990: Indian Peace Keeping Force (IPKF) and the Indo-Sri Lanka Accord

The Accord and Arrival of IPKF

- On **29 July 1987**, Indian Prime Minister **Rajiv Gandhi** and Sri Lankan President **J.R. Jayewardene** signed the **Indo-Sri Lanka Accord**, aiming to end the ethnic conflict.
- India deployed the **IPKF**, a force that peaked at **100,000 troops**, to enforce peace and disarm Tamil militant groups, especially the LTTE.

From Peacekeeping to Combat

- The LTTE initially agreed to disarm but soon reneged, leading to **Operation Pawan** in **October 1987**, where the IPKF launched a full-scale assault on **Jaffna**.
- The IPKF became embroiled in intense urban and jungle warfare against the LTTE, suffering **over 1,200 fatalities**.
- Allegations of **human rights abuses** and **civilian casualties** tarnished India's image.

Operation Pawan: The Battle for Jaffna (October 1987)

Operation Pawan was launched by the IPKF to **disarm the LTTE** and **take control of Jaffna**, the symbolic and operational heart of Tamil separatism.

- It followed the **Indo-Sri Lanka Accord** signed on **29 July 1987**, which mandated India to enforce peace and oversee the disarmament of Tamil militant groups.
- The LTTE initially agreed but soon **refused to surrender arms**, prompting India to shift from peacekeeping to combat operations.

Timeline of Key Events

DATE	EVENT
9–10 Oct 1987	IPKF raided LTTE radio and TV stations; destroyed printing presses
11 October	LTTE ambushed IPKF patrols, escalating hostilities
12 October	**Jaffna University Helidrop**: A disastrous commando raid aimed at capturing LTTE leadership
15–16 October	IPKF halted advance to regroup; massive airlift of reinforcements including tanks and BMPs

| Late October | Full-scale assault resumed; IPKF captured Jaffna after three weeks of brutal urban warfare |

The Jaffna University Helidrop: A Tactical Misstep

- Planned as a **quick strike** to capture LTTE leaders believed to be at **Jaffna University**.
- Involved **17 commandos** from the **10 Para Regiment** and **30 troops** from the **13 Sikh Light Infantry**.
- LTTE had **intercepted IPKF radio transmissions**, setting up a deadly ambush.
- Result: **29 of 30 Sikh LI troops** and **2 commandos** were killed; only one Sikh LI soldier survived and was taken prisoner.

Urban Warfare and Resistance

- The LTTE used **snipers, IEDs, claymore mines**, and **anti-tank weapons** to stall IPKF advances.
- Fighting occurred in **densely populated areas**, with civilians often caught in the crossfire.
- IPKF troops faced difficulty distinguishing **combatants from civilians**, as LTTE fighters blended into the population.
- The **Indian Navy** enforced a **300-mile blockade** to cut LTTE supply lines.

Reinforcements and Adaptation

- IPKF brought in **T-72 tanks, BMP-1 infantry vehicles**, and **Mi-25 helicopter gunships**.
- The **Indian Air Force** flew over **2,200 tactical transport sorties** and **800 helicopter missions** to support ground troops.
- Troops adapted by removing rank insignia and changing gear to avoid sniper targeting.

Outcome

- IPKF **captured Jaffna** but suffered **heavy casualties**: over **214 killed, 700 wounded**, and **36 missing**.
- LTTE lost around **2,000 fighters**, but many leaders escaped, prolonging the conflict.

Operational Challenges

- **Dense Urban Terrain**: Narrow streets and civilian presence limited use of heavy artillery.
- **LTTE Tactics**: Guerrilla warfare, sniper nests in coconut palms, and disguised fighters.
- **Communication Disruption**: LTTE mined IPKF communication lines and ambushed patrols.

Outcome

- After **three weeks of intense fighting**, the IPKF captured **Jaffna Peninsula**.
- LTTE suffered heavy losses but retained leadership and regrouped in jungle areas.
- The operation exposed flaws in planning and intelligence but demonstrated adaptability under fire.

Strategic Map Overview: Jaffna Campaign (October 1987)

While I can't display the actual map here, here's how the battlefield was laid out:

Key Locations

AREA	STRATEGIC ROLE
Palaly Airbase	IPKF's main operational HQ; staging ground for reinforcements
Jaffna University	Target of the heliborne assault to capture LTTE leadership
Jaffna Fort	Held by 1 Maratha Light Infantry; later linked with advancing IPKF units
Navanthurai Coastal Road	Cleared by Indian Marine Commandos to enable troop movement
Point Pedro & Elephant Pass	LTTE escape routes into jungle terrain
Kokkuvil & Tavadi	LTTE radio and TV stations; seized early in the operation

Axis of Advance

The IPKF launched a **five-pronged assault** into Jaffna:

1. **91st Brigade** advanced from **Palaly** toward the city center.
2. **72nd Brigade** moved from the west, aiming to link up with heliborne troops.
3. **41st Brigade** pushed from the east, securing coastal roads.
4. **340th Independent Brigade** supported beach reconnaissance and flank security.
5. **Marine Commandos (IMSF)** secured the coastline and cleared mines.

Tactical Highlights

- **Heliborne Assault on Jaffna University**: Intended to capture LTTE leadership; ambushed due to intercepted radio transmissions.
- **Urban Combat**: LTTE used snipers, IEDs, and claymore mines extensively in built-up areas.
- **Naval Blockade**: Indian Navy enforced a 300-mile blockade to cut LTTE supply lines.
- **Air Support**: Mi-25 gunships and Mi-8 helicopters provided close air support and troop transport.

Outcome

- After **three weeks of intense fighting**, the IPKF captured **Jaffna Peninsula**.
- LTTE suffered heavy losses but retained leadership and regrouped in jungle areas.

- The operation exposed flaws in planning and intelligence but demonstrated adaptability under fire

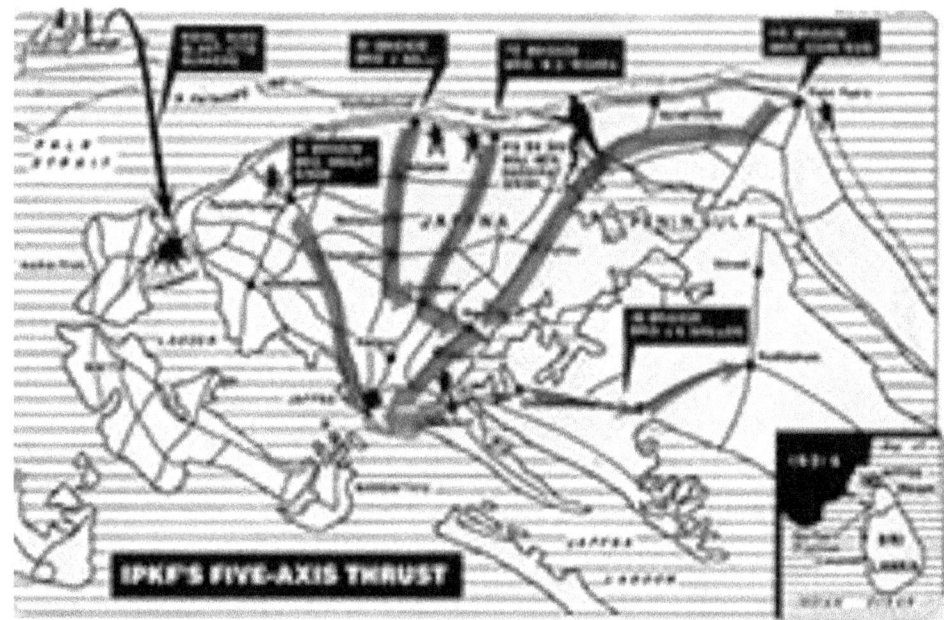

(Images in this article are AI generated)

References
everything.explained.today
www.bharat-rakshat.com
testbook.com
en.wikipedia.org
military-history.fandom.com

38

The 1987 Grenade Attack on Sri Lanka's Parliament: A Political Flashpoint

The Indo-Sri Lanka Accord, signed on **29 July 1987** between Indian Prime Minister **Rajiv Gandhi** and Sri Lankan President **J.R. Jayewardene**, was intended to bring an end to the ethnic conflict between the Sinhalese majority and Tamil minority. However, the accord sparked fierce opposition from Sinhalese nationalist groups, particularly the **Janatha Vimukthi Peramuna (JVP)**, a Marxist-Leninist party that viewed the agreement as a betrayal of Sri Lankan sovereignty.

The Incident

On **18 August 1987**, less than three weeks after the accord was signed, a dramatic attack unfolded inside **Committee Room A** of the Sri Lankan Parliament. During a routine meeting of the ruling United National Party (UNP) parliamentary group, an assailant hurled **two hand grenades** into the room where **President Jayewardene**, **Prime Minister Ranasinghe Premadasa**, and over **120 legislators** were gathered.

- The grenades bounced off the table where the President and PM were seated and exploded near **National Security Advisor Lalith Athulathmudali** and **Matara District MP Keerthisena Abeywickrama**.
- **Abeywickrama** died on the way to the hospital, while **Norbert Senadeera**, a parliamentary staff member, succumbed to head injuries days later.
- **16 others** were injured, including several senior ministers.

The Perpetrators

Responsibility was claimed by the **Deshapremi Janatha Viyaparaya (DJV)**, the armed wing of the **JVP**, which was then engaged in a violent insurgency against the government.

The attack was widely interpreted as retaliation for the Indo-Sri Lanka Accord, which the JVP saw as a capitulation to Indian influence and a threat to Sinhalese nationalism.

- The prime suspect was **Ajith Kumara**, a catering service worker inside Parliament and a known JVP activist.
- He evaded capture for nearly eight months before being arrested in **April 1988** during an unrelated police raid in **Naula**.
- Kumara and four others were indicted on multiple counts, including conspiracy to assassinate the President. However, all were **acquitted in 1990** due to lack of evidence.

Political and Social Impact

The attack underscored the deep divisions within Sri Lankan society and the volatility of its political landscape:

- It exposed the vulnerability of even the highest levels of government to insurgent violence.
- The incident intensified the government's crackdown on the JVP, which escalated into a brutal counterinsurgency campaign during the **1987–1989 JVP insurrection**.
- The Indo-Sri Lanka Accord itself failed to bring lasting peace, as the **Liberation Tigers of Tamil Eelam (LTTE)** rejected its terms and continued their armed struggle.

Though the grenade attack did not achieve its intended political assassination, it remains one of the most audacious acts of domestic terrorism in Sri Lanka's post-independence history. It marked a turning point in the JVP's insurgency and highlighted the perilous intersection of ethnic conflict, foreign diplomacy, and radical nationalism.

39

Vijaya Kumaratunga: Star, Statesman, and Martyr of Sri Lanka

Early Life and Rise to Stardom

Kovilage Anton Vijaya Kumaratunga was born on **October 9, 1945**, in Ragama, British Ceylon, into a Roman Catholic family. He was the youngest of four siblings and received his education at **St. Benedict's College** and **De Mazenod College**, where he excelled in drama, singing, and public speaking.

His cinematic debut came in **1969** with the film *Hanthane Kathawa*, which catapulted him into national fame. Over the next two decades, he starred in **over 120 films**, becoming one of the most beloved actors in Sri Lankan cinema. His roles often portrayed the struggles of ordinary people, and his charisma made him a household name.

Artistic Legacy

Beyond acting, Vijaya was a **playback singer**, recording over **100 songs**, and even produced films such as *Waradata Danduwam* and *Samawa*. His performances in *Bambaru Avith*, *Ganga Addara*, and *Baddegama* are considered cinematic milestones. He won multiple **Sarasaviya Most Popular Actor Awards** and posthumously received accolades for his singing.

Political Awakening

In **1974**, Vijaya entered politics through the **Lanka Sama Samaja Party (LSSP)**. He later joined the **Sri Lanka Freedom Party (SLFP)** and became its vice secretary. His political journey was marked by idealism and a commitment to social justice. In **1983**, he survived an assassination attempt during a by-election in Mahara, highlighting the volatility of Sri Lankan politics.

Vijaya Kumaratunga's marriage to **Chandrika Bandaranaike** was both a personal and political union that captured the imagination of Sri Lanka.

They married on **20 February 1978**, in a modest ceremony attended by close friends, including film director Lester James Peries and politician Hector Kobbekaduwa. Chandrika, the daughter of two former prime ministers—**S.W.R.D. Bandaranaike** and **Sirimavo Bandaranaike**—was already steeped in political legacy. Vijaya, a beloved film star and rising political figure, brought charisma and mass appeal to the partnership.

Their relationship was rooted in shared ideals and long conversations about national and international politics. After marriage, they lived in several homes across Colombo, including Rosemead Place and Polhengoda Road. Together, they had **two children**, **Yasodhara** and **Vimukthi**, both of whom later became doctors in the UK.

Disillusioned with mainstream politics, he founded the **Sri Lanka Mahajana Party (SLMP)** in **1984**, advocating for peace and reconciliation during the escalating civil conflict. He was one of the few Sinhala politicians to visit **Jaffna**, then under LTTE control, and openly called for dialogue with Tamil groups.

The couple's bond was tragically cut short by Vijaya's assassination in 1988. Chandrika, devastated but resolute, entered politics soon after and eventually became **Sri Lanka's first female Executive President**—continuing the legacy they had envisioned together.

Assassination and National Mourning

On **February 16, 1988**, Vijaya was **shot dead outside his home in Polhengoda, Colombo**, by **Lionel Ranasinghe**, a member of the **Deshapremi Janatha Viyaparaya (DJV)**—the militant wing of the **Janatha Vimukthi Peramuna (JVP)**. The assassin used a **Type 56 assault rifle**, and the attack was politically motivated, targeting Vijaya for his support of the **Indo-Sri Lanka Accord** and his criticism of the JVP insurgency.

His death sent shockwaves across the nation. The funeral, held at **Independence Square**, was the **first to be broadcast live on Sri Lankan television**, and drew massive crowds. The day became known as **"The Darkest Tuesday"** in Sri Lankan history.

Vijaya's assassination marked a turning point in Sri Lankan politics. He was mourned not just as a politician, but as a **symbol of unity, compassion, and courage**. His widow, **Chandrika Bandaranaike Kumaratunga**, later became **President of Sri Lanka**, continuing his vision for peace.

A **Presidential Commission** later implicated high-ranking officials, including **President Ranasinghe Premadasa** and **Minister Ranjan Wijeratne**, in suppressing the investigation, though direct involvement was never conclusively proven.

40

LTTE'S MOST NOTABLE INCIDENTS & GOVERNMENT OPERATIONS (1991-2000)

1991: Assassination of Rajiv Gandhi

On **21 May 1991**, former Indian Prime Minister **Rajiv Gandhi** was killed by an **LTTE suicide bomber** during an election rally in Tamil Nadu. The assassination shocked the region and made the LTTE a **globally recognized terrorist group**. India officially banned the LTTE, and Sri Lankan Tamils faced increasing stigma abroad.

1992: Deaths of Senior Military Commanders

One of the most significant incidents involving the deaths of top Sri Lankan military personnel in Jaffna occurred on **8 August 1992**, and it profoundly impacted the course of the civil war.

The Kayts Landmine Explosion: Deaths of Senior Military Leaders

On that day, **Lieutenant General Denzil Kobbekaduwa**, one of Sri Lanka's most respected military strategists, was killed along with several senior officers when their **Land Rover hit a landmine** on the island of **Kayts**, off the coast of Jaffna.

(Pic: Free Social Encyclopaedia)

Key Personnel Killed

The explosion claimed the lives of:

- **Lt. Gen. Denzil Kobbekaduwa** – Overall Operations Commander, Northern Sector
- **Brigadier Wimalaratne** – Deputy Commander
- **Lt. Colonel G.H. Ariyaratne** – Battalion Commander
- **Lt. Colonel A. Palipahana** – Battalion Commander
- **Lt. Colonel H.R. Stephen** – Battalion Commander
- **Lieutenant Commander Asanga Lankathilaka**
- **Lieutenant Commander C.B. Wijepura**
- **Major Nalin S. De Alwis**
- **General's Aide-de-camp**
- **Corporal Jagath Wickramaratna**

These officers were part of a high-level team preparing to launch **Operation Final Countdown**, a major offensive to recapture the Jaffna Peninsula from the LTTE.

Circumstances of the Attack

- The team was conducting a **reconnaissance mission** on Kayts Island.
- Their vehicle struck a **remotely detonated landmine**, believed to have been planted by the **LTTE**.
- The explosion was devastating, killing most of the occupants instantly and critically wounding others.

Strategic Impact

- The deaths were a **severe blow** to the Sri Lankan military, both tactically and emotionally.

  Lt. Gen. Kobbekaduwa was widely regarded as a brilliant commander, having led successful operations like **Operation Liberation (Vadamarachchi)** in 1987.

- His loss disrupted the momentum of planned offensives and led to a **reassessment of military strategy** in the north.

Legacy

- Kobbekaduwa is remembered as a **national hero**, and memorials have been erected in his honor.
- His death marked a turning point in the war, highlighting the LTTE's capability to target high-ranking officials and the vulnerability of even elite military units.

Operation Final Countdown: A Halted Offensive

Operation Final Countdown was planned as a decisive military move to **reclaim the Jaffna Peninsula**, which had become a strategic and symbolic stronghold of the **LTTE**.

- Kobbekaduwa and his top commanders were conducting final assessments and site surveys on **Kayts Island**, just off the coast, to orchestrate the offensive.
- It was intended to be a **coordinated, multi-pronged attack**, involving land, air, and sea forces, possibly the most ambitious since Operation Liberation in 1987.
- The objective was not just territorial: it aimed to **dislodge LTTE leadership**, disrupt their logistics, and restore government control in the north.

The plan, however, was **never executed**, following the tragic assassination of Kobbekaduwa and his team. Their deaths created a vacuum of military leadership and morale that stalled forward movement.

The Strategic Brilliance of Denzil Kobbekaduwa

Often hailed as **Sri Lanka's most gifted battlefield tactician**, Kobbekaduwa:

- Championed **joint operations** between branches of the military.
- Was known for **meticulous planning**, emphasizing intelligence and terrain familiarity.
- Had previously led **Operation Vadamarachchi** in 1987, which nearly crushed the LTTE before Indian intervention.

He also maintained **strong rapport with troops**—a rare quality for commanders. Soldiers under him viewed him not just as a leader but as a **symbol of patriotic duty and decency**.

After his death:

- Annual memorials are held on **August 8** to honor the fallen military heroes.
- **Denzil Kobbekaduwa Mawatha**, a major street in Colombo, and several monuments bear his name.
- His leadership style remains a **benchmark** for military cadets and strategists to this day.

His death reminded Sri Lankans of the high cost of war—and the valor of those willing to shape its outcome with integrity.

41

1993: Killing of President Premadasa

Ranasinghe Premadasa, Sri Lanka's President and architect of a hardline approach against the LTTE, was assassinated in a **May Day bombing** on **1 May 1993**. The LTTE placed a suicide bomber close to the stage where he was addressing crowds. His death brought uncertainty but also paved the way for fresh attempts at negotiation.

President Premadasa was a polarizing figure in Sri Lankan politics. By 1993, he had survived an impeachment attempt and was facing mounting criticism over alleged corruption and his handling of the civil war. His decision to **arm the LTTE** in the late 1980s to counter the Indian Peace Keeping Force (IPKF) had backfired, as the LTTE later turned against the Sri Lankan government.

The **Liberation Tigers of Tamil Eelam (LTTE)**, known for their suicide bombings and targeted assassinations, viewed Premadasa as a threat to their separatist ambitions. His increasing military pressure on the LTTE and his role in the withdrawal of the IPKF made him a prime target.

Planning the Assassination

The suicide bomber was **Kulaveerasingam "Babu" Veerakumar**, a 23-year-old LTTE operative from **Gurunagar, Jaffna**. His infiltration into Premadasa's inner circle was meticulous and patient:

- Babu befriended **E.M.P. Mohideen**, Premadasa's trusted valet, exploiting his **fondness for liquor** to gain access to the president's residence, **Sucharitha**.
- He opened a **grocery shop** near the residence and ran a **trucking service** between Colombo and Jaffna, allegedly used to smuggle explosives.
- Babu was seen traveling with **Advance Presidential Security Teams**, suggesting deep penetration into the president's entourage.

- Despite warnings from CID officials about a possible poisoning attempt, no serious action was taken to vet domestic staff or tighten security.

Execution on May Day

On **May 1, 1993**, the **United National Party** organized a **May Day rally** in Colombo. Premadasa was supervising the procession near **Armour Street and Grandpass Road**.

- At **12:45 PM**, Babu approached Premadasa's **Range Rover** on a **bicycle**, carrying **0.91 kg of plastic explosives** strapped to his body.
- Security personnel tried to stop him, but **Mohideen signaled them to let him through**, trusting Babu implicitly.
- Once within **8–10 feet** of the president, Babu **detonated the suicide vest**, killing:
  - President Premadasa
  - Mohideen
  - SSP Ronnie Gunasinghe
  - 20 others, including most of Premadasa's personal staff
- **38–60 people** were injured, with several in critical condition.

Aftermath and Investigation

- The blast site was **cleaned within hours**, before a proper forensic investigation could be conducted—allegedly to prevent communal violence.
- Confusion reigned for hours; Premadasa's death was only confirmed when his **ring and watch** were identified on body parts in the morgue.
- An **island-wide curfew** was imposed, and **Prime Minister D.B. Wijetunga** was sworn in as acting president on **May 7, 1993**.

  23 individuals were arrested, including members of the president's domestic staff and security detail.

- Despite the arrests, **no one was convicted**, and the case was eventually dropped due to lack of evidence.

The assassination remains one of the most **brazen and tragic political killings** in Sri Lanka's history.

While the LTTE was widely blamed, some critics questioned whether **internal political rivalries** played a role.

Premadasa's death came just **eight days after the assassination of Lalith Athulathmudali**, another prominent politician—fueling speculation about deeper conspiracies.

1995: Capture of Jaffna and LTTE Retaliation

Under President **Chandrika Kumaratunga**, the Sri Lankan Army launched **Operation Riviresa**, capturing **Jaffna town**—a major LTTE stronghold—in **late 1995**. Though hailed as a victory, it came at great cost:

- **Thousands of Tamil civilians** were displaced.
- LTTE regrouped in **jungles and eastern areas**.

Retaliation followed swiftly:

In **October 1996**, the **Palliyagodella massacre** saw the LTTE kill over **120 Muslim villagers** in the East, accusing them of siding with the government.

1996: Central Bank Bombing

On **31 January 1996**, the LTTE carried out one of the deadliest bombings in Sri Lanka's history:

- A suicide truck bomb destroyed part of the **Central Bank** in **Colombo**.
- Nearly **100 people were killed**, and **1,400 injured**.
- The attack caused **mass panic** and **international condemnation**.

1997–1999: Failed Peace Efforts and Escalating Violence

President Kumaratunga attempted peace talks and constitutional reforms:

- A **devolution package** was proposed but stalled in Parliament.
- The LTTE continued attacks, including ambushes and assassinations.

In **December 1999**, Kumaratunga barely survived an **LTTE suicide bombing** during her campaign rally:

- She was **badly injured**, losing sight in one eye.
- The incident reflected the LTTE's refusal to accept compromise.

A Nation Changed

By the year **2000**, Sri Lanka had endured:

- **Multiple assassinations** of top leaders.
- **Tens of thousands of civilian casualties**.
- A refugee crisis with **hundreds of thousands displaced**.
- A fractured political landscape with **public fatigue**, **fear**, and **anger** growing.

The LTTE had evolved into a **powerful military force** with air and naval capability, while the government continued to oscillate between military campaigns and political negotiation—neither yielding lasting peace.

Between **1983 and 2000**, Sri Lanka was **transformed by war**. Cities, villages, and families across ethnic lines were drawn into the vortex. The loss of life, shattered dreams, and lost opportunities during this period shaped not just policy but the very psyche of a nation.

42

Lalith Athulathmudali – A Politician who could have become the President

Lalith Athulathmudali |
Statesman & Briliant Visionary

The Making of a Visionary — Lalith Athulathmudali

In the annals of Sri Lankan political history, few names evoke the same reverence and intellectual admiration as **Lalith William Samarasekera Athulathmudali**. Born on **26 November 1936** in **Colombo**, into a family steeped in legal and political tradition, Lalith was destined to leave an indelible mark on the nation's governance and public life. His father, **D.D. Athulathmudali**, was a member of the **State Council of Ceylon**, and his mother, **Srimathi Samarasekera**, nurtured a household that valued education, discipline, and civic duty.

Early Life and Education

Lalith's academic journey began at **St. John's College, Panadura**, followed by **Royal Primary School**, and then **Royal College, Colombo**, where he quickly distinguished himself as a scholar and athlete. He won numerous prizes for literature, history, and public speaking, and was a decorated sportsman—captaining teams in athletics and cricket. His intellectual brilliance earned him the **Governor-General's Prize**, among many others, foreshadowing a future of leadership and reform.

In 1955, Lalith entered **Jesus College, Oxford**, to read **Jurisprudence**, graduating with a **BA**, **MA**, and **BCL**. He became the **first Sri Lankan President of the Oxford Union**, a prestigious debating society that shaped many global leaders. He later earned an **LL.M. from Harvard University** in 1963, where his thesis was accepted into the university's permanent collection—a rare honor.

Legal and Academic Career

Before entering politics, Lalith built a formidable career in law and academia:

- Admitted to the **Gray's Inn** as a **Barrister** in 1959
- Served as a **law lecturer** and **Associate Dean** at the **University of Singapore**
- Guest lecturer at **Hebrew University (Israel)**, **University of Edinburgh**, and **University of Allahabad**
- Returned to Sri Lanka in 1964 to practice law and lecture at **Ceylon Law College**
- Appointed **President's Counsel** in 1985

His fluency in **Sinhala, English, German, and French** made him a rare intellectual force in both domestic and international circles.

Political Ascent

Lalith entered politics in the early 1970s, joining the **United National Party (UNP)** and its **Policy Planning Committee**. In the **1977 general election**, he was elected MP for **Ratmalana**, and later for **Colombo District**, securing a record **235,447 preferential votes** in 1989.

His ministerial career was marked by innovation and reform:

- **Minister of Trade and Shipping (1977–1984)**: Introduced **Intellectual Property Law**, established the **Sri Lanka Export Development Board**, and modernized the **Colombo Port**
- **Founder of the Mahapola Scholarship Scheme (1981)**: A transformative initiative that provided financial aid to thousands of underprivileged university students
- **Minister of National Security and Deputy Minister of Defence (1984–1989)**: Oversaw military expansion and led the successful **Vadamarachchi Operation** against the LTTE
- **Minister of Agriculture and Education (1989–1991)**: Advocated for export-oriented farming and educational modernization

Lalith was widely regarded as one of the most **intellectually gifted and principled politicians** of his time. His speeches in Parliament were masterclasses in logic, clarity, and conviction. He was admired for his **discipline**, **punctuality**, and **unwavering commitment to national progress**.

Despite his brilliance, Lalith's career was not without turbulence. His **attempt to impeach President Premadasa** in 1991 led to his expulsion from the UNP. He then co-founded the **Democratic United National Front (DUNF)**, positioning himself as a reformist alternative.

Tragically, his life was cut short on **23 April 1993**, when he was **assassinated** during a campaign rally in **Kirulapana**. His death remains one of the most controversial and mourned events in Sri Lankan political history.

Earlier Attempts on His Life

Between **1991 and 1992**, Athulathmudali survived **multiple attacks** believed to be politically motivated:

- **November 2, 1991 – Pannala**: Assaulted during a public meeting.
- **April 23, 1992 – Madapatha**: Targeted exactly one year before his assassination.
- **August 7, 1992 – Fort Railway Station**: Attacked by alleged thugs linked to rival political factions.
- **August 29, 1992 – Dehiwala**: Another violent disruption of his campaign.

These incidents occurred after he led an **impeachment motion against President Ranasinghe Premadasa** in 1991, accusing him of abuse of power. The motion failed, but it deepened the rift between the two leaders.

Final Days and Political Climate (1993)

In **March 1993**, the government dissolved provincial councils and announced elections for **May 17**. Athulathmudali, now leader of the **Democratic United National Front (DUNF)**, was campaigning to become **Chief Minister of the Western Province**.

- On **April 23, 1993**, he addressed rallies in **Borella**, **Aluthkade**, and finally **Kirulapana**, where he was **fatally shot** at around **8:10 PM** while speaking to a crowd of over 1,000 people.
- His **bodyguard**, Thilak Shantha, was also wounded in the exchange of gunfire with the assassin.

The Assassination and Aftermath

- The next morning, police found the body of **Appiah Balakrishnan alias Ragunathan**, a Tamil youth, 200 meters from the stage. He had allegedly died by **cyanide poisoning**, a method associated with **LTTE operatives**.
- Initial investigations blamed the **LTTE**, citing Ragunathan's supposed affiliation and suicide capsule. However, **no conclusive evidence** linked him to the group.
- A **Presidential Commission** later implicated **President Premadasa** and members of his security apparatus in orchestrating the murder, suggesting the LTTE narrative was a **cover-up.**

Legacy and Controversy

- Athulathmudali's death came **just eight days before Premadasa himself was assassinated** by an LTTE suicide bomber on **May 1, 1993**.
- The **Scotland Yard investigation** supported the LTTE theory, but its findings were widely criticized as politically influenced.

- The **1997 Presidential Commission** concluded that **underworld figures** linked to Premadasa were responsible, and that Ragunathan was **not the assassin**, but a **planted body** to mislead investigators.

Lalith Athulathmudali's assassination remains a haunting reminder of Sri Lanka's volatile political landscape. His vision for reform and national unity was extinguished in a moment of violence that still sparks debate and suspicion.

Presidential Commission of Inquiry (1994–1997)

After years of public skepticism and conflicting reports, **President Chandrika Kumaratunga** appointed a **Special Presidential Commission of Inquiry** in **1994** to investigate the assassination. The commission was chaired by **Justice Tissa Dias Bandaranayake** and included **Justice G.W. Edirisuriya**.

The commission was tasked with examining:

- The **circumstances of the assassination** on April 23, 1993
- The **identity of the perpetrators**
- The **role of public officials** in failing to provide security
- The **validity of the LTTE involvement theory**
- The **possible political conspiracy** behind the murder

Findings and Implications

The commission's final report, submitted in **October 1997**, made **explosive claims**:

- **Former President Ranasinghe Premadasa** was **implicated** as the **mastermind** behind the assassination.
- His close associate, **Minister Sirisena Cooray**, was recommended for **civic disability** due to his alleged involvement.

- The commission rejected the **LTTE theory**, stating that the Tamil youth **Ragunathan**, found dead near the crime scene, was **not the assassin** but a **planted body** to mislead investigators.
- The actual assassin was identified as **Janaka Priyankara Jayamanna**, alias **Wellampitiye Sudumahattaya**, a known **underworld figure**.
- Several **security force members** and **underworld operatives** were arrested and charged with conspiracy, but **three were killed** during prosecution, raising further doubts.

The commission's findings **directly contradicted** earlier investigations:

- A **Scotland Yard report**, commissioned by Premadasa's government, had concluded that **Ragunathan was the assassin** and had committed suicide via cyanide.
- The commission dismissed this as a **cover-up**, citing **forensic inconsistencies**, lack of motive, and **political interference** in the investigation.

- The commission's report led to **legal challenges**, including a **Supreme Court case** by Sirisena Cooray, who argued the findings violated principles of natural justice.
- The court ruled that **commission reports are subject to judicial review**, reinforcing the importance of due process.
- ⬜ Despite the Commission's conclusions, **no convictions** were secured, and the case remains **officially unresolved**.

Two Potential Future Sri Lankan Presidents – Gamini Dissanayake & Lalith Athulathmudali

43

The JVP Insurrection (1987–1989): A Violent Chapter in Sri Lanka's History

The **Janatha Vimukthi Peramuna (JVP)**, led by **Rohana Wijeweera**, launched its second armed uprising between **1987 and 1989**. Unlike the 1971 revolt, this was a **low-intensity guerrilla war** marked by **assassinations, sabotage, and terror tactics**. The JVP opposed the **Indo-Lanka Accord** and the presence of **Indian Peace Keeping Forces (IPKF)** and aimed to overthrow the government and establish a Marxist state.

Major Killings by the JVP?

The JVP targeted **government officials, military personnel, political figures, and civilians**. Some of the most notable assassinations included:

- **Jinadasa Weerasinghe**, MP for Tangalle – killed on the first day of the uprising.
- **Public servants**: Over **487** were murdered.
- **Police officers**: More than **342** killed.
- **Military personnel**: At least **209** assassinated.
- **Political leaders**: **16** killed, mostly from the **UNP**.
- **Civilians**: Nearly **5,000**, including:

- **30 Buddhist monks**
- **2 Catholic priests**
- **52 school principals**
- **18 estate superintendents**
- **27 trade unionists**
- Family members of **93 policemen** and **69 servicemen**

The JVP also used **child s soldiers**, such as the infamous case of "Kantale Bonikki," a 13-year-old girl used to kill a 70-year-old UNP supporter.

Government Hunt down: Operation Combine

In response, the government launched **Operation Combine**, a brutal counter-insurgency campaign led by **State Minister for Defence Ranjan Wijeratne**. The operation included:

- **Death squads** like the **Black Cats** and **Eagles of the Central Hills**.
- Use of the **Prevention of Terrorism Act (PTA)** to arrest and detain suspects without trial.
- **Extrajudicial killings** and mass disappearances—estimated at **60,000 to 80,000 deaths**, with **20,000+ missing**.
- Bodies were often mutilated, burned, or dumped in rivers to instill fear.

The Last Days of Rohana Wijeweera

Capture

Wijeweera was living under the alias **Nimal Kirthisiri Attanayake** in **Ulapane**, Kandy.

- On **12 November 1989**, he was arrested by a military team led by **General Janaka Perera**.

He was brought to **Operation Combine HQ** in Colombo for interrogation.

Interrogation and Video Recording

Wijeweera was filmed giving a **final statement**, where he:

- *Denied involvement in certain killings.*
- *Criticized the government's support for the LTTE.*
- *Called for youth to lay down arms and return to democracy.*

Execution

- On **13 November 1989**, Wijeweera was **executed**, though the exact method remains disputed:

- **Official version**: He was shot by fellow JVP leader **H.B. Herath**, prompting security forces to kill both.
- **Unofficial accounts**: He was **shot on the Colombo Golf Course** and **cremated alive or while unconscious**.

Who Was Behind It?

The man most responsible for the crackdown was **Ranjan Wijeratne**, the **State Minister for Defence**.

- He masterminded **Operation Combine**.

- He oversaw the **capture, interrogation, and elimination** of JVP leaders.
- He later vowed to use similar tactics against the LTTE before being **assassinated in 1991**.

The **1987–1989 JVP Insurrection** and its violent suppression changed Sri Lanka's political image forever. It exposed:

- The **fragility of democracy**.
- The **brutality of state power**.
- The **depth of youth disillusionment**.

While the JVP later re-entered mainstream politics, the scars of this era remain deep. The death of **Rohana Wijeweera** marked the end of a revolutionary dream—but also the beginning of a long debate about justice, accountability, and reconciliation.

44

The Assassination of Gamini Dissanayake and UNP Leaders — October 24, 1994

In 1994, Sri Lanka was preparing for a pivotal **Presidential Election**. Gamini Dissanayake, a seasoned statesman and visionary leader of the **United National Party (UNP)**, had emerged as a top contender. He was widely respected for his role in national development, especially the **Mahaweli Project**, and was seen as a potential unifier during a time of civil unrest.

The country was also in the midst of **peace negotiations** with the **Liberation Tigers of Tamil Eelam (LTTE)**, who had a history of targeting political figures.

The Attack

- **Date & Time**: 24 October 1994, around **12:10 AM**
- **Location**: Thotalanga, northern Colombo
- **Event**: A late-night campaign rally for the UNP

As Dissanayake concluded his speech and bid the crowd "good morning," a **female suicide bomber**, allegedly sent by the LTTE, detonated explosives near the stage.

Casualties

- **Total killed: 52 people**
- **Injured**: Over **200**, with **75 critically wounded**

Among the deceased were several high-ran ranking UNP members:

NAME	POSITION
Gamini Dissanayake	Leader of the Opposition, UNP presidential candidate
Dr. Gamini Wijesekera	UNP General Secretary
G. M. Premachandra	Minister of Labour and Vocational Training
Weerasinghe Mallimarachchi	Member of Parliament
Ossie Abeygunasekera	Member of Parliament
K.B. Christie Perera	Deputy Mayor of Colombo
K.B. Sriyani Gunasekera	Daughter of Christie Perera

The blast was so powerful that it sprayed **ball bearings and shrapnel**, causing widespread devastation.

Aftermath and Impact

- The assassination occurred **just two weeks before the presidential election**, throwing the UNP into disarray.
- The party nominated **Srima Dissanayake**, Gamini's widow, as a replacement candidate. She lost in a **landslide** to **Chandrika Kumaratunga**, who became Sri Lanka's first female president.
- President D.B. Wijetunga **reimposed a state of emergency** and **canceled peace talks** scheduled for later that day in Jaffna.

Gamini Dissanayake's death was a **national tragedy**. He was remembered as a **visionary leader**, a **champion of development**, and a **gentleman politician**. His assassination, along with the loss of other key figures, marked a turning point in Sri Lanka's political landscape and underscored the LTTE's brutal tactics.

45

1994 General Elections

The political climate leading up to the **1994 Sri Lankan General Elections** was charged with public frustration, deepening ethnic tensions, and a yearning for democratic renewal after **17 years of United National Party (UNP) rule**.

Political Climate Before the 1994 Elections

Authoritarian Legacy: The UNP governments under **J.R. Jayewardene** and **Ranasinghe Premadasa** had been accused of suppressing opposition, manipulating media, and using state violence against both the **LTTE** and **JVP** insurgencies.

Civil War Fatigue: The ongoing conflict with the LTTE had drained national morale. Citizens were weary of war, repression, and economic hardship.

Assassinations & Instability: President Premadasa was assassinated in 1993, followed by the killing of opposition leader **Lalith Athulathmudali** and later **Gamini Dissanayake**, the UNP's presidential candidate. These events created a vacuum of leadership and heightened public anxiety.

Demand for Change: There was a strong public desire for peace, democratic reform, and a more inclusive government. The UNP's credibility had eroded due to allegations of corruption and authoritarianism.

Key Political Players

NAME	ROLE & AFFILIATION	SIGNIFICANCE
Chandrika Bandaranaike Kumaratunga	Leader of the **People's Alliance (PA)**, daughter of two former prime ministers	Symbol of democratic revival and reconciliation with Tamils
D.B. Wijetunga	Incumbent **UNP President** (1993–1994)	Took office after Premadasa's assassination; chose not to run for re-election
Gamini Dissanayake	UNP's original presidential candidate	Assassinated by LTTE during campaign; replaced by his wife **Srima Dissanayake**
Sirimavo Bandaranaike	Former Prime Minister; nominal leader of SLFP	Played a symbolic role in the PA coalition led by her daughter
Sri Lanka Muslim Congress (SLMC)	Minority party allied with PA	Helped PA secure a parliamentary majority
LTTE	Tamil separatist group	Continued armed struggle; responsible for high-profile assassinations

Held on **16 August 1994**, with a **76.2% turnout**.

The **People's Alliance** won **105 seats**, forming a government with support from SLMC and other minority parties.

Marked the **end of UNP's 17-year rule** and ushered in a new era of coalition politics and hopes for peace.

Campaign Promises: A Battle of Visions

People's Alliance (PA) – Led by *Chandrika Bandaranaike Kumaratunga*

- Promised **democratic reform** and an end to authoritarianism.
- Advocated **peace talks** with Tamil groups, including the LTTE, without preconditions.
- Vowed to **abolish the Executive Presidency**, transferring more power to Parliament and the Prime Minister.
- Supported the **open-market economy**, but with a "human face":
  o Fairer privatization
  o Support for small producers
  o Expanded welfare for the poor
- Focused on **reducing inflation** and the **cost of living**.
- Emphasized **ethnic reconciliation**, especially with Tamil and Muslim minorities.

United National Party (UNP) – Led by *D.B. Wijetunga*

- Highlighted its **economic development record**:
  - Mahaweli River Project
  - Infrastructure expansion
- Industrial growth
- Defended its **free-market reforms** and privatization efforts.

- Warned against the PA's lack of experience and leftist leanings.
- Downplayed the ethnic conflict, framing it as a **terrorism issue** rather than a political crisis.

Election Results

PARTY	VOTES (%)	SEATS WON
People's Alliance	48.94%	105
United National Party	44.04%	94
Sri Lanka Muslim Congress	1.80%	7
Tamil United Liberation Front	1.67%	5

- **Turnout**: 76.24%
- PA formed a government with support from **SLMC** and **independent Tamil MPs**, reaching the required **113-seat majority**.

The election marked the **end of 17 years of UNP rule**, restoring faith in electoral democracy.

- Chandrika Kumaratunga became **Prime Minister**, later winning the **Presidency** in November 1994.
- Despite promises, the **Executive Presidency was not abolished**, and the civil war continued.
- The PA's initial peace overtures to the LTTE failed, leading to renewed military conflict.
- The election was seen as a **vote for good governance** but hopes for sweeping reform were only partially fulfilled.

Evolution of Key Campaign Promises under Kumaratunga

Peace Negotiations with the LTTE

- Initially engaged in talks with the LTTE in 1995, leading to a temporary ceasefire.
- Talks collapsed after the LTTE attacked naval vessels in Trincomalee.
- The government then launched **Operation Riviresa**, recapturing Jaffna in late 1995.

Executive Presidency Reform

- Although she pledged to abolish the powerful Executive Presidency, it remained intact throughout her tenure.
- Attempts at constitutional reform were hampered by political resistance and lack of parliamentary consensus.

Economic and Social Welfare

- Continued market-oriented policies but introduced **Samurdhi**, a rural-focused poverty alleviation program.
- Efforts to humanize economic reforms were partially successful but plagued by bureaucratic inefficiencies.

War Years and Shifting Strategy

- After initial setbacks in peacebuilding, Kumaratunga's administration shifted toward **military containment** of the LTTE.
- Launched **multi-pronged offensives**, but sustained peace remained elusive.

Public Sentiment

- The assassination attempt in 1999 dramatically shaped her second term—consolidating her image as a resilient, peace-seeking leader.
- Despite mixed success in achieving reforms, she maintained a reputation for **integrity**, **intellectual rigor**, and **courage** in the face of violence.

46

The Sri Lanka Muslim Congress: Voice of a Marginalized Community

"Birth of a Political Party for Muslims"

Origins and Founding Vision

The **Sri Lanka Muslim Congress (SLMC)** was founded in **1981** in **Kattankudy**, Eastern Province, by **Mohammed Hussain Mohammed Ashraff**, a lawyer and visionary leader. At the time, Sri Lankan Muslims—especially in the east—felt politically alienated and vulnerable amid the growing ethnic conflict between the Sinhalese and Tamils.

Ashraff's goal was to create a **distinct political platform** that could:

- Represent the **Muslim minority's interests**
- Prevent Muslim youth from joining militant groups like the **LTTE**
- Advocate for **peaceful coexistence** and **multiracial harmony**

Initially a **socio-cultural movement**, the SLMC was formally declared a political party in **1986**, with Ashraff as its charismatic leader.

M.H.M. Ashraff: The Architect of Muslim Political Identity

(Pic: colombotimes.net)

Ashraff's leadership transformed the SLMC into a **national political force**. His achievements include:

- Championing the **Mahapola Scholarship Scheme**
- Establishing the **Southeastern University of Sri Lanka**
- Advocating for **Muslim rights** in Parliament and peace talks

- Serving as **Minister of Shipping, Ports, Rehabilitation and Reconstruction** under President Chandrika Kumaratunga

Ashraff's eloquence, legal acumen, and deep understanding of Tamil and Islamic traditions made him a **bridge-builder** between communities. His untimely death in a helicopter crash in **September 2000** left a vacuum in Muslim politics that remains palpable.

Transition and Leadership of Rauff Hakeem

After Ashraff's death, **Rauff Hakeem**, a lawyer and SLMC's General Secretary, assumed leadership. Hakeem's tenure was marked by **strategic alliances** and **political pragmatism**:

- Joined the **People's Alliance (PA)** government in 1994
- Later aligned with the **United National Front (UNF)** in 2001

Served in multiple ministerial roles including:

- **Minister of Ports and Shipping**
- **Minister of Justice**
- **Minister of Urban Development and Water Supply**

Hakeem's ability to **negotiate coalition deals** made SLMC a **kingmaker** in several elections, especially in **1994**, when it helped the PA form a government.

Political Influence and Challenges

SLMC's influence peaked in the 1990s and early 2000s, when it:

- Secured **multiple parliamentary seats**
- Became a **decisive force** in coalition politics
- Gave Muslims a **strong voice** in national decision-making

However, internal divisions and shifting alliances led to:

- Fragmentation of the party post-Ashraff
- Criticism over **opportunistic crossovers**
- Declining electoral performance in recent years

Despite these challenges, SLMC remains the **largest Muslim political party** in Sri Lanka.

The SLMC's legacy lies in its role as:

- A **protector of Muslim identity and rights**
- A **moderating force** during ethnic tensions
- A **symbol of political empowerment** for a marginalized community

While its relevance has waned in recent years, the SLMC's foundational ideals—**equality, justice, and unity**—continue to resonate.

The Death of M.H.M. Ashraff: A Tragedy Shrouded in Mystery

On the morning of **16 September 2000**, **M.H.M. Ashraff**, then **Minister of Ports, Shipping, Rehabilitation and Reconstruction**, boarded a **Sri Lanka Air Force (SLAF) Mi-17 helicopter** from the Police Grounds in **Bambalapitiya**, Colombo. His destination was **Ampara District**, his political stronghold in the Eastern Province.

- On board were **14 others**: nine SLMC officials, three bodyguards, and two SLAF crew members.
- The flight path was to pass over **Kandy**, **Randenigala**, **Maha Oya**, and **Iginiyagala**.

Approximately **45 minutes after takeoff**, the helicopter lost radio contact. It was later discovered to have **crashed into Bible Rock (Urakanda)** near **Aranayake**, in **Kegalle District**. All **15 passengers perished**, and their bodies were recovered from the burning wreckage.

Weather and Initial Reports

- The weather was reportedly **clear and calm**, ruling out poor visibility or storms as contributing factors.
- Initial government statements cited **engine failure**, but this explanation was met with skepticism due to the aircraft's maintenance history and the absence of distress signals.

Government Response

- A **Presidential Commission of Inquiry** was appointed in **January 2001** by President **Chandrika Kumaratunga** to investigate the crash.
- Despite extensive probing, **no conclusive cause** was determined. The commission failed to establish whether the crash was due to mechanical failure, sabotage, or foul play.

Suspicious Circumstances

- Just days before the crash, Ashraff had **resigned from the government**, citing irreconcilable differences with the **People's Alliance (PA)**. Though President Kumaratunga refused to accept the resignation, Ashraff had sent faxes to media outlets declaring that the **SLMC and National Unity Alliance (NUA)** were severing ties with the PA.
- He had also **returned from a pilgrimage to Mecca**, reportedly reinvigorated and politically resolute.
- Some observers noted that Ashraff had **received threats** and was increasingly **isolated within the cabinet**, especially due to tensions with fellow Muslim ministers and PA leadership.

The lack of definitive answers has fueled **decades of speculation**:

- Was the crash a **technical failure**, or was it **deliberately orchestrated**?
- Did Ashraff's **political realignment** and growing influence threaten powerful interests?
- Why was the **wreckage cleared so quickly**, and why were **no survivors or distress signals** reported?

To this day, **no one has been held accountable**, and the mystery remains unresolved.

Impact on Muslim Politics

Ashraff's death created a **vacuum in Muslim leadership** that has never truly been filled. His vision for a **united, inclusive Sri Lanka** and his ability to **bridge ethnic divides** made him a rare figure in Sri Lankan politics.

His widow, **Ferial Ashraff**, entered politics and became the **first Muslim woman cabinet minister**, but the SLMC's internal cohesion and national influence waned in the years following his death.

To this day, **no one has been held accountable**, and the mystery remains unresolved.

The Udathalawinna Massacre — December 5, 2001

Udathalawinna massacre, a deeply troubling incident that occurred during the **2001 general elections** in Sri Lanka, when **General Anuruddha Ratwatte** was serving as **Deputy Minister of Defence** under the People's Alliance government.

On the evening of **December 5, 2001**, ten Muslim youth—supporters of the **Sri Lanka Muslim Congress (SLMC)**—were **shot dead at point-blank range** in **Udathalawinna**, near **Katugastota in Kandy District**.

Circumstances of the Attack

- The victims were **escorting election officials** transporting a ballot box from **Madawala polling station** to the counting center in Kandy.
- Their vehicle was allegedly **intercepted by armed men**, described as a **"thug squad"** linked to **Lohan Ratwatte, son of General Anuruddha Ratwatte**.
- The attackers **forced the vehicle off the road**, crashed it into a lamppost, and **opened fire**, killing all ten occupants instantly.

Victims

The deceased were all young SLMC supporters, aged between 19 and 31. Their names included:

- T.M. Fisar (24)
- F.M. Rizwan (27)
- M.R.M. Nazir (25)
- A.M.M. Mohideen (31)
- Z.M. Nazar (19)

- M.I.M. Ashwar (26)
- And others

Legal Proceedings and Controversy

- **General Ratwatte**, along with his sons **Lohan** and **Chanuka**, were **charged with aiding and abetting** the murders.
- A **Trial-at-Bar** was held in Kandy, but in **2006**, all three were **acquitted** due to lack of direct evidence.
- **Five army personnel** were initially **convicted and sentenced to death**, but in **2009**, the **Supreme Court acquitted them**, citing procedural flaws and insufficient evidence.

Political and Social Impact

- The massacre was w ⬚ widely condemned as **politically motivated violence**, targeting Muslim voters during a tense election.
- It highlighted the **impunity** often enjoyed by powerful political figures and the **vulnerability of minority communities**.
- The incident remains a **symbol of electoral brutality** and **unresolved justice**, with no one held accountable despite multiple investigations.

SLMC's Response to the Udathalawinna Massacre

The **Udathalawinna killings** on **December 5, 2001**, in which **ten Muslim youth** affiliated with the SLMC were murdered during the general election, sent shockwaves through the Muslim community. The victims were escorting ballot boxes when they were ambushed and shot at point-blank range by a group allegedly linked to **Lohan Ratwatte**, son of then Deputy Defence Minister **General Anuruddha Ratwatte**.

SLMC's Immediate Reaction

- SLMC leaders, including **Rauff Hakeem**, condemned the killings as **politically motivated** and demanded a **full investigation**.
- The party called for **international attention**, with organizations like **OMCT** and **Amnesty International** urging accountability and justice.
- SLMC joined civil society groups in alleging that the perpetrators were shielded by political power and that the massacre was part of a broader pattern of **electoral violence and voter suppression** targeting minorities.

Legal Proceedings and Disillusionment

- Although **General Ratwatte** and his sons were charged, they were **acquitted in 2006** by the High Court.
- Five army personnel were initially convicted and sentenced to death, but the **Supreme Court acquitted them in 2009**, citing lack of evidence.
- SLMC leaders and Muslim activists expressed **deep frustration** over the **failure to secure justice**, viewing the acquittals as emblematic of **impunity for powerful figures**.

Impact on Muslim Political Representation

SLMC's Strategic Shift

- The massacre galvanized SLMC's resolve to **assert Muslim rights** more forcefully in Parliament.
- SLMC continued to play a **kingmaker role** in coalition politics, aligning with both the **People's Alliance** and later the **United National Front**, depending on strategic interests.
- Rauff Hakeem emerged as a **key negotiator** in peace talks and constitutional reform discussions, advocating for **minority protections**.

Broader Political Consequences

- The massacre highlighted the **vulnerability of Muslim voters** during elections and led to increased calls for **electoral reform** and **security guarantees**.
- SLMC pushed for **independent election monitoring**, **minority-inclusive policing**, and **legal safeguards** against political violence.

Despite setbacks, the party maintained a **visible presence** in Parliament and continued to influence national policy on **ed ⬜ education**, **land rights**, and **reconciliation**.

47

1999 Assassination Attempt on President Chandrika Bandaranaike Kumaratunga

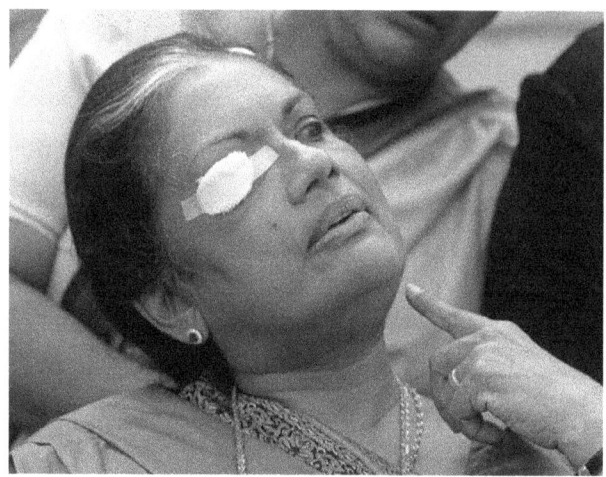

One of the most dramatic moments in Sri Lanka's political history

On **December 18, 1999**, just two days before the presidential election, President Chandrika Kumaratunga was targeted in a **suicide bombing** orchestrated by the **Liberation Tigers of Tamil Eelam (LTTE)**. The attack occurred at her **final campaign rally** held at **Town Hall in Colombo**, the capital of Sri Lanka.

The Attack

- As President Kumaratunga exited the rally and walked toward her vehicle, an **unidentified female suicide bomber** attempted to leap over a barricade.
- Security personnel restrained her, but she detonated the **explosive vest** strapped to her body.
- The explosion was captured on live television, blinding many nearby and causing widespread panic.

Injuries and Casualties

- Kumaratunga suffered **severe facial injuries**, including permanent damage to her **optic nerve**, resulting in **blindness in her right eye**. She now wears a glass eye.
- **34 people** were killed, including:
  - Her chauffeur
  - Several security guards

- Sri Lanka's most senior policeman, **T. N. De Silva**
  - Three government ministers
  - Over **105 others** were injured, including foreign journalists.

Coordinated Attacks

- On the same day, another suicide bombing targeted the **opposition United National Party (UNP)** rally in **Ja-Ela**, killing **12 people**, including **Major General Lucky Algama**, and injuring over **70**.
- Both attacks were attributed to the LTTE, which opposed Kumaratunga's peace initiatives and viewed her as a threat to their separatist goals.

Aftermath and Response

- Despite her injuries, Kumaratunga remained composed and urged the public to **stay calm and avoid retaliatory violence**. She requested that people **pray for peace** at their places of worship.
- She won the **presidential election** on **December 21, 1999**, and was sworn in for her **second term** on **December 22**.
- The government imposed an **indefinite curfew** in Colombo and surrounding districts, deploying troops to prevent further unrest.

Legal Proceedings

- Two individuals, **Velayutham Varatharajah** and **Chandra Ragupathy**, were convicted for aiding and abetting the attack and sentenced to **30 years in prison**.
- In **2021**, they were **pardoned** by President **Ranil Wickremesinghe**, with Kumaratunga's consent.

Strengthening Leadership Through Crisis

The attempt on Kumaratunga's life just days before her re-election didn't weaken her resolve—it amplified her image as a resilient and determined leader. Public sympathy surged, and her calm, measured response in the aftermath demonstrated poise under pressure.

- Despite suffering severe injuries and losing sight in one eye, she returned to political duties swiftly.
- Her victory in the **December 1999 Presidential Election** was in part a reflection of national unity and support during a time of crisis.

Her Peace Agenda vs. Reality

Kumaratunga came to office in 1994 on a platform of **peace and reconciliation** with the Tamil minority. The bombing deepened her recognition that the LTTE would not easily come to the negotiating table.

- Prior to the attack, she had initiated **peace talks** and supported **constitutional reforms** aimed at devolving power to Tamil regions.

- Post-attack, her administration shifted toward a tougher **military stance** against the LTTE, especially after failed negotiations.

Escalation of the Civil War

The assassination attempt marked a turning point in Sri Lanka's civil war trajectory:

- It reaffirmed the LTTE's strategy of targeting top political leaders, stoking fear and instability.
- The government, under Kumaratunga, launched **renewed military offensives**, which included retaking key northern territories.
- Trust between the government and Tamil representatives eroded further, complicating future reconciliation efforts.

Legacy of Leadership

Despite the violence, Kumaratunga's presidency maintained a focus on long-term peace:

- She laid the groundwork for future peace talks by advocating for a **federal system** and **inclusive national policies**.
- Her experience surviving the attack became symbolic of Sri Lanka's endurance during decades of strife.

48

Secret Arms Transfers to LTTE (1989–1990)

Strategic Motivation

After the **Indo-Sri Lanka Accord** of 1987, the **Indian Peace Keeping Force (IPKF)** was deployed in Sri Lanka to disarm Tamil militant groups. However, the IPKF soon clashed with the LTTE, leading to widespread violence and civilian casualties. President Premadasa, elected in **1988**, viewed the IPKF as a **foreign occupying force** and sought to **expel them**—even if it meant **arming the LTTE**, his government's former enemy.

Key Figures Involved

NAME	ROLE
Ranasinghe Premadasa	President of Sri Lanka; authorized the arms transfers
General Sepala Attygalle	Defence Secretary; oversaw logistics and coordination
Colonel T.M. Bohran	Army Civil Co-ordinating Officer at Weli Oya; facilitated deliveries
SSP Lionel Karunasena	Commandant of the Special Task Force; involved in handovers
General Cyril Ranatunge	Head of Operational HQ; issued direct orders
Ranjan Wijeratne	Deputy Defence Minister; allegedly justified the transfers as anti-IPKF strategy

Nature of the Arms Supplied

- **Thousands of rifles**
- **Hundreds of RPGs**
- **Hundreds of thousands of rounds of ammunition**
- **Communication equipment**
- **Handcuffs and restraints** (used in LTTE detention camps)

Deliveries were made at **multiple jungle locations**, often in secrecy, bypassing standard military channels. Officers were instructed to **keep operations confidential**, even from their immediate superiors.

Reaction from the LTTE

The LTTE, having suffered heavy losses against the IPKF, welcomed the arms with **mocking gratitude**. According to military accounts, LTTE leaders **hugged and thanked** Sri Lankan officers, while hinting that the weapons would eventually be used **against the very soldiers handing them over**.

India's Reaction

India was **fully aware** of the arms transfers. The LTTE used the weapons to **intensify attacks on the IPKF**, especially in **Valvettithurai** and **Mannar** in **August 1989**, breaching ceasefires and provoking Indian reprisals.

- Indian officials were **deeply angered** but **restrained** in their response, partly due to **domestic political pressures** from Tamil Nadu parties sympathetic to the LTTE.
- The arms transfer **undermined India's credibility** and contribute to the **IPKF's withdrawal** in **March 1990**.
- The episode strained **Indo-Sri Lankan relations**, and India later **distanced itself** from direct involvement in Sri Lanka's conflict.

Controversy

- The operation was seen by many Sri Lankan officers as **treacherous and demoralizing**.
- It violated the **Prevention of Terrorism Act** and **military protocols**, yet no one was held accountable.
- The LTTE later turned its weapons against the Sri Lankan state, leading to **Eelam War II**.

Political Fallout and Withdrawal

- The mission became deeply unpopular in both Sri Lanka and India.
- In **1990**, under pressure from Sri Lankan President **Ranasinghe Premadasa** and India's new government, the IPKF withdrew completely.
- The LTTE emerged stronger, and India's involvement culminated in the **assassination of Rajiv Gandhi** by an LTTE suicide bomber in **1991**.

49

Eelam Wars II & III

Eelam War II refers to the **second phase** of the Sri Lankan civil war, fought between the **Sri Lankan government** and the **Liberation Tigers of Tamil Eelam (LTTE)** from **June 1990 to January 1995**. It was a period marked by intense military confrontations, devastating civilian massacres, and a dramatic shift in LTTE tactics.

How It Started

- The war began after the **breakdown of peace talks** between President **Ranasinghe Premadasa** and the LTTE.
- Ironically, Premadasa had previously **supplied arms to the LTTE** to help them fight the Indian Peace Keeping Force (IPKF), which withdrew in **March 1990**.
- Just weeks later, the LTTE turned on the government, triggering full-scale war.

Key Military Events

- **Massacre of 774 police officers** in the Eastern Province (June 1990) after they surrendered to the LTTE.
- **Siege of Jaffna Fort**: LTTE surrounded the garrison until it was relieved by **Operation Thrividha Balaya**.
- **First Battle of Elephant Pass** (July–August 1991): LTTE deployed 5,000 cadres to besiege a strategic army base; broken by **Operation Balavegaya**.
- **Battles of Janakapura and Pooneryn** (1993): Major LTTE offensives causing heavy army casualties and loss of equipment.

Civilian Atrocities

- **Palliyagodella Massacre** (1992): LTTE killed over 100 Muslim civilians using grenades and machetes.
- **Batticaloa Massacre** (1990): Sri Lankan Army killed at least 184 Tamil refugees, including children and infants.
- **Kokkadichcholai Massacre** (1991): 152 Tamil civilians killed by the army following a landmine attack.

Strategic Shifts

- LTTE transitioned from guerrilla tactics to **conventional warfare**, using large formations and heavy weapons.
- Sri Lankan military responded with **amphibious operations**, air support, and limited offensives to regain territory.

End of the Phase

- The war ended inconclusively in **January 1995**, just before the start of **Eelam War III**, which began after a brief ceasefire and the LTTE's attack on navy vessels.

Eelam War III

Eelam War III was the **third phase** of the Sri Lankan civil war, fought between the **Sri Lankan government** and the **Liberation Tigers of Tamil Eelam (LTTE)** from **April 19, 1995, to February 22, 2002**. It followed the collapse of a brief ceasefire and marked a period of intense military operations, territorial shifts, and devastating civilian impact.

How It Began

- In early 1995, President **Chandrika Kumaratunga** initiated peace talks with the LTTE.
- After a **100-day ceasefire**, the LTTE abruptly ended negotiations by **blowing up two Sri Lankan Navy gunboats**—SLNS *Sooraya* and *Ranasuru*—on **April 19, 1995**, triggering full-scale war.

Major Military Operations

OPERATION	DESCRIPTION
Operation Riviresa (1995)	Government forces recaptured **Jaffna Peninsula** from the LTTE.
Battle of Mullaitivu (1996)	LTTE overran the army base, killing over **1,600 soldiers** and capturing large quantities of weapons.
Operation Jayasikurui (1997–1998)	Aimed to open a land route to Jaffna via the A9 highway; ultimately failed after 18 months.
Operation Unceasing Waves II & III	LTTE offensives that recaptured **Kilinochchi** and **Oddusuddan**, and later **Elephant Pass**, a strategic base.

Civilian Impact

- **Navaly Church Bombing** (1995): Over **140 Tamil civilians** killed by Sri Lankan Air Force bombs.
- **Kumarapuram Massacre** (1996): **26 Tamil civilians**, including children, killed by army troops.
- **Gonagala Massacre** (1999): LTTE cadres hacked to death over **50 Sinhalese villagers**, many of them women and children.
- Over **800,000 people displaced**, with widespread shortages of food and medicine.

Tactical Shifts

- LTTE introduced **Stinger missiles**, downing Sri Lankan aircraft.
- Developed **Sea Tigers**, a naval wing that challenged the Sri Lankan Navy.
- Used **female suicide bombers** and launched **behind-enemy-lines operations**, notably under **Brigadier Balraj**.

Ceasefire and End of Phase

- LTTE declared a **unilateral ceasefire** in **December 2000**, which ended in **April 2001**.
- The war officially ended with the **Permanent Ceasefire Agreement** signed on **February 22, 2002**, brokered by **Norway**.

1990–2001: Eelam War III - Escalation

Renewed Hostilities

- After the IPKF's exit, the LTTE launched **Eelam War III**, marked by:

- The **Mullaitivu base massacre** (1996): Over **1,000 soldiers killed**.
- The **Central Bank bombing** (1996): Over **100 civilians killed**.
- The **Temple of the Tooth attack** (1998): A sacred Buddhist site bombed.

Government Response

- President **Chandrika Kumaratunga** initiated peace talks in **1995**, but they collapsed after LTTE attacks.
- The government launched **Operation Riviresa**, recapturing **Jaffna** in **December 1995**.

2002–2005: Ceasefire and Political Shifts

Norwegian-Brokered Ceasefire

- In **February 2002**, Prime Minister **Ranil Wickremesinghe** signed a **ceasefire agreement** with the LTTE.
- The LTTE temporarily dropped its demand for a separate state, agreeing to explore federal solutions.

Breakdown and Assassinations

- Talks stalled in **2003**, and violence resumed.
- In **2004**, LTTE commander **Karuna Amman** defected, weakening the group's Eastern control.
- In **August 2005**, Foreign Minister **Lakshman Kadirgamar** was assassinated, ending hopes of reconciliation.

50

Ranjan Wijeratne: A Life of Service and a Death That Shook a Nation (1991)

Early Life and Career

Born on **April 4, 1931**, Ranjan Wijeratne hailed from a distinguished family with ties to Sri Lanka's political elite. Educated at **S. Thomas' College**, he excelled in academics, sports, and agriculture. His early professional life was rooted in the **plantation sector**, where he rose to prominence as a tea planter and held leadership roles in several industry associations.

In the 1970s, Wijeratne transitioned into the **public sector**, serving as Permanent Secretary to the Ministry of Agricultural Development and Research. His administrative acumen earned him key positions in state-run agricultural enterprises, including the **Sri Lanka State Plantations Corporation** and **Pelwatta Sugar Company**.

Military and Political Rise

In 1984, Wijeratne was commissioned as a **Lieutenant Colonel** in the Sri Lanka Army Volunteer Force and became the founding commander of the **2nd Battalion, Sri Lanka Rifle Corps**, which drew personnel from the plantation sector.

By 1988, he had entered active politics, becoming **Chairman and later General Secretary of the United National Party (UNP)**. He played a crucial role in securing **Ranasinghe Premadasa's presidential victory** and was appointed **Minister of Foreign Affairs** and **State Minister of Defence** in 1989.

Confronting Insurgency

Wijeratne was known for his **hardline stance** against both the **Janatha Vimukthi Peramuna (JVP)** and the **Liberation Tigers of Tamil Eelam (LTTE)**. He masterminded **Operation Combine**, which nearly crushed the JVP insurgency in 1989. His approach to the LTTE was equally uncompromising, famously declaring in Parliament, "I am going all out for the LTTE. I never do anything in half measures".

Despite criticism for his militaristic methods, Wijeratne was respected for his **straight-talking leadership** and **unwavering support for the armed forces**. He regularly visited troops on the front lines and was seen as a man who took full responsibility for his actions.

Assassination and Aftermath

On **March 2, 1991**, while traveling to his office in Colombo, Wijeratne was killed in a **remote-controlled car bomb blast** on Havelock Road. The explosion claimed the lives of **19 people**, including five of his bodyguards and several civilians. The **LTTE was widely blamed**, although questions lingered about whether they acted alone.

His death left a vacuum in Sri Lanka's defense leadership. The military lost a trusted ally, and the government struggled to maintain momentum in its fight against insurgency. Wijeratne was **posthumously promoted to General** and honored with an **LLD (Honoris Causa)** by the Kotelawala Defence Academy.

Ranjan Wijeratne remains a **symbol of patriotic sacrifice** in Sri Lanka's modern history. His life embodied a rare blend of **agricultural expertise, military discipline, and political resolve**. Though controversial, his leadership during one of the country's most turbulent periods left an indelible mark on its fight against terrorism and its pursuit of national unity.

51

Echoes of Explosions – A City Under Siege: From 1996 to 2006, when the air in Colombo trembled!

Explosions arrived like thunderclaps from unseen storms—unpredictable, unrelenting. In crowded train stations, serene banks, quiet streets, and bustling markets, death hid behind ordinary moments.

A child clutched his schoolbag a second too late. A vendor turned to greet a friend and never spoke again. These bombings were not mere acts of war—they were punctuations in the lives of thousands, severing futures, fracturing families, rewriting love into loss. The sounds of sirens and weeping replaced laughter. Sri Lankans clung to a fragile rhythm, rebuilding from rubble, only to be struck again.

Outside the island, the world watched with a mixture of horror and helplessness as headlines etched Sri Lanka's pain into global memory. But inside Colombo, survival was no longer heroic—it was habitual.

1996 – Central Bank Bombing

Pic: cbsl.gov.lk

The tranquility of a bustling weekday morning was shattered on **January 31, 1996**, when a truck packed with high explosives slammed into the Central Bank of Sri Lanka in the heart of Colombo's financial district. The blast tore through eight buildings, killing **91 people** and wounding over **1,400 others**, many of whom were innocently walking to work or waiting for buses. Windows shattered across several blocks, and chaos reigned as rescuers sifted through rubble, searching for survivors. The LTTE claimed responsibility, asserting it was retaliation against government military operations. In the weeks following, **Sri Lanka's tourism industry collapsed**, with travel advisories issued globally, and the psychological scar on the city remained long after the debris was cleared.

1996 – Dehiwala Train Bombing

(Pic: srilankaguasrdian.org)

Just six months later, on **July 24**, the LTTE carried out another devastating strike at the **Dehiwala railway station**. This time, **suitcase bombs** had been planted in multiple compartments of a commuter train, targeting unsuspecting passengers during rush hour. The coordinated detonation killed **64 people** and injured over **400**, most of them office workers, students, and vendors returning home. The blast illuminated how fragile public spaces had become. Commuters began avoiding trains, fearing the next attack. Surveillance at transportation hubs intensified, and routine travel transformed into a nervous ritual.

1997 – World Trade Centre Suicide Bombing

On **October 15, 1997**, suicide bombers struck Colombo again—this time at the city's iconic **World Trade Centre towers**, symbols of economic ambition and resilience. A truck bomb detonated at the entrance, killing **18 people** and injuring over **100**. Flames engulfed surrounding buildings as smoke billowed into the skyline, creating eerie visuals reminiscent of a war zone. Though the LTTE denied involvement, the attack bore their unmistakable tactical signature. In response, security protocols hardened around financial institutions, and the business community feared Colombo was no longer a safe haven for commerce.

1998 – Maradana Twin Blasts

The dual explosions at **Maradana Railway Station** on **March 5, 1998**, came during the peak of evening rush hour. Twin devices planted near crowded platforms exploded in succession, killing **11** and injuring more than **80**. The coordinated nature of the attack suggested a ruthless desire to maximize civilian casualties. Panic swept through the city as families searched for loved ones and emergency responders raced to triage the wounded. In the aftermath, Colombo witnessed sweeping crackdowns, increased checkpoints, and the rise of paramilitary patrols throughout its metropolitan area.

2001 – Airport Attack

(Pic: BBC)

On **April 21, 2001**, LTTE suicide bombers infiltrated the outskirts of **Bandaranaike International Airport**, targeting military aircraft and strategic infrastructure. Though the death toll—**9 killed, 30+ wounded**—was relatively lower, the psychological and logistical impact was enormous. International flights were grounded, and Sri Lanka's only major airport became synonymous with vulnerability. It signaled a new phase of the conflict, where the LTTE expanded their reach beyond civilian targets to directly challenge military strongholds and international gateways.

2004 – Kollupitiya Assassination Bombing

A political assassination attempt in the upscale district of **Kollupitiya** on **July 24, 2004**, claimed **4 lives** and injured **10 others**. The attack aimed at a prominent minister underscored how even Sri Lanka's elite and diplomatic zones were no longer safe. Security details were reinforced across government buildings, and whispers of internal conspiracies filled the air. The blast reverberated through political circles, and fear rippled down from corridors of power to ordinary citizens who increasingly felt caught in a dangerous crossfire.

April 25, 2006 – Suicide Attack on Army Head Quarters Compound

It was a quiet Tuesday morning in Colombo, the kind that carried the scent of sea breeze and routine. But at **10:30 AM**, the city's pulse was shattered by a deafening explosion that echoed across neighborhoods. A **female suicide bomber**, posing as a pregnant woman seeking medical care, had infiltrated the **Army Headquarters compound** and detonated herself near the military hospital. The blast killed **at least eight people**, wounded **27 others**, and left **General Sarath Fonseka**, the Army Commander, fighting for his life.

I was home on vacation from Oman with my wife, miles away from the blast site, yet the tremor reached us—not just through sound, but through fear. Our first thought was our children. **Thurstan College**, where your sons studied, was near the epicenter.

We didn't hesitate. She took the wheel, her knowledge of Colombo's streets guiding me through the chaos. But when wenarrived, the school had already closed. Our sons were nowhere to be found. The road to the Army Headquarters was sealed, traffic diverted and panic thick in the air. The roads were full of traffic and panicky.

Then came the second wave of dread—your **five-year-old daughter**, who attended a Muslim school on **Fareed Place near Galle Road in Bambalapitiya**. We turned toward the junction, only to see her standing alone, crying, abandoned in the street. My heart sank. I ran to her, scooped her up, shielding her from a world that had suddenly become unrecognizable. The school had closed its gates and sent even the youngest children out into the streets. Even now, the memory of that decision burns with anger.

When we finally returned home, the gate was locked—but our sons had somehow climbed over it. They were huddled outside the front door, visibly shaken yet thankfully unharmed. Like us, they had heard the deafening blast, a sound that tore through the morning calm and reverberated across the city like a warning bell.

They described how the tremors had rattled their classroom walls—and how shards of bomb shrapnel had rained down on the roof of Thurstan College. For a moment, chaos had replaced curiosity, and panic swept through the students and teachers. The fear was palpable. Even in the supposed safety of school walls, war had found a way to intrude. The city was in lockdown. The military launched retaliatory airstrikes against LTTE positions in the east. The ceasefire that had held since 2002 was now a ghost. Colombo, once a city of resilience, was now a city of barricades and sirens.

52

2001 General Elections: Another Turning Point in Sri Lankan Politics & Events that Churned Sri Lanka from 2001 to 2005

The **2001 parliamentary elections**, held on **5 December**, came just **14 months** after the previous general election in **October 2000**. The early dissolution of Parliament was triggered by a **loss of majority** by the ruling **People's Alliance (PA)**, led by President **Chandrika Bandaranaike Kumaratunga**. The PA had suffered defections, notably from the **Sri Lanka Muslim Congress (SLMC)** and several senior ministers, including **G.L. Peiris** and **S.B. Dissanayake**, who crossed over to the opposition.

The country was also grappling with:

- A **worsening economy**, burdened by high defense spending and inflation
- A **stalemated civil war** with the **LTTE**
- Failed peace talks and rising public frustration
- A surge in **political violence**, with over **1,300 incidents** reported during the campaign

Key Political Players

LEADER	PARTY/ALLIANCE	ROLE
Ranil Wickremesinghe	United National Party (UNP) / United National Front (UNF)	Opposition Leader; PM candidate
Chandrika Kumaratunga	Sri Lanka Freedom Party (SLFP) / People's Alliance (PA)	Incumbent President
Somawansa Amarasinghe	Janatha Vimukthi Peramuna (JVP)	Marxist party leader
R. Sampanthan	Tamil National Alliance (TNA)	Tamil nationalist coalition leader
Rauff Hakeem	Sri Lanka Muslim Congress (SLMC)	Muslim minority leader; defected from PA to UNF

The **UNF** coalition included the **UNP**, **SLMC**, **Ceylon Workers Congress**, and other minority parties. The **PA** attempted to retain power by courting the **JVP**, but this alienated moderate allies and further weakened its base.

Challenges and Election Violence

The election was marred by:

- **60 deaths**, including **14 on polling day**
- Allegations of **intimidation, fraud,** and **partisan policing**
- A suicide bombing attempt targeting **PM Ratnasiri Wickremanayake**
- Over **2,700 incidents** of violence reported by the **Centre for Monitoring Election Violence (CMEV)**

Despite these challenges, voter turnout was **76.03%**, reflecting strong public engagement.

Election Results

PARTY/ALLIANCE	VOTES (%)	SEATS WON
United National Front (UNF)	45.62%	109
People's Alliance (PA)	37.19%	77
Janatha Vimukthi Peramuna (JVP)	9.10%	16
Tamil National Alliance (TNA)	3.89%	15
Sri Lanka Muslim Congress (SLMC)	1.18%	5

- The **UNF** secured a **parliamentary majority** and formed the government.
- **Ranil Wickremesinghe** was sworn in as **Prime Minister** on **9 December 2001**.
- The **President and Prime Minister** now belonged to **rival parties**, leading to **cohabitation tensions** and eventual dissolution of Parliament in **2004**.

Aftermath

- The new government-initiated **peace talks with the LTTE**, leading to the **2002 ceasefire agreement**.
- The election marked a **shift toward coalition politics**, with minority parties playing kingmaker roles.
- It exposed the **fragility of Sri Lanka's democratic institutions**, especially in managing violence and political polarization.

Between **2001 and 2005**, Sri Lanka's **Northern and Eastern provinces** experienced a volatile mix of **ceasefire optimism**, **internal fragmentation**, and **escalating violence**, despite the formal halt in hostilities between the government and the LTTE.

Ceasefire and Hope (2002–2003)

- In **February 2002**, the Sri Lankan government and the LTTE signed a **Norwegian-brokered Ceasefire Agreement (CFA)**, halting military operations and allowing LTTE political offices in government-controlled areas.
- The **Sri Lanka Monitoring Mission (SLMM)** was established to oversee compliance.
- Roads reopened, commercial flights resumed, and civilians in war-torn areas experienced a brief respite.
- Six rounds of peace talks were held, focusing on **federalism** and **self-governance** for the North and East.

Violations and LTTE Expansion

- Despite the ceasefire, the LTTE committed **over 3,800 violations**, including **targeted killings**, **extortion**, and **child recruitment**.
- Anti-LTTE Tamil political parties, forced to disarm under the CFA, became vulnerable to attacks.
- The LTTE used its political offices to **recruit underage fighters**, **collect intelligence**, and **eliminate dissent**.

On **December 26, 2004**, nature delivered a tragedy even the most hardened war zones couldn't anticipate. The **Indian Ocean tsunami** ravaged Sri Lanka's eastern coastline. Entire villages were swallowed; families lost not only loved ones but the little infrastructure war hadn't claimed.

Relief coordination between the LTTE and government faltered under layers of mistrust. The **Post-Tsunami Operational Management Structure (P-TOMS)**, a joint mechanism, was proposed but collapsed amid political resistance. The **TMVP**, still militarized, commandeered aid in some areas and banned LTTE-affiliated NGOs.

In the grief-stained terrain of Batticaloa and Trincomalee, disaster relief became **territorial negotiation**.

Timeline: North & East Sri Lanka (2001–2005)

2001

- **December 5**: General elections held; **UNF coalition wins**, and **Ranil Wickremesinghe** becomes Prime Minister.
- LTTE begins consolidating control in areas under their de facto administration in the North and East.

2002

- **February 22**: Government and LTTE sign the **Permanent Ceasefire Agreement (CFA)**, brokered by **Norway**.

- **March–October**: LTTE opens political offices in government-controlled zones, particularly in the East.
- LTTE continues recruitment and targeted assassinations despite the ceasefire.
- SLMM (Sri Lanka Monitoring Mission) established to monitor CFA violations.

2003

- **April**: LTTE **withdraws from peace talks** after six rounds, citing inadequate government proposals.
- Tamil groups opposing the LTTE (e.g., EPDP, PLOTE) become targets of systematic elimination.
- The government begins international consultations with donor nations to fund post-war recovery.

2004

- **March**: **Colonel Karuna Amman**, LTTE's Eastern commander, **breaks away**, claiming discrimination against Eastern cadres.
- Karuna takes about **6,000 fighters** and sets up base near Batticaloa.
- LTTE accuses Karuna of treachery and begins **purges**, including child soldiers and civilian sympathizers.
- **April**: Parliamentary elections bring **UPFA** into power; **Mahinda Rajapaksa** appointed Prime Minister.
- **December 26**: **Indian Ocean tsunami** devastates the East, killing **tens of thousands**, especially in Trincomalee, Batticaloa, and Ampara.
- Relief efforts complicated by government–LTTE mistrust, particularly over management of joint aid (P-TOMS).

2005

- LTTE and Karuna faction engage in **low-intensity battles** in the East. Civilians face threats from both groups.
- UN agencies report **ongoing child recruitment** by the LTTE despite international condemnation.
- **August 12**: Foreign Minister **Lakshman Kadirgamar** assassinated in Colombo, widely blamed on the LTTE.
- **November**: Presidential elections held; **Mahinda Rajapaksa** wins and adopts a **hardline stance** toward LTTE.

Summary of Impact

- **Ceasefire optimism** in 2002 gave way to disappointment as violence surged in politically fragile areas.
- The **Karuna split** transformed the Eastern war theater, creating new tensions and factional violence.
- Civilians remained trapped between LTTE authoritarian control, Karuna's militancy, and state security operations.
- The **tsunami disaster** exposed the deep mistrust between the LTTE and Colombo, even in the face of shared tragedy.

Pic: commons.wikimedia.org

On December 26, 2004, Sri Lanka witnessed the **deadliest train disaster in history** when the Matara Express was struck by a massive tsunami near the village of Peraliya. The train, packed with over 1,500 passengers, had halted on the coastal tracks when the first wave hit. Locals, believing the train to be safe, climbed aboard or sheltered behind it.

Minutes later, a towering wave—estimated at **7.5 to 9 meters high**—lifted the train off its tracks and hurled it into nearby trees and buildings. All eight carriages were destroyed, and most passengers drowned inside the flooded compartments. The death toll is believed to be **over 1,700**, with only about 150 survivors.

This tragedy unfolded during the **Boxing Day Tsunami**, which devastated coastal regions across the Indian Ocean. The wreck site has since become a memorial, with restored train parts and annual ceremonies honoring the lives lost.

53

Lakshman Kadirgamar: Statesman, Diplomat, and Martyr for Peace

Early Life and Education

Born on **12 April 1932** in **Manipay, Jaffna**, Lakshman Kadirgamar hailed from a distinguished Tamil Protestant family. His father, **Samuel J.C. Kadirgamar Sr.**, was a prominent lawyer and founder of the **Law Society of Ceylon**. Lakshman was the youngest of six siblings, including **Rajan Kadirgamar**, who became **Commander of the Royal Ceylon Navy**.

- Attended **Trinity College, Kandy**, where he excelled in academics and sports.
- Won the **Ryde Gold Medal** for best all-round student in 1950.
- Studied law at the **University of Ceylon**, graduating with honors.
- Became an **Oxford Union President** in 1959 while at **Balliol College, Oxford**—a rare honor for a Sri Lankan.

Legal and International Career

Before entering politics, Kadirgamar built a formidable career in law and international diplomacy:

- Practiced commercial and constitutional law in Sri Lanka and London.
- Served as a **consultant to Amnesty International** and the **International Labour Organization**.
- Held senior positions at the **World Intellectual Property Organization (WIPO)**, including **Director for Asia and the Pacific**.

His legal writings appeared in journals like the *Modern Law Review* and *South African Law Journal*, showcasing his intellectual depth.

Political Career and Foreign Policy Legacy

Kadirgamar entered politics in **1994** as a **national list MP** for the **People's Alliance**. He was appointed **Foreign Minister** under President **Chandrika Kumaratunga**, serving from **1994–2001** and again from **2004 until his death**.

Achievements as Foreign Minister

- Spearheaded efforts to **ban the LTTE internationally**, securing proscription in the **US (1997)** and **UK (2001)**.
- Strengthened Sri Lanka's diplomatic ties with **India**, **China**, **the US**, and **Europe**.
- Advocated for **multilateralism**, **human rights**, and **regional cooperation** through **SAARC** and **IOR-ARC**.
- Proposed **Vesak Day** as an international observance at the **UN General Assembly** in 1999.

Despite being Tamil, he was a **fierce critic of the LTTE**, condemning their use of child soldiers and political assassinations.

Assassination and Aftermath

On **12 August 2005**, Kadirgamar was **shot by an LTTE sniper** while exiting his swimming pool at his private residence in **Colombo**.

Details of the Attack

- The sniper fired from a **neighboring house**, using a **high-powered rifle** mounted on a custom tripod.
- Kadirgamar was hit **three times**—in the head, neck, and chest.
- He was rushed to the **National Hospital** but succumbed to his injuries after emergency surgery.

Security Lapses

- Despite being one of the **most heavily guarded ministers**, the sniper infiltrated a **toilet on the first floor** of a nearby house.
- Investigators found **sniper gear**, **food supplies**, and **waste bags**, indicating a **long surveillance operation**.

Global Reaction

The assassination drew **international condemnation**:

- **UN Secretary-General Kofi Annan** called it a "criminal and senseless act."
- **US Secretary of State Condoleezza Rice** praised him as a man of "dignity, honor, and integrity."

- **Norwegian peace monitors** warned the killing could jeopardize the **2002 ceasefire agreement**.

President Kumaratunga declared a **state of emergency**, and the LTTE denied involvement—though the method and motive strongly pointed to them.

Lakshman Kadirgamar was posthumously awarded **Sri Lankabhimanya**, the nation's highest civilian honor. His legacy includes:

- Elevating Sri Lanka's global standing.
- Advocating for **peace through strength**, not appeasement.
- Serving as a **symbol of unity**, transcending ethnic divisions.

His assassination marked a turning point in Sri Lanka's conflict, underscoring the LTTE's continued threat and the fragility of peace.

54

The Karuna Split and Eastern Turmoil
(2004–2005)

Shattered Soil: The Eastern Rebellion

The Eastern Province, long overshadowed by the northern epicenter of Tamil militancy, underwent a profound shift in 2004 when the iron grip of the Liberation Tigers of Tamil Eelam (LTTE) was shattered from within. The defection of **Vinayagamoorthy Muralitharan**, better known as **Colonel Karuna Amman**, redefined the balance of power and reshaped not just battlefield dynamics, but the rhythm of everyday life for civilians caught in the crossfire.

A Break from the North: The Rise of the Karuna Faction

In March 2004, Karuna Amman, the LTTE's most senior commander in the East, publicly split from the northern leadership. The justification was not ideological—it was deeply personal and regional. Karuna accused LTTE chief **Velupillai Prabhakaran** of sidelining Eastern cadres and exploiting them disproportionately in northern-led operations. With him defected an estimated **6,000 armed fighters**, many of whom had family ties in Batticaloa and Ampara.

Almost overnight, the LTTE's Eastern monopoly collapsed into a patchwork of **guerrilla skirmishes**, **targeted purges**, and **covert alliances**. What followed was not a conventional war—it was a **shadow conflict**, where uniforms blurred, allegiances shifted, and civilians became bargaining chips between factions.

Intelligence and Shadows: Colombo's Calculated Embrace

Recognizing an opportunity, the Sri Lankan government and its intelligence agencies moved swiftly to **support Karuna's faction**, albeit covertly. Though officially unacknowledged, state actors provided **logistical assistance**, **safe havens**, and **military cover** for Karuna's operatives.

For Colombo, Karuna's breakaway was a **strategic wedge**—a way to fracture the LTTE's unified command structure and weaken its eastern support base. For Karuna, the alliance was survival—bolstered by men, arms, and legitimacy that would eventually evolve into the **Tamil Makkal Viduthalai Pulikal (TMVP)**, his fledgling political front.

Living Between Flags

For civilians, especially in villages like **Kiran**, **Vavunathivu**, and **Thirukkovil**, the split translated into sheer terror:

- Parents hid children from both factions—LTTE conscription and TMVP retaliation were relentless.
- Farmers paid "taxes" twice, to different guns pointed at their gates.
- TMVP established informal courts and curfews, replacing what little state infrastructure existed.
- The LTTE accused Karuna loyalists of betrayal, executing captured cadres and suspected informants.

Eastern Tamils—long marginalized—found themselves prisoners of geography. The North no longer spoke for them, but the South didn't protect them.

The War of Propaganda

Both factions engaged in media warfare. LTTE publications condemned Karuna as a traitor, accusing him of collaborating with "Sinhala occupiers." The TMVP portrayed itself as a **grassroots liberation movement**, releasing communiqués in Tamil newspapers and even conducting staged public hearings.

This war of words extended to the diaspora. Eastern Tamil communities abroad struggled with division—remittances became politicized, and fundraising split along factional lines.

Aftermath: The East as a New Battleground

By 2005, the East had become a testing ground for a **proxy war**—not fought with frontal assaults, but with assassinations, intelligence, and localized terror:

- Karuna's men, often operating in civilian dress, targeted **LTTE informants** and **former fighters**.
- The LTTE responded with **bombings, public executions**, and **blunt warnings to sympathizers**.
- Tamil civilians were forced into a **double life**, performing loyalty to both sides while privately seeking protection from neither.

What began as a strategic schism became a **humanitarian fragmentation**, exposing the limits of ceasefires and peace declarations when the fault lines ran deeper than politics.

The Karuna split did more than divide fighters—it forced open a conversation about **regional Tamil identities**, **Northern hegemony**, and **state opportunism**. It questioned the LTTE's ability to represent all Tamils and exposed their intolerance for dissent. It also demonstrated the Sri Lankan state's willingness to **co-opt militancy** as a counterinsurgency tool.

55

The Rise of the Rajapaksa Dynasty and 2005 Presidential Election

Origins of a Political Family

The **Rajapaksa family** hails from **Medamulana**, a rural village in **Hambantota District**, Southern Sri Lanka. Their political lineage began with **Don Alwin Rajapaksa**, a founding member of the **Sri Lanka Freedom Party (SLFP)** and a parliamentarian in the 1950s and '60s. His sons—**Chamal**, **Mahinda**, **Gotabaya**, and **Basil**—would later become central figures in Sri Lanka's political landscape.

While the family had long held influence in the **southern Sinhalese heartland**, it was **Mahinda Rajapaksa** who catapulted the clan to national prominence.

Mahinda Rajapaksa's Political Ascent

- Entered Parliament in **1970** as the youngest MP at the time.
- Rose through SLFP ranks, serving as **Minister of Labour**, **Minister of Fisheries**, and **Leader of the Opposition**.
- Appointed **Prime Minister** in **2004** under President **Chandrika Kumaratunga**, setting the stage for his presidential bid.

Mahinda cultivated a **populist image**, portraying himself as a man of the people, deeply rooted in Buddhist-Sinhalese nationalism. His charisma and rural appeal resonated with voters disillusioned by elite politics and prolonged civil conflict.

The 2005 Presidential Election

Held on **17 November 2005**, the election was a **watershed moment** in Sri Lankan politics.

Leading Candidates

CANDIDATE	PARTY/ALLIANCE
Mahinda Rajapaksa	SLFP / United People's Freedom Alliance (UPFA)
Ranil Wickremesinghe	UNP / United National Front (UNF)

Results

- **Mahinda Rajapaksa**: 4,887,152 votes (**50.29%**)
- **Ranil Wickremesinghe**: 4,706,366 votes (**48.43%**)
- Turnout: **73.73%**
- Margin of victory: ~180,000 votes

Key Factors Behind Mahinda's Victory

- **LTTE-enforced boycott** in Tamil-majority areas suppressed votes that likely favored Wickremesinghe.
- Mahinda secured endorsements from **Janatha Vimukthi Peramuna (JVP)** and **Jathika Hela Urumaya (JHU)** by rejecting federalism and promising to renegotiate the ceasefire.
- Promoted **economic nationalism**, opposing privatization and pledging rural development.

Consolidation of the Dynasty

Following his victory, Mahinda began embedding his family into the state apparatus:

FAMILY MEMBER	ROLE – POST-2005 ELECTION
Gotabaya Rajapaksa	Secretary of Defence; architect of war strategy
Basil Rajapaksa	Economic Development Minister
Chamal Rajapaksa	Speaker of Parliament; later Minister
Namal Rajapaksa	Entered Parliament in 2010; later Minister of Sports

The Rajapaksas controlled **key ministries**, **security forces**, and **economic portfolios**, transforming governance into a **family enterprise**.

Legacy of the 2005 Election

- Marked the beginning of **Eelam War IV**, culminating in the **defeat of the LTTE in 2009**.

- Cemented the Rajapaksas as **national war heroes** among the Sinhalese majority.
- Set the foundation for **authoritarian tendencies**, **nepotism**, and **centralized power**.
- Triggered a decade of **dynastic rule**, with Mahinda serving until **2015**, and Gotabaya later elected president in **2019**.

The **2005 presidential election** was not just a political contest—it was the **birth of a dynasty**. Mahinda Rajapaksa's narrow victory reshaped Sri Lanka's trajectory, ushering in a family-led era that would dominate the island's politics, economy, and military for years. The Rajapaksas' rise was built on **populism**, **nationalism**, and **strategic alliances**, but it also sowed the seeds of **controversy and eventual backlash**.

(Pic: L-R: Basil, Mahinda and Gotabaya Rajapasa)

56

The Iron Fist and the Final War: Rajapaksa's Road to Victory (2005–2009)

The election of **Mahinda Rajapaksa** in November 2005 marked a decisive shift in Sri Lanka's approach to the civil war. His presidency ushered in an era of **centralized power**, **militarized governance**, and **family-led administration**, culminating in the **defeat of the Liberation Tigers of Tamil Eelam (LTTE)** in 2009. This chapter traces the transformation of the state, the war strategy, and the consequences of the final phase of conflict—**Eelam War IV**.

Building the Rajapaksa State

Rajapaksa's governance style was rooted in **populist nationalism**, **rural symbolism**, and **dynastic consolidation**. His manifesto, *Mahinda Chinthana*, promised economic development, national unity, and a hardline stance against separatism.

Key appointments solidified the family's grip:

NAME	ROLE
Gotabaya Rajapaksa	Secretary of Defence; war strategist
Basil Rajapaksa	Presidential Advisor; later Minister of Economic Development
Chamal Rajapaksa	Speaker of Parliament
Namal Rajapaksa	Groomed for future leadership

The **Ministry of Defence**, under Gotabaya, became the **nerve center** of war planning, intelligence, and media control. The Rajapaksas cultivated a **cult of personality**, portraying Mahinda as the **"father of victory"** and Gotabaya as the **"architect of peace."**

Eelam War IV: The Final Confrontation (2006–2009)

The war reignited in **July 2006**, when the LTTE blocked the **Mavil Aru sluice gates**, cutting water to thousands of civilians. The government responded with **Operation Watershed**, marking the start of **Eelam War IV**.

Key Military Campaigns

OPERATION/BATTLE	OUTCOME
Operation Riviresa II (2006–07)	Recapture of Eastern Province
Battle of Thoppigala (2007)	End of LTTE control in the East
Northern Offensive (2008–09)	Capture of Kilinochchi, Elephant Pass, and Mullaitivu
Final Battle at Nandikadal Lagoon (May 2009)	Death of LTTE leader **Velupillai Prabhakaran**

The military expanded rapidly, growing from **125,000 to over 300,000 personnel**. The government invested in **air power**, **naval blockades**, and **intelligence networks**, often aided by **defectors from the LTTE**, notably **Colonel Karuna Amman**.

Civilian Toll and Humanitarian Crisis

The final months of the war saw **intense fighting** in the **Vanni region**, where **300,000 civilians** were trapped. Both sides were accused of **human rights violations**:

- LTTE used civilians as **human shields** and forcibly recruited **child soldiers**.
- Government forces were accused of **indiscriminate shelling**, including in **No Fire Zones**.
- The **UN estimated** up to **40,000 civilian deaths**, though figures remain contested.

Despite international pressure, Rajapaksa refused a ceasefire, insisting on **total military victory**.

Media, Messaging, and Morale

The government tightly controlled war narratives:

- **State media** portrayed soldiers as heroes and the LTTE as terrorists.
- **Independent journalists** faced intimidation, censorship, and exile.
- **Victory parades** and **memorials** reinforced the image of a **unified Sinhala nation**.

Rajapaksa's popularity soared among the Sinhalese majority, while Tamil voices were marginalized.

International Dynamics

- **India** maintained a cautious stance, providing **intelligence support** but avoiding direct intervention.
- **China and Pakistan** supplied **arms and military training**, deepening strategic ties.
- Western nations condemned **civilian casualties** but failed to halt the offensive.

The war's end was hailed domestically as a **historic triumph**, but abroad it triggered calls for **accountability and reconciliation**.

Aftermath: Victory and Consolidation

On **May 19, 2009**, Sri Lanka declared victory. The LTTE was annihilated, its leadership dead or captured. Rajapaksa emerged as a **national icon**, and the Rajapaksa dynasty entered its **golden era**.

Immediate consequences:

- **Emergency laws** remained in place.
- **Tamil political representation** was weakened.
- **Reconstruction** began in the North and East, but **militarization persisted**.

The government promised reconciliation, but **transitional justice** was slow and selective.

The years **2005 to 2009** marked the **militarization of governance**, the **centralization of power**, and the **defeat of the LTTE**. Rajapaksa's leadership was hailed as decisive, but it came at the cost of **civil liberties**, **ethnic trust**, and **international scrutiny**. The war's end closed one chapter—but opened another, filled with questions about **justice**, **memory**, and **the future of pluralism** in Sri Lanka.

Timeline of Journalist Killings in Sri Lanka (2004–2025)

DATE	JOURNALIST	AFFILIATION	DETAILS
May 31, 2004	Aiyathurai A. Nadesan	Tamil daily *Eelanaadu*	Shot dead in Batticaloa; known for pro-Tamil reporting.
Apr 28, 2005	Dharmaratnam "Taraki" Sivaram	*TamilNet, Daily Mirror*	Abducted near Parliament, body found hours later near Diyawanna Oya.

Jan 24, 2007	Subramaniam Suhirtharajan	*Sudar Oli*	Shot dead in Trincomalee after photographing prison abuse.
Feb 15, 2007	Subramaniam Ramachandran	*Yarl Thinakkural*	Disappeared in Jaffna after military detention.
May 28, 2008	Paranirupasingham Devakumar	*NewsFirst* (Jaffna)	Stabbed to death after critical reporting on LTTE and government.
Jan 8, 2009	Lasantha Wickrematunge	*The Sunday Leader*	Murdered in broad daylight; exposed corruption in defense ministry.
Jan 24, 2010	Prageeth Ekneligoda	*Lanka e News*	Disappeared after investigating chemical weapons use.

The killings of journalists in Sri Lanka remain a haunting testament to the dangers of speaking truth to power. Despite international outcry and sporadic investigations, justice has largely eluded the victims and their families. Cases like those of Lasantha Wickrematunge and others were marred by political interference, missing evidence, and stalled legal proceedings. While some suspects were arrested, many were released without charges, and key witnesses either disappeared or died under suspicious circumstances. The culture of impunity persists, with press freedom advocates continuing to call for accountability and reform. Until these cases are resolved transparently and perpetrators held accountable, the shadow over Sri Lanka's media landscape will remain.

(Prageeth Ekneligoda)

Lasantha Wickrematunge

Editor of *The Sunday Leader*, fearless critic of government corruption.

What happened: On Jan 8, 2009, he was ambushed by motorcycle-riding assailants while driving to work. He was bludgeoned to death near a school in Mount Lavinia.

Why it matters: Lasantha had been investigating a $14M MiG aircraft deal involving then-Defense Secretary Gotabaya Rajapaksa. He predicted his own death in a chilling editorial published posthumously: "And Then They Came For Me".

Aftermath:

- His notebook and phone disappeared from the crime scene.
- Investigations were repeatedly stalled or transferred between departments.
- A military intelligence unit, the **Tripoli Platoon**, was later linked to the murder.
- In 2025, Sri Lanka's top prosecutor sought to discharge key suspects without explanation.

Dharmaratnam "Taraki" Sivaram

Former Tamil militant turned respected journalist and political analyst.

What happened: Abducted on April 28, 2005, outside a restaurant near Bambalapitiya police station. His body was found hours later near Parliament, shot twice.

Why it matters: Sivaram was a prominent voice on Tamil issues and the civil war. His murder sent shockwaves through the media community.

Aftermath:

A PLOTE member was arrested for possessing Sivaram's SIM card but later released.

A shadowy group called *Theraputthabhaya Balakaya* claimed responsibility, threatening other journalists.

Patterns of Impunity

- **Tamil journalists** were disproportionately targeted.
- **Investigations** often stalled, manipulated, or abandoned.
- **International pressure** (UN, CPJ, Hague Tribunal) has called for justice, but convictions remain elusive.

57

The Final War - Strategic Command and Leadership

During the final phase of Sri Lanka's civil war—**Eelam War IV (2006–2009)**—a number of senior military leaders played pivotal roles in planning, executing, and overseeing operations that led to the defeat of the LTTE. Here's a breakdown of the **key military personnel** who shaped the outcome:

General Sarath Fonseka

- **Position**: Commander of the Sri Lanka Army
- **Role**: Architect of the overall ground strategy; oversaw troop expansion and offensive coordination.
- **Legacy**: Credited with transforming the army into a modern, mobile force; later became Chief of Defence Staff.

Surviving the Shadows: Assassination Attempts on General Sarath Fonseka

The **only confirmed assassination attempt** on General Fonseka occurred on **April 25, 2006,** in a meticulously planned suicide bombing at the Army Headquarters in Colombo. This attack remains one of the most brazen and high-profile strikes by the LTTE against Sri Lanka's military leadership.

- **Time & Place:** 10:30 AM, Army Headquarters, Colombo

- **Attacker:** Anoja Kugenthirarasah, a female LTTE suicide bomber disguised as a pregnant woman seeking medical care at the military hospital
- **Casualties:** 9 killed, 27 injured
- **Target Outcome:** Fonseka sustained critical abdominal injuries and underwent emergency surgery. He was later flown to Singapore for advanced treatment and resumed command in July 2006

The attack was part of the LTTE's broader strategy to destabilize the military hierarchy by eliminating its top commanders. Fonseka's survival was considered miraculous and became a rallying point for the armed forces. His return to duty marked a renewed and intensified phase of the war effort, culminating in the LTTE's defeat in May 2009.

Were There Other Attempts?

Despite widespread speculation and persistent threats, **no other assassination attempts on Fonseka have been officially confirmed**. Intelligence reports during his tenure frequently warned of planned ambushes, sniper attacks, and explosive devices targeting his motorcade or residence. However, these plots were either thwarted or never materialized into actionable attacks.

The **2006 bombing remains the sole documented attempt** on his life, and it continues to be the subject of legal proceedings in Sri Lanka. As of July 2025, the trial against three accused individuals has been postponed to August 4, with charges filed under the Prevention of Terrorism Act and Emergency Regulations.

Fonseka's resilience in the face of mortal danger elevated his stature both within the military and among the public. His survival not only preserved the continuity of command but also galvanized the troops under his leadership. The failed assassination attempt became symbolic of the LTTE's desperation and marked a turning point in the conflict's trajectory.

Gotabaya Rajapaksa

(Pic: newsweek.com)

- **Position**: Secretary of Defence
- **Role**: Civilian head of defence; coordinated inter-service strategy and intelligence.
- **Legacy**: Played a central role in war logistics, media control, and international diplomacy; later elected President in 2019.

Division Commanders and Battlefield Leaders

NAME	DIVISION/ROLE	CONTRIBUTION
Major General Shavendra Silva	Commander, 58 Division	Led key offensives in the Western and Northern fronts; captured Kilinochchi and Puthukkudiyiruppu
Major General Kamal Gunaratne	Commander, 53 Division	Spearheaded final assault near Nandikadal Lagoon; oversaw Prabhakaran's elimination
Major General Prasanna de Silva	Commander, 59 Division	Advanced from the southeast; captured Mullaitivu, the LTTE's last stronghold
Major General Jagath Dias	Commander, 57 Division	Led operations in Vanni region; instrumental in isolating LTTE forces
Major General Mahinda Hathurusinghe	Commander, Task Force 3	Secured flanks and cleared remaining LTTE pockets in the East

Air and Naval Leadership

Air Marshal Roshan Goonetileke

- **Position**: Commander of the Sri Lanka Air Force
- **Role**: Provided close air support, reconnaissance, and strategic bombing of LTTE infrastructure.

(Pic: businesstoday.lk)

Position: Commander of the Sri Lanka Navy

- **Role**: Enforced naval blockades, intercepted LTTE arms shipments, and neutralized Sea Tiger units.

Intelligence and Special Operations

- **Military Intelligence Corps** and **Long-Range Reconnaissance Patrols (LRRP)** played critical roles in:

- Targeting LTTE leadership
- Mapping terrain and bunkers
- Disrupting supply lines

Many operatives remain unnamed due to the classified nature of their missions.

Each division closed in like concentric jaws, pushing LTTE fighters into a narrowing pocket near **Nandikadal Lagoon**, where the final confrontation occurred.

Strategic Landmarks

- **Kilinochchi**: LTTE's administrative capital; fell in January 2009
- **Elephant Pass**: Vital gateway; recaptured, severing north-south movement
- **Mullaitivu**: Last stronghold; captured by 59 Division in final days

- **Nandikadal Lagoon**: Site of Prabhakaran's death and total LTTE defeat

58

The Final Commanders:

LTTE Leadership During Eelam War IV

Velupillai Prabhakaran — Supreme Leader and Commander-in-Chief

(wallpaperaccess.com)

- **Role**: Founder and undisputed head of the LTTE; directed all military and political strategy.
- **Legacy**:
  - ○ Created a **cult of personality** around himself.
  - ○ Oversaw the development of the **Black Tigers**, **Sea Tigers**, and **Air Tigers**.
  - ○ Refused compromise or federal solutions, insisting on full Tamil Eelam.
- **Death**: Killed on **May 18, 2009** near **Nandikadal Lagoon**, marking the end of the LTTE.

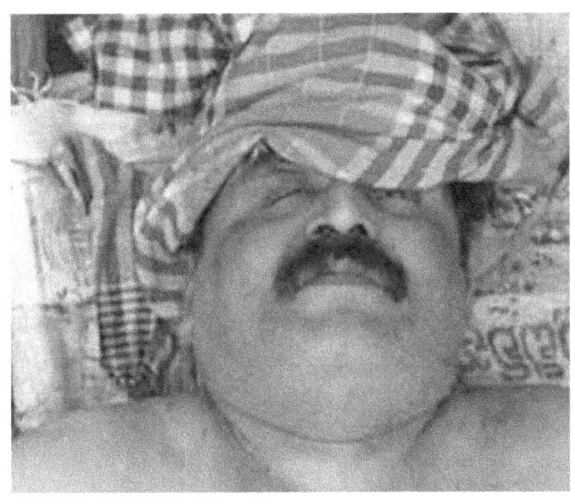

(Pic – New Indian Express)

Pottu Amman (Shanmugalingam Sivashankar) — Intelligence Chief

(Pic: oneindia)

- **Role**: Head of the **Tiger Intelligence Division** and **Black Tigers** (suicide commandos).
- **Notable Actions**:
  - Masterminded high-profile assassinations, including **Rajiv Gandhi** and **Lakshman Kadirgamar**.
  - Oversaw internal purges and counter-intelligence.
- **Death**: Reported killed during final battles in May 2009.

Soosai (Thillaiyampalam Sivanesan) — Sea Tigers Commander

(Pic: yarl,com)

- **Role**: Led the LTTE's **naval wing**, responsible for amphibious assaults and maritime logistics.
- **Impact**:
  - Developed suicide boat tactics and challenged Sri Lankan naval supremacy.
  - Played a key role in smuggling arms and personnel.
- **Death**: Killed during the final offensive in Mullaitivu.

Charles Anthony — Air Tigers Leader

Charles Anthony son of Velupillai Prabakharan (1954-2009)

- **Role**: Head of the LTTE's **air wing** and son of Prabhakaran.
- **Contribution**:
  - Oversaw limited aerial attacks using light aircraft.
  - Symbolized dynastic succession within the LTTE.
- **Death**: Killed in combat during the final days of the war.

- **Role**: Head of the LTTE's **political office**; former Sri Lankan police officer.
- **Responsibilities**:
  - ○ Acted as LTTE's spokesperson during peace talks.
  - ○ Managed diplomatic outreach and ceasefire negotiations.

Death: Killed in May 2009; circumstances remain controversial.

Castro (Veerakathy Manivannan) — International Operations Chief

(Pic: dailymotion.com)

- **Role**: Ran the LTTE's **global network**, including fundraising and propaganda.
- **Reach**:
  - ○ Coordinated diaspora activities across Europe, Canada, and Australia.
  - ○ Managed front organizations and media outlets.
- **Death**: Believed to have died in the final phase of the war.

Brigadier Balraj — Elite Field Commander (died before final war)

(Pic: Tamil Guardian)

- **Role**: Led the **Charles Anthony Regiment**, LTTE's elite conventional force.
- **Legacy**:

- Known for battlefield innovation and discipline.
- Died of illness in **May 2008**, weakening LTTE's ground leadership before the final offensive.

Leadership Collapse and Strategic Failure

The LTTE's leadership structure was **centralized and rigid**, with Prabhakaran making all final decisions. This lack of flexibility contributed to:

- **Failure to adapt** to changing battlefield realities.
- **Missed opportunities** for negotiated settlement.
- **Overreliance on suicide tactics** and human shields.

By May 2009, nearly all senior leaders were **killed or captured**, and the LTTE ceased to exist as a military force.

After the Guns Fell Silent: Diaspora Networks and the Legacy of LTTE Leadership

The **defeat of the LTTE in May 2009** ended its military operations within Sri Lanka—but its ideological footprint persisted across Tamil diasporic communities scattered across **Canada, the UK, Australia, France, Switzerland, Norway**, and parts of **South India**. For some, the movement's end marked closure. For others, it sparked **reimagining, martyrdom narratives**, and new forms of activism.

Transformation of the Global Network

Under leaders like **Castro** (Veerakathy Manivannan), the LTTE had built a sophisticated international infrastructure:

- **Fundraising and remittances** under humanitarian guises

- **Front organizations** (e.g., Tamil Coordinating Committee, Tamil Rehabilitation Organization)
- **Media outlets**, such as TamilNet and satellite television channels
- **Youth wings** and cultural forums in major Western cities

Following the war:

- Many organizations were **rebranded** or dissolved, as Sri Lanka lobbied host governments to **proscribe pro-LTTE entities**.
- Countries like **Canada, the UK, and India** kept the LTTE designated as a **terrorist organization**, restricting its formal revival.

Nevertheless, **commemorations**, **memorials**, and **academic forums** emerged, reframing the LTTE leadership as **freedom fighters and martyrs**, particularly Prabhakaran and Pottu Amman.

Commemoration and Cultural Preservation

- Annual events like **Maaveerar Naal (Heroes' Day)** are held across diaspora hubs, paying tribute to fallen fighters.
- **Portraits of Prabhakaran**, Charles Anthony, and Balraj are displayed in community halls and Tamil temples.
- Diaspora media continues to highlight **LTTE anniversaries**, framing the defeat not as closure but as **a pause in resistance**.

These events often draw criticism from host nations and human rights groups, but for many Tamils, they offer **communal healing**, especially for those with family lost or displaced during the war.

The LTTE's leadership is far from universally revered within the Tamil community:

- **Critics**, especially in **India and moderate diaspora circles**, argue the LTTE squandered peace opportunities and committed grave abuses.

  Survivors of child soldier recruitment, torture, and suppression of dissent within Tamil society speak out against romanticization.

- **New political movements**, such as the Transnational Government of Tamil Eelam (TGTE), aim to continue the cause through diplomacy and advocacy, while distancing from militancy.

Surveillance and Continued Scrutiny

- Sri Lanka's security agencies maintain active watch on diaspora activity, tracking possible remnants of militant funding or organizing.
- **Interpol red notices** were issued for surviving LTTE members, though most were later cancelled or expired.

Diaspora-based activism remains potent, especially in lobbying foreign parliaments, UN bodies, and human rights commissions to investigate alleged war crimes committed in the final phase of war.

Though the LTTE's military defeat in 2009 was unequivocal, the lives and legacies of its final leaders—**Prabhakaran, Pottu Amman, Balraj, Soosai, Charles Anthony**—live on in **cultural memory, political discourse, and ransnational identity**. Their portraits hang in homes, their speeches echo in exile forums, and their symbolism fuels a diaspora grappling with the meaning of defeat, dignity, and Tamil nationhood.

Some **of key LTTE figures** from the earlier phases of the movement—primarily spanning the **1970s to the 1990s**—whose contributions laid the foundation for the organization's rise, but who are often overshadowed by later wartime commanders:

Uma Maheswaran

- Early LTTE leader and head of the **People's Liberation Organisation of Tamil Eelam (PLOTE)** after being expelled by Prabhakaran
- His split in 1980 marked the beginning of factionalism among Tamil militant groups

N.S. Krishnan

- LTTE's **first international representative**, based in London
- Introduced Prabhakaran to Anton Balasingham
- Played a key role in building the LTTE's **diaspora network**

Urmila Kandiah

- One of the **first female members** of the LTTE
- Active in the **TULF youth wing** before joining the Tigers

  Her relationship with ⬚ Maheswaran led to internal disciplinary action, reflecting LTTE's strict code of conduct

Kuttimani (Selvarajah Yogachandran)

- Co-founder of **Tamil Eelam Liberation Organization (TELO)**
- Advocated for Tamil independence through armed struggle
- Executed in prison during the **1983 Welikada prison massacre**

Ponnuthurai Sivakumaran

- Early Tamil militant and founder of **Tamil Manavar Peravai (Students League)**
- Committed suicide in 1974 to avoid capture—becoming a **martyr figure** for Tamil youth

(Pic: cbc.ca)

S.P. Thamilselvan was one of the most prominent and charismatic figures in the LTTE's leadership, especially during its political and diplomatic phase.

Early Life and Entry into Militancy

- Born in **Chavakachcheri, Jaffna**, in **1967**, Thamilselvan joined the LTTE at age **16**, shortly after the **1983 anti-Tamil pogrom**.
- Trained in **Tamil Nadu**, India, and initially served as **Prabhakaran's personal bodyguard**.
- Rose through the ranks to become **Jaffna area commander** during the IPKF intervention.

Political Role and Diplomacy

- After sustaining a **leg injury** in 1993, he transitioned from combat to politics.
- Appointed **LTTE's Political Commissar** in **1994**, succeeding Anton Balasingham as the **chief negotiator** during peace talks in **2002–2003**.
- Known for his **media-savvy demeanor**, **calm articulation**, and **diplomatic presence** in Geneva and Kilinochchi.
- Became the **international face of the LTTE**, especially as Prabhakaran remained reclusive.

Dual Role in Final Years

- In **2007**, he was assigned **military duties** in **Pooneryn**, while continuing political responsibilities.

- His presence in both political and military spheres made him a **symbol of LTTE's hybrid leadership model**.

Death and Impact

- Killed on **2 November 2007** in a **Sri Lankan Air Force precision strike** on a fortified bunker near Kilinochchi.
- The attack also killed five other senior LTTE cadres and was seen as a **major psychological blow** to the movement.
- Posthumously promoted to **Brigadier** by Prabhakaran — the **first LTTE member** to receive that rank.

Legacy and Mourning

- His death was mourned across the **Tamil diaspora**, with **25,000 attending his funeral** in Kilinochchi.
- LTTE leader Prabhakaran called him a **"peace dove"**, lamenting the loss of a man who embodied the movement's diplomatic aspirations.

His widow and children surrendered in 2009 and were held under protective custody until 2011.

Thamilselvan's legacy is unique: he was both a **warrior and a diplomat**, a **symbol of Tamil resilience**, and a **bridge between battlefield and negotiation table**. His assassination marked the end of the LTTE's political engagement and foreshadowed the all-out military finale.

59

A Silence of Tigers: The Final Days of the LTTE

(Pic: srilankaguardian.org)

For nearly three decades, the name **Liberation Tigers of Tamil Eelam** (LTTE) stirred fear, devotion, condemnation, and sacrifice. To its adherents, it symbolized Tamil resistance. To its critics—both domestic and international—it embodied tyranny and terror. By **May 2009**, the movement that once held de facto control over a third of Sri Lanka dissolved under relentless firepower, territorial collapse, and the severing of its leadership spine.

But the end of the LTTE was not simply a battlefield conclusion. It was **a rupture in memory, belonging, and identity**.

The Final March

In those last weeks—hemmed into a sliver of land between the **Nandikadal Lagoon** and the **Indian Ocean**—civilians moved like ghosts. **Child soldiers clutched rifles too heavy for their arms**, elderly mothers dragged sacks of rice soaked in seawater, and commanders scribbled orders in the dark knowing they would never be read.

As artillery roared and fire crept closer, the LTTE's final leaders—**Prabhakaran, Pottu Amman, Soosai, Charles Anthony, B. Nadesan**—gathered for what would be their last hours. There were no trumpets. No final speeches. No filmed defiance. The jungle that had once sheltered revolutionaries now concealed corpses.

One by one, they fell—some in direct combat, others in controversial surrender attempts. The lagoon swallowed the story. What emerged from its waters was **a nation changed**, **a people divided**, and **a legacy contested**.

The Question of Memory

Across much of the world, the LTTE remained branded as a **terrorist organization**, a designation earned through:

- The assassination of **Rajiv Gandhi** (India)
- Suicide bombings targeting civilians and Buddhist holy sites
- Forced recruitment and suppression of Tamil political dissent

Yet for segments of the **Tamil diaspora**, the LTTE had given voice to communities silenced for generations. They mourned the loss of fighters as **martyrs**, not militants. They lit candles on **Maaveerar Naal**, not in celebration of bloodshed—but in tribute to sacrifice.

In Kilinochchi, **the once-proud Tiger flags were burned or buried**, and in refugee camps, mothers wept not only for sons who had fought—but for a cause that had vanished, leaving only **questions of dignity**, **identity**, and **belonging**.

Aftermath and Absence

With the LTTE gone, what remained was a **landscape of scars**. The North and East bore the imprints of bunkers, mass graves, and orphaned generations. The Sri Lankan government celebrated victory—but reconciliation lagged behind ceremony.

Former cadres wandered between silence and stigma. Some surrendered. Others disappeared. Many remain unnamed in death, their stories washed away by politics and propaganda.

The diaspora, too, fractured. Some clung to r remembrance. Others embraced new futures—**post-LTTE activism**, **academic discourse**, and **grassroots reconciliation**. But everywhere, there was a **longing to understand** what the war had truly taken—and what it had left behind.

Epilogue: Echoes

The final chapter of the LTTE is not clean. It is not heroic. It is not wholly tragic. It is the sound of **a cause that burned too hot to survive**, led by men who chose **violence over compromise**, and undone by both **military defeat** and **strategic rigidity**.

And yet, in the faded murals in Tamil homes, in the speeches of activists abroad, and in the dreams of youth who were born after the bullets ceased—**the echo of that movement persists**. Not in war, but in the question: *"What does freedom mean when the voice that fought for it has been silenced?"*

60

Role of Anton Balasingam in LTTE

Anton Stanislaus Balasingham was the **chief political strategist, ideologue, and international spokesperson** of the Liberation Tigers of Tamil Eelam (LTTE). Often referred to as **"Bala Annai"** (elder brother) by LTTE cadres, he played a pivotal role in shaping the movement's diplomatic posture and articulating its political vision to the world.

Strategic Role in the LTTE

- **Political Advisor to Prabhakaran**: Balasingham was one of the few individuals whom LTTE leader **Velupillai Prabhakaran** trusted implicitly. He was described as a "source of unwavering strength" and "the voice of the nation" by the LTTE.
- **Chief Negotiator**: He led the LTTE delegation in nearly all major peace talks, including:
    - **Thimpu Talks (1985)**
    - **Premadasa-LTTE negotiations (1990)**
    - **Kumaratunga-era talks (1994–95)**
    - **Norwegian-brokered peace process (2002–2003)**
- **Diplomatic Liaison**: Maintained close ties with international mediators, especially **Norwegian envoy Erik Solheim**, and was instrumental in securing the **2002 Ceasefire Agreement**.

Ideological Contributions

- Authored several works, including *War and Peace: Armed Struggle and Peace Efforts of Liberation Tigers* (2004), which became required reading for LTTE cadres.

- Taught **Marxist theory**, Tamil nationalism, and political strategy to LTTE members during training sessions.
- Articulated LTTE's position in English, serving as Prabhakaran's voice to the international community: "I do all the thinking and planning in the LTTE. As I am bad in English, Balasingham articulates my views," Prabhakaran once said.

International Presence and Influence

- Lived in **London**, where he became the LTTE's de facto representative in Europe.
- Played a key role in **diaspora mobilization**, media outreach, and shaping global perceptions of the Tamil struggle.
- Despite being denied re-entry into India after 1987, he continued to describe India as the "fatherland of Sri Lankan Tamils" and sought its engagement in peace efforts.

Final Years and Legacy

- Suffered from **renal failure** and later **bile duct cancer**, which led to his death on **14 December 2006** in London.
- His passing was considered an **irreplaceable loss** by the LTTE, especially as it coincided with rising international pressure and internal fragmentation.
- After his death, the LTTE struggled to find a political figure with comparable diplomatic skill and ideological clarity.

Anton Balasingham's legacy is complex: he was both a **bridge to the outside world** and a **pillar of LTTE orthodoxy**. His absence left a vacuum in the movement's political wing, and many analysts believe that without his moderating influence, the LTTE became increasingly isolated in its final years

61

From Triumph to Tension: Southern Euphoria and 2010 Presidential Election

Victory and Euphoria in the South

On **May 19, 2009**, Sri Lanka declared victory over the **Liberation Tigers of Tamil Eelam (LTTE)**, ending a brutal 26-year civil war. In the **southern heartland**, the mood was euphoric. Streets filled with jubilant crowds waving national flags, lighting firecrackers, and chanting slogans of unity and triumph. For many Sinhalese citizens, the war's end was not just a military success—it was a **national rebirth**, a moment of liberatiion after decades of fear, bombings, and uncertainty.

The **Rajapaksa family**, led by **President Mahinda Rajapaksa**, was hailed as the architects of victory. His brothers—**Gotabaya Rajapaksa** (Defence Secretary) and **Basil Rajapaksa** (Presidential Advisor)—were credited with strategic coordination, logistics, and international diplomacy. The media, largely state-controlled, amplified this narrative, portraying Mahinda as the **"father of peace"** and Gotabaya as the **"guardian of the nation."**

The Sidelining of General Sarath Fonseka

Yet behind the scenes, tensions simmered. **General Sarath Fonseka**, Commander of the Sri Lanka Army, had played a **decisive role** in the battlefield victory. His leadership, tactical innovation, and relentless drive were instrumental in dismantling the LTTE's conventional and guerrilla capabilities.

However, post-war, Fonseka found himself **marginalized**:

- He was **moved** from Army Commander to **Chief of Defence Staff**, a ceremonial role with limited operational authority.
- Rumors circulated that the Rajapaksas feared Fonseka's **growing popularity** and **potential political ambitions**.
- Fonseka alleged that the government **mistrusted him**, even suspecting him of plotting a coup.

In **November 2009**, Fonseka **resigned** from the military and announced his candidacy for the upcoming **Presidential Election**, positioning himself as the **"common candidate"** of a broad opposition coalition.

The 2010 Presidential Election

Held on **January 26, 2010**, the election was the **first post-war presidential contest**, and it was fiercely competitive.

Main Candidates

CANDIDATE	PARTY/ALLIANCE
Mahinda Rajapaksa	United People's Freedom Alliance (UPFA)
Sarath Fonseka	New Democratic Front (NDF), backed by UNP, JVP, SLMC, TNA

Results

CANDIDATE	VOTES	PERCENTAGE
Mahinda Rajapaksa	6,015,934	57.88%
Sarath Fonseka	4,173,185	40.15%

- **Turnout**: 74.5% of registered voters
- Rajapaksa won **decisively**, securing a **second term**.
- Fonseka carried many **Tamil-majority districts** but failed to sway the Sinhalese south.

Aftermath and Fallout

Following the election:

- Fonseka was **arrested** in February 2010 on charges of **political conspiracy and military misconduct**.
- He was **court-martialed**, stripped of his rank, and imprisoned—sparking international concern over **democratic backsliding**.
- The Rajapaksa family further consolidated power, with **Gotabaya** and **Basil** assuming expanded roles in governance.

The **initial euphoria** of war victory gave way to **polarization**, as the state tightened control over media, civil society, and dissent.

The **southern celebration of victory** in 2009 was genuine and deeply felt. But beneath the surface, it masked a **power struggle** that would define Sri Lanka's post-war politics. The sidelining of General Fonseka and the 2010 election revealed the **fragility of democratic institutions** in the face of triumphalism and dynastic ambition. The Rajapaksas emerged stronger—but at the cost of **pluralism, accountability**, and the very unity the war's end had promised.

The post-war political fallout surrounding **General Sarath Fonseka** is not only compelling, it's crucial to understanding how Sri Lanka transitioned from military triumph to dynastic consolidation and democratic contention. The following chapter builds on the events following the **2010 presidential election**, capturing Fonseka's **imprisonment, political resurrection**, and broader implications for Sri Lanka's governance.

62

From Battlefield Glory to Prison Cell: The Rise, Fall, and Return of General Sarath Fonseka

The War Hero Turned Challenger

After leading the Sri Lankan Army to victory against the LTTE in 2009, **General Sarath Fonseka** was revered as a **National Hero**. His battlefield success and tactical brilliance had delivered what decades of negotiations could not: total military defeat of separatism.

Yet, his war-time glory soon collided with politics. Feeling **sidelined** by the Rajapaksa administration, and accusing them of attempting to **claim sole credit**, Fonseka resigned from the military and declared his candidacy for the **2010 presidential election**, challenging **President Mahinda Rajapaksa**, his former commander-in-chief.

Though supported by a broad opposition alliance, including the **UNP**, **JVP**, and **Tamil minority parties**, Fonseka lost decisively. But his entry into civilian politics shattered long-standing notions of **military detachment** from political life.

Arrest and Controversy

Just weeks after the election, Fonseka was **arrested on February 8, 2010**, while dining with opposition allies. The charges were dramatic:

- Allegedly plotting to overthrow the government
- Misusing military funds and equipment during his service
- Leaking sensitive information to journalists

Two **military courts-martial** followed, where Fonseka was **stripped of his rank, denied his pension**, and sentenced to **30 months imprisonment**. His trial was **closed-door**, his defenders were silenced, and his name became taboo in military circles.

For many, this was not justice—it was **retribution**. International human rights groups and Western governments expressed alarm over the erosion of **due process** and the weaponization of the judiciary.

The Political Awakening Behind Bars

Fonseka did not remain silent. In prison, he declared himself a **prisoner of conscience**, accused the government of corruption and war crimes cover-ups, and vowed to continue his political fight.

By 2012, pressure mounted:

- Protests gathered momentum outside Welikada prison.
- The opposition rallied around his image.
- Western governments quietly lobbied for his release.

In **May 2012**, Fonseka was released via **presidential pardon** but still faced civil restrictions. His resurgence was slow—but resilient.

Return to Parliament and Redemption

In the lead-up to the **2015 presidential election**, Fonseka backed **Maithripala Sirisena**, a defector from the Rajapaksa camp. Sirisena won, and the new government restored Fonseka's **military rank**, **pension**, and public standing.

Fonseka returned to Parliament via the **Democratic Party**, later aligning with the UNP. Though his party didn't gain traction, he was appointed a **Minister Without Portfolio** and held an advisory role on national security.

His transformation—from war general, to prisoner, to politician—became symbolic of Sri Lanka's **turbulent post-war democracy**.

The sidelining of General Sarath Fonseka after 2009 revealed cracks in Sri Lanka's political maturity:

- Victory bred **centralization**, not pluralism.
- Dissent—especially from national heroes—was punished, not debated.
- The **military's credibility** became entwined with political loyalty.

Fonseka's fall and rise remain a study in resilience. His presence served as a **counterweight** to dynastic power, a reminder that those who fight wars often emerge changed—not just in body, but in conviction.

63

Sri Lanka (2010–2015): Politics, Economic Mismanagement, and Corruption

Political Landscape

Between 2010 and 2015, Sri Lanka was governed by **President Mahinda Rajapaksa**, who had secured a second term following the military defeat of the **Liberation Tigers of Tamil Eelam (LTTE)** in 2009. This victory gave Rajapaksa immense popularity and political capital, which he used to consolidate power.

Key political developments included:

- **18th Amendment to the Constitution (2010)**: Removed presidential term limits and expanded executive powers.
- **Centralization of authority**: Rajapaksa appointed family members to key positions, including his brothers Gotabaya (Defense Secretary) and Basil (Economic Development Minister).
- **Suppression of dissent**: Critics, journalists, and opposition figures faced intimidation and surveillance.

Despite the appearance of stability, the political climate was increasingly authoritarian, with democratic institutions weakened and checks on executive power eroded.

Economic Mismanagement

Sri Lanka's post-war economy initially showed signs of growth, with GDP averaging over 7% annually. However, this growth was **heavily reliant on public investment and foreign debt**, masking deeper structural issues.

Major economic missteps included:

- **Debt-fueled infrastructure projects**: The government borrowed heavily to fund large-scale projects like the **Hambantota Port**, **Mattala Rajapaksa International Airport**, and **Colombo Port City**, many of which were criticized for poor returns on investment.
- **Rising external debt**: Debt-to-GDP ratio rose from 86.9% in 2010 to over 100% by 2015.
- **Fiscal indiscipline**: Populist spending, including public sector salary hikes and subsidies, widened the budget deficit.
- **Weak export performance**: Despite infrastructure growth, exports stagnated, and the trade deficit expanded.
- **Overreliance on remittances and tourism**: These sectors were vulnerable to external shocks and failed to offset the growing import bill.

By 2015, Sri Lanka faced mounting pressure on foreign reserves, inflationary risks, and a deteriorating balance of payments.

Corruption and Governance Failures

Corruption was a pervasive issue during this period, undermining public trust and economic efficiency.

Notable concerns included:

- **"Helping Hambantota" scandal**: Allegations that **tsunami relief funds** were diverted to a private account linked to Rajapaksa.
- **Nepotism and cronyism**: Family members and loyalists were appointed to key positions, including the **Chairman of SriLankan Airlines**, which was later investigated for misuse of resources during Rajapaksa's 2015 campaign.
- **Lack of transparency in procurement**: Public contracts were often awarded without competitive bidding, raising concerns of kickbacks and inflated costs.
- **Weak anti-corruption enforcement**: The **Commission to Investigate Allegations of Bribery or Corruption (CIABOC)** was seen as ineffective due to political interference.
- **Media suppression**: Investigative journalism was stifled, and whistleblowers lacked protection, further enabling corrupt practices.

Transparency International's **Corruption Perceptions Index** showed a decline in Sri Lanka's score during this period, reflecting growing concerns over governance.

During the 2010–2015 period in Sri Lanka, several key political and administrative figures were frequently cited in connection with allegations of corruption, misuse of public funds, and abuse of power. Here's a breakdown of the most prominent individuals and their roles:

Key Figures Allegedly Linked to Corruption (2010–2015)

Mahinda Rajapaksa – President (2005–2015)

- Accused of centralizing power and enabling widespread nepotism.
- Allegations include misuse of tsunami relief funds via the *Helping Hambantota* scheme.
- His administration was linked to numerous questionable infrastructure deals and state resource abuse.

Gotabaya Rajapaksa – Secretary of Defence

- Oversaw military operations and procurement during the post-war period.
- Criticized for lack of transparency in defense spending and alleged involvement in land acquisitions.

Basil Rajapaksa – Minister of Economic Development

- Managed large-scale development projects funded by foreign loans.
- Accused of mismanaging funds and favoring politically connected contractors.

Ajith Nivard Cabraal – Governor of the Central Bank

- Allegedly facilitated questionable financial transactions and was linked to money laundering claims involving billions of rupees.

Nishantha Wickramasinghe – Chairman of SriLankan Airlines

- Rajapaksa's brother-in-law; accused of misusing airline resources for political campaigns.

Notable Scandals

- **SriLankan Airlines Misuse**: State resources allegedly used for Rajapaksa's 2015 campaign.
- **Port City Deal**: China Harbour Engineering Company was investigated for offering bribes to secure contracts.
- **Military Aircraft Abuse**: Rajapaksa family reportedly used Air Force planes for personal travel, costing millions in public funds.

These figures were part of a broader system where **institutional checks were weakened**, and **anti-corruption bodies lacked independence**. While investigations were launched after 2015, many cases remain unresolved or politically contested.

Timeline of Key Figures & Corruption-Linked Events (2010–2015)

YEAR	EVENT/SCANDAL	INDIVIDUALS INCOLVED	NOTES/ALLEGATIONS
2010	Helping Hambantota revived	Mahinda Rajapaksa	Alleged diversion of Tsunami relief funds
2011	SriLankan Airlines irregularities	Nishantha Wickramasinghe	Misuse of airline resources linked to campaigns.
2012	Hambantota Port expansion scrutiny	Basil Rajapaksa, Gotabaya Rajapaksa	Accusations of inflated contracts and debt traps.
2013	Colombo Port City deal	Mahinda Rajapaksa, Basil Rajapaksa	Chinese firm allegedly offered bribes for access.
2014	Military transport misuse	Gotabaya Rajapaksa	Personal use of Air Force aircraft.
2015	Election campaign financing questions	Mahinda Rajapaksa, Ajith Nivard Cabraal	Alleged laundering of state funds.

The period from 2010 to 2015 in Sri Lanka was marked by **authoritarian consolidation**, **economic overreach**, and **systemic corruption.** While post-war optimism fueled ambitious development, poor fiscal management and governance failures led to long-term economic strain. The 2015 political transition reflected a public yearning for accountability and reform, though the road to recovery remained complex.

A Review of Political and Extrajudicial Killings in Sri Lanka (2010–2015)

Between 2010 and 2015, under the presidency of **Mahinda Rajapaksa**, Sri Lanka witnessed a troubling surge in **politically motivated violence, extrajudicial killings**, and **enforced disappearances**. These acts were often attributed to **state security forces, paramilitary groups**, and **individuals aligned with the ruling regime**, creating a climate of fear and impunity.

Key Patterns and Incidents

- **Extrajudicial Killings in Custody**
  - Over **200 suspects** were reportedly killed while in police custody during this period.
  - Victims included **Makandure Madush, Kosgoda Tharaka**, and **Dineth Melan**, all allegedly shot during staged operations while handcuffed or under detention orders.
  - Legal experts and human rights lawyers condemned these killings as **fabricated encounters**, often justified by police as attempts to recover weapons or prevent escape.
- **Targeting of Journalists and Activists**
  - The **murder of Lasantha Wickrematunge**, editor of *The Sunday Leader*, in 2009 set the tone for continued suppression of dissent.
  - Journalists and civil society members faced **harassment, abduction, and intimidation**, with many forced into exile or silence.
- **Political Killings and Election Violence**
  - The **2010 presidential election** saw at least **five politically linked murders**, including supporters of both Rajapaksa and opposition candidate Sarath Fonseka.

    Election monitoring groups described it as **the most violent election in two decades**, with over **800 incidents** reported.

- **Prison Massacres**

- Notable incidents include the **Welikada Prison massacre (2012)**, where **27 inmates were killed**, and the **Mahara Prison killings (2020)**, which claimed **11 lives**.
- These events were linked to **state-sanctioned violence** and **lack of accountability**.

Culture of Impunity

- Despite widespread documentation, **no senior officials** were held accountable during Rajapaksa's tenure.
- Investigations were often stalled, manipulated, or dismissed.
- The **Lessons Learnt and Reconciliation Commission (LLRC)**, set up by the government, was criticized for **whitewashing abuses** and lacking independence.

Impact and Legacy

- These years entrenched a **culture of fear**, especially among **minority communities**, **opposition voices**, and **human rights defenders**.
- The **2015 presidential election**, which saw Maithripala Sirisena defeat Rajapaksa, was partly driven by public outrage over these abuses.
- However, many victims and families still await justice, and the **cycle of impunity** remains a challenge for Sri Lanka's democratic institutions.

Echoes of Silence — A Reckoning with Sri Lanka's Culture of Impunity

Between 2010 and 2015, Sri Lanka witnessed a disturbing pattern of **political violence**, **enforced disappearances**, and **murders**—many of which remain unresolved. Two of the most emblematic cases are those of **Prageeth Eknaligoda** and **Wasim Thajudeen**, both of which shook the conscience of the nation and exposed the deep-rooted culture of impunity.

Prageeth Eknaligoda – The Vanished Voice of Dissent

Prageeth's vanishing, just days before the 2010 presidential elections, struck like a lightning bolt through Sri Lanka's journalistic community. His crime? Drawing cartoons that questioned the regime and investigating military abuses. His case—linked to army intelligence—remains unresolved. His wife, Sandya, embodies resilience, having turned personal tragedy into global advocacy. Her voice is the heartbeat of this chapter.

- **Disappearance Date**: January 24, 2010, just two days before the presidential election.
- **Profession**: Political cartoonist, journalist, and activist.
- **Affiliation**: Supported opposition candidate Sarath Fonseka and contributed to *Lanka e News*.
- **Circumstances**:

  - Previously abducted in 2009 and released.
  - Investigated alleged use of chemical weapons by the military.
  - Last seen heading to meet a former LTTE member turned intelligence informant.

Investigation:

- CID linked his disappearance to **military intelligence units**.
- Nine intelligence officers were indicted in 2019.
- The case has faced **political interference**, **witness intimidation**, and **delays**.
- His wife, **Sandya Eknaligoda**, continues to fight for justice and was honored internationally for her activism.

Wasim Thajudeen – A Murder Disguised as a Crash

A celebrated rugby player found dead, with injuries too brutal for any accident to explain. Allegations of political involvement swirled, suggesting he crossed paths with the powerful and paid the ultimate price. Years of obstruction followed, even as forensic evidence screamed murder. To this day, justice remains elusive.

- **Death Date**: May 17, 2012.
- **Profession**: National rugby player and former captain of Havelock Sports Club.
- **Initial Claim**: Died in a car crash near Shalika Grounds, Narahenpita.
- **Emerging Evidence**:
  - Injuries inconsistent with a crash—**broken bones, signs of torture**, and **body found in passenger seat**.
  - Alleged conflict with a **powerful political figure**, possibly over control of the rugby club.

Investigation:

- CID declared it a **murder** in 2015.
- Several police and security officials were arrested for **covering up evidence**.
- A **Defender jeep** linked to the Rajapaksa family's charity was allegedly used in the abduction.
- Despite forensic confirmation of murder, **no convictions** have been made to date.

Other Notable Cases (2010–2015)

- **Lasantha Wickrematunge** (2009): Editor of *The Sunday Leader*, assassinated in broad daylight. His murder remains unsolved. He predicted his death in an open letter.

- **Nadarajah Raviraj** (2006): Tamil MP, shot dead in Colombo. Several navy personnel were charged years later.

-
- **Five Trincomalee students** (2006): Executed on the beach; suspects were re-arrested in 2015.
- **Joseph Pararajasingham** (2005): Tamil MP killed during Christmas Mass; suspects include former paramilitary members.

These cases reflect a **systemic failure of justice**, where **political influence**, **military involvement**, and **lack of accountability** have obstructed truth and closure. Each case connects through common threads—manipulated investigations, suppressed evidence, and the absence of accountability.

In the shadow of victory and peace, Sri Lanka's post-war years from 2010 to 2015 were riddled with pain few dared to name. Beneath grand political speeches and polished international forums lay an unsettling truth: silence had become a weapon, wielded to obscure injustice and erase dissent.

This chapter delves into the stories that linger—not on newspaper front pages, but in grieving homes and unfinished investigations. It is not just an account of lost lives. It is a revelation of a system that not only failed to protect its people, but in many cases, enabled their persecution.

Impunity: The True Architect of Fear

These stories are not historical footnotes—they are unfinished chapters etched in grief, in courtroom delays, and in the quiet resolve of families who refuse to forget. Each disappearance, each murder, each cover-up stains the nation's conscience and reminds us that justice postponed is justice denied. Sri Lanka cannot afford to build its future on denial and amnesia. It must face the voices it silenced, the lives it stole, and the truths it buried. Only then can it hope to rise—not as a land of fractured memory, but as a place where dignity is restored and silence no longer stands in for surrender.

64

2015 Presidential Election & Political Shift

In the tense buildup to the Presidential Elections, Sri Lanka found itself at a political crossroads. The atmosphere, once marked by resignation and political fatigue, suddenly shifted. The electorate—wounded by the unchecked corruption, entrenched nepotism, and oppressive governance of the Mahinda Rajapaksa administration—began to stir. For many, this was more than an election; it was a rare and precious chance to reclaim their voice and challenge a regime that had, for years, operated with impunity.

Behind the scenes, whispers of injustice had long grown louder: politically motivated assassinations, kidnappings that left families shattered, and a culture of intimidation where thuggery had seeped into the fabric of daily life. Trust had eroded. The country's democratic spirit, battered and bruised, demanded renewal.

Yet, in this moment of urgency, the main opposition—the **United National Party led by Ranil Wickremesinghe**—appeared hesitant to face the challenge head-on. Many viewed Wickremesinghe's reluctance to contest as a lack of courage, especially given his history of abstaining from the 2010 Presidential race. Then too, instead of running himself, he backed General Sarath Fonseka—a war hero turned politician—as the Common Candidate.

In 2015, history repeated itself. Rather than stepping forward, Wickremesinghe orchestrated a strategic defection from within the ruling party, elevating a prominent SLFP figure, **Maithripala Sirisena**, to lead the opposition. This move, though politically unconventional, was hailed by many as ingenious—a means of defeating Rajapaksa from within his own ranks. It reignited hope among the disenfranchised and became a rallying point for change.

For millions disillusioned with the status quo, this realignment offered a glimmer of possibility: that perhaps the cycle of abuse could be broken, and a new chapter—however uncertain— could begin. It underscored how, in Sri Lankan politics, courage did not always wear the badge of candidacy. Sometimes, it revealed itself in the boldness to reconfigure the playing field entirely.

Political Shift in 2015

In **January 2015**, **Maithripala Sirisena**, a former ally of Rajapaksa, contested the presidential election as the **Common Opposition Candidate**. Running on a platform of **"Yahapalanaya" (Good Governance)**, he won a surprise victory, signaling public rejection of authoritarianism and corruption.

His government promised:

- **Constitutional reforms**: The **19th Amendment** reintroduced term limits and reduced presidential powers.

- **Anti-corruption investigations**: Probes into Rajapaksa-era deals and misuse of state resources were launched.
- **Improved transparency**: Efforts were made to strengthen institutions and restore democratic norms.

Sri Lanka's 2015 Presidential Election: A Turning Point in History

On **January 8, 2015**, Sri Lanka held its **7th presidential election**, marking a dramatic shift in the country's political landscape. **Maithripala Sirisena**, who defected from the ruling party to become the **Common Candidate** of the opposition, won with **6,217,162 votes (51.28%)**, defeating incumbent **Mahinda Rajapaksa**, who secured **5,768,090 votes (47.58%)**.

This result stunned many observers. Rajapaksa, once seen as politically invincible after ending the civil war in 2009, conceded defeat peacefully the next day. Sirisena was sworn in as the **6th executive president** of Sri Lanka on **January 9, 2015**, at Independence Square in Colombo.

Aftermath and Political Shifts

The election outcome triggered a wave of political and institutional changes:

- **End of Rajapaksa's decade-long rule**: His defeat marked the first time an incumbent president lost a re-election bid in Sri Lanka.
- **Rise of a reformist coalition**: Sirisena led a diverse alliance of 49 parties, promising a "100-Day Programme" focused on:
    - Reducing presidential powers
    - Restoring rule of law
    - Tackling corruption and nepotism
    - Improving governance and transparency
- **Minority support played a key role**: Tamil and Muslim communities overwhelmingly backed Sirisena, reflecting deep dissatisfaction with Rajapaksa's handling of ethnic tensions and extremist violence.
- **Economic promises**: Sirisena pledged salary increases for public servants and reductions in fuel prices, though budgetary constraints made implementation difficult.
- **Allegations of a coup attempt**: Days after the election, the new government announced an investigation into an alleged attempt by Rajapaksa to retain power through unconstitutional means.

The 2015 election was more than a political contest—it was a referendum on authoritarianism, communal politics, and democratic accountability. It showed that even entrenched regimes can be challenged when public will converges with strategic opposition.

65

Sri Lanka's Political Landscape (2015–2019): Hope, Discord, and Missed Opportunities

Pic of The President & Prime Minister

The period between 2015 and 2019 was one of **high expectations and deep disillusionment** in Sri Lankan politics. It began with a historic shift in power and ended in a constitutional crisis that exposed the fragility of coalition governance.

Maithripala Sirisena: A Presidency of Promise and Paralysis

Maithripala Sirisena came to power in 2015 as the **"Common Candidate"** backed by a broad coalition of opposition forces. His victory over Mahinda Rajapaksa was seen as a triumph for democracy, transparency, and reconciliation. However, his tenure was marked by:

Successes:
Restoration of **media freedom** and **judicial independence**
Creation of **independent commissions** (e.g., Elections, Police, Public Service)
Efforts to **curb executive powers** through the 19th Amendment
Initiatives for **reconciliation** with minority communities

Failures:
Inability to deliver on transitional justice and war crimes accountability
Weak economic performance and rising debt
Poor coordination with **Prime Minister Ranil Wickremesinghe**

Easter Sunday attacks (2019), which exposed severe lapses in national security and intelligence sharing

Sirisena's leadership was often described as **indecisive**, and his later attempts to delay the 2019 elections and re-align with the Rajapaksas further eroded public trust.

Ranil Wickremesinghe: The Strategist Behind the Curtain

Ranil Wickremesinghe, leader of the United National Party (UNP), served as Prime Minister during this period. His political maneuvering was both praised and criticized:

Strategic Moves:

Orchestrated Sirisena's candidacy to defeat Rajapaksa in 2015

Pushed for **economic liberalization** and **fiscal reforms**, including a surplus in the primary budget

Advocated for **international reconciliation mechanisms**, including co-sponsoring UNHRC Resolution 30/1

Controversies:

- **Alienated nationalist factions** and faced resistance from business and political elites
- **Failed to deliver on the 100-Day Programme**, leading to public frustration
- **Clashed with Sirisena**, culminating in the 2018 constitutional crisis when Sirisena attempted to replace him with Mahinda Rajapaksa

Wickremesinghe's technocratic style and reliance on international diplomacy often made him appear **out of touch with grassroots sentiment**, despite his long-standing political experience.

Political Atmosphere (2015–2019): Coalition Chaos and Rising Tensions

This era was defined by **coalition governance**, which initially promised unity but quickly unraveled:

- **Coalition Fragility**: The UNP-SLFP alliance was riddled with ideological differences and personal rivalries
- **Rise of Sinhala-Buddhist Nationalism**: Undermined reconciliation efforts and fueled communal tensions
- **Economic Struggles**: Growth slowed, debt increased, and public dissatisfaction grew
- **Security Failures**: The Easter Sunday bombings in 2019 were a tragic culmination of political dysfunction and intelligence breakdowns

Sri Lanka's **Parliamentary General Election** was held on **August 17, 2015,** ten months ahead of schedule, to elect **225 members** to the 15th Parliament. The election followed the presidential victory of **Maithripala Sirisena** earlier that year and was seen as a test of his reformist agenda and the strength of the opposition coalition.

Key Results

Political Alliance/Party	Seats Won	Vote Shate (%)
United National Front for Good Governance (UNFGG) – led by UNP	106	45.66%
United People's Freedom Alliance (UPFA)	95	42.38%
Tamil National Alliance (TNA)	16	4.62%
Janatha Vimukthi Peramuna (JVP)	6	4.87%
Sri Lanka Muslim Congress (SLMC)	1	-
Eelam People's Democratic Party (EPDP)	1	-

Ranil Wickremesinghe, leader of the UNP, was reappointed **Prime Minister,** forming a **national unity government** with support from UPFA MPs loyal to President Sirisena.

Aftermath and Political Dynamics

- The election **ended Mahinda Rajapaksa's bid to return as Prime Minister,** despite his contesting under the UPFA banner.
- Sirisena's **dual role** as SLFP leader and President created internal tensions, as many SLFP members remained loyal to Rajapaksa.
- The **UNFGG coalition,** though short of an outright majority, gained enough support to push forward constitutional reforms, including the **19th Amendment,** which curtailed presidential powers.
- The **Tamil and Muslim vote** played a decisive role, especially in the Northern and Eastern provinces, favoring reformist and minority-friendly candidates.

66

The 2018 Sri Lankan Constitutional Crisis: A Parliamentary Coup and Its Aftermath

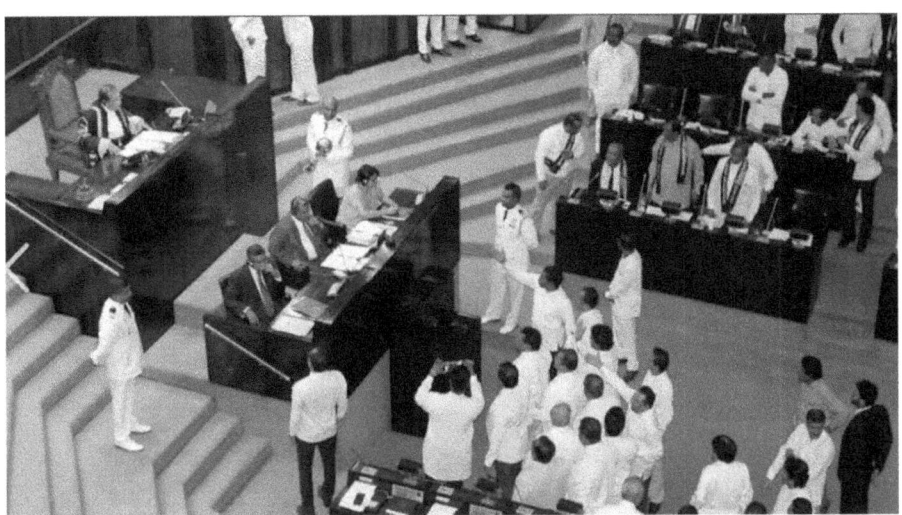

(Pic: onmanorama.com)

On **October 26, 2018**, Sri Lanka plunged into a dramatic political crisis when **President Maithripala Sirisena** abruptly dismissed **Prime Minister Ranil Wickremesinghe** and appointed **former President Mahinda Rajapaksa** in his place. This move, widely condemned as unconstitutional, triggered a seven-week standoff that tested the resilience of Sri Lanka's democratic institutions and exposed deep fissures within its political landscape.

Background and Political Tensions

The seeds of the crisis were sown in the uneasy coalition between Sirisena's **Sri Lanka Freedom Party (SLFP)** and Wickremesinghe's **United National Party (UNP)**, formed after the 2015 presidential election. Sirisena had campaigned as a reformist, promising to curb executive powers and promote transparency. However, by 2018, tensions between the two leaders had escalated over economic policy, corruption allegations, and investigations into wartime abuses.

Sirisena accused Wickremesinghe of mismanaging the economy and obstructing investigations into an alleged assassination plot against him. These grievances culminated in Sirisena's decision to **sack Wickremesinghe** and install **Mahinda Rajapaksa**, a controversial figure known for his authoritarian rule and close ties to China.

The Coup and Dual Premiership

The appointment of Rajapaksa was met with immediate resistance. Wickremesinghe refused to vacate his official residence, claiming still held a parliamentary majority. This led to an unprecedented situation where **Sri Lanka had two rival prime ministers**, each backed by different factions.

In an attempt to consolidate Rajapaksa's position, Sirisena **suspended Parliament**, delaying a vote that could have tested Rajapaksa's legitimacy. When it became clear that Rajapaksa lacked majority support, Sirisena **dissolved Parliament** and called for snap elections—a move later ruled **unconstitutional** by the Supreme Court.

The crisis sparked widespread protests, legal challenges, and international concern. The **Court of Appeal** issued an interim order preventing Rajapaksa and his cabinet from functioning. The **Supreme Court** upheld this decision, declaring that the dissolution of Parliament violated the 19th Amendment to the Constitution, which limits presidential powers.

Amid mounting pressure and legal setbacks, **Rajapaksa resigned** on **December 15, 2018**, ending his short-lived tenure of just seven weeks. Wickremesinghe was reinstated as Prime Minister, restoring constitutional order. The crisis had severe economic repercussions:

- **Foreign reserves** dropped by over **$1 billion**
- The **Sri Lankan rupee** depreciated by **3.8%**
- **Foreign aid** from countries like the U.S. and Japan was frozen
- **Industrial activity** declined sharply

Politically, the episode damaged Sirisena's credibility and exposed vulnerabilities in Sri Lanka's governance. It also galvanized public discourse around constitutional reform and the need for stronger checks on executive power.

The 2018 constitutional crisis stands as a cautionary tale of executive overreach and political opportunism. While the judiciary ultimately upheld democratic norms, the events underscored the fragility of Sri Lanka's institutions and the importance of constitutional safeguards. The brief premiership of Mahinda Rajapaksa, born of a parliamentary coup, ended not with triumph but with a reaffirmation of the rule of law.

Parliamentary Mayhem: November 2018

Following President Maithripala Sirisena's controversial dismissal of Prime Minister Ranil Wickremesinghe and appointment of Mahinda Rajapaksa, Parliament became the epicenter of a fierce political showdown.

Scenes of Unprecedented Disorder

- On **November 15**, Parliament descended into **physical brawls**. Lawmakers exchanged punches, hurled water bottles, books, and even **chili powder mixed with water** to disrupt proceedings.
- MPs loyal to Rajapaksa **occupied the Speaker's chair**, attempting to block votes and intimidate opposition members.

- Some MPs who fell to the floor were **kicked by rivals**, and one was hospitalized after trying to rip out a microphone.
- The Speaker was **physically surrounded and protected** by opposition MPs as tensions escalated.

Speaker Karu Jayasuriya's Defiant Role

Amid the chaos, **Speaker Jayasuriya emerged as a constitutional bulwark**, determined to uphold parliamentary integrity.

His Key Actions and Statements

Declared that **Sri Lanka had no legitimate government**, as neither Rajapaksa nor Wickremesinghe had proven a majority.

Refused to recognize Rajapaksa as Prime Minister, citing the lack of parliamentary support and procedural violations.

Conducted a **voice vote** to pass a no-confidence motion against Rajapaksa's government, despite fierce resistance.

Faced accusations of bias but **stood firm**, stating his actions were guided by constitutional principles and legal advice.

Urged dissenting MPs to bring a **no-confidence motion against him** if they disagreed, rather than resorting to intimidation.

The Speaker's unwavering stance helped:

- **Expose Rajapaksa's lack of majority** in Parliament.
- Reinforce the authority of the **judiciary**, which later ruled the dissolution of Parliament unconstitutional.
- Restore **Ranil Wickremesinghe** as Prime Minister, ending the crisis after seven weeks of turmoil.

67

The Eelam People's Democratic Party (EPDP): A Contested Force in Sri Lankan Tamil Politics

Origins and Evolution

The **Eelam People's Democratic Party (EPDP)** was founded in **November 1987** by **Douglas Devananda**, a former member of the **Eelam Revolutionary Organisation of Students (EROS)** and later the **Eelam People's Revolutionary Liberation Front (EPRLF)**. Initially conceived as a **militant Tamil nationalist group**, the EPDP emerged from a splinter faction of the EPRLF and briefly aligned with the **Eelam National Democratic Liberation Front (ENDLF)** before establishing its independent identity.

Following the **Indo-Lanka Accord of 1987**, the EPDP abandoned its armed struggle against the Sri Lankan state and instead **aligned with government forces** against the **Liberation Tigers of Tamil Eelam (LTTE)**. This marked a pivotal shift—from insurgency to **paramilitary collaboration and political participation**.

Paramilitary Role and Allegations

Throughout the **Sri Lankan Civil War**, the EPDP functioned as a **pro-government paramilitary group**, particularly active in the **Jaffna peninsula and northern regions**. It was accused of:

- **Kidnappings and extortion** of Tamil civilians
- **Enforced disappearances and torture**
- **Sexual exploitation and child trafficking**, including allegations of prostitution rings involving Tamil girls
- **Election violence and vote rigging**, especially during the 2000s

A leaked **US embassy cable** described the EPDP as a **feared paramilitary group** with **non-official control** over parts of Jaffna, operating with **tacit approval from the Sri Lankan Army**. Despite claims of disarmament post-2009, reports suggest the EPDP retained **armed cadres** and continued to exert influence through **intimidation and criminal networks**

Political Participation and Government Alliances

The EPDP entered electoral politics in **1994**, winning **nine parliamentary seats** from Jaffna District, largely due to low voter turnout in LTTE-controlled areas. Over the years, it became a **consistent ally of ruling coalitions**, including:

- **People's Alliance (PA)** under President Chandrika Kumaratunga
- **United People's Freedom Alliance (UPFA)** under Mahinda Rajapaksa

- **New Democratic Front** in more recent years

Douglas Devananda held various **ministerial portfolios**, including:

- **Minister of Rehabilitation and Reconstruction of the North**
- **Minister of Social Services and Welfare**
- **Minister of Traditional Industries and Small Enterprise Development**

Despite electoral setbacks, the EPDP maintained a **presence in local government**, particularly in **Jaffna**, and continued to contest elections under broader coalition banners.

Controversies and Criticism

The EPDP's dual identity—as a **political party and paramilitary force**—has drawn widespread criticism:

- **Human rights organizations** such as Amnesty International and Human Rights Watch have documented its involvement in **abductions, killings, and extortion**
- **Journalists and civil society activists** have accused the EPDP of **media suppression and intimidation**
- Allegations of **land grabs**, **illegal business monopolies** and **corruption** have persisted, particularly in post-war reconstruction efforts
- Douglas Devananda himself has faced **criminal charges in India**, including **kidnapping and murder**, though he continues to serve in Sri Lankan politics.

Legacy and Contemporary Role

- Today, the EPDP remains a **polarizing force** in Sri Lankan Tamil politics. While it positions itself as a **moderate alternative** to separatist movements, its **history of collaboration with state forces**, **accusations of abuse**, and **limited grassroots support** have undermined its credibility among many Tamils.

- Nonetheless, its **strategic alliances**, **ministerial access**, and **organizational resilience** have allowed it to persist in the political landscape—especially in **Jaffna and northern districts**.

The EPDP's journey from **militant insurgency to political integration** reflects the **complex interplay of survival, ideology, and power** in post-war Sri Lanka. Its legacy is marred by **controversy**, yet its continued relevance underscores the **fragmented nature of Tamil representation** and the **challenges of reconciliation** in a deeply divided society.

68

Communal Politics and Anti-Muslim Violence in Sri Lanka — Roots, Agents, and Consequences

Bing Image – Aluthgama violence

Introduction: A Nation Divided by Identity Politics

Sri Lanka, a multi-ethnic and multi-religious island nation, has long grappled with the politics of identity. While the country's post-independence history is often framed around the Sinhala-Tamil divide, the **Muslim minority**—comprising nearly 10% of the population—has increasingly become a target of **communal hostility**, especially in the post-war era. The rise of **Sinhala-Buddhist nationalism**, coupled with political opportunism and state complicity, has fueled a wave of **violence, discrimination, and marginalization** against Muslims that continues to shape Sri Lanka's political landscape.

Historical Context: From Marginalization to Targeting

- **1990 Northern Expulsion**: The **LTTE forcibly expelled over 70,000 Muslims** from the Northern Province, accusing them of collaborating with the state. This act of ethnic cleansing remains largely unacknowledged in national reconciliation efforts.
- **Eastern Massacres**: Attacks on mosques in **Kattankudy and Eravur** in 1990 left hundreds dead, marking the beginning of systematic violence against Muslims during the civil war.

- **Post-War Shift**: After the war ended in 2009, **anti-Muslim sentiment shifted from Tamil militants to Sinhala-Buddhist nationalist groups**, who began portraying Muslims as economic and cultural threats.

Communal Politics: The Rise of Sinhala-Buddhist Nationalism

- **Ideological Roots**: Sinhala-Buddhist nationalism promotes the idea of Sri Lanka as a **Buddhist homeland**, marginalizing other religious communities. This ideology has been weaponized to consolidate political power and suppress dissent.
- **Political Exploitation**: Successive governments have **used anti-Muslim rhetoric** to distract from economic failures and rally Sinhala voters. The slogan "One Country, One Law" became a dog whistle for discriminatory policies targeting Muslims.

Key Organizations and Leaders Behind Anti-Muslim Campaigns

ORGANIZATION	ROLE	NOTABLE FIGURES	ACTIVITIES
Bodu Bala Sena (BBS)	Leading anti-Muslim group	**Galagoda Aththe Gnanasara**	Incited riots, spread hate speech, lobbied for niqab and madrasa bans
Sinhala Ravaya	Militant nationalist group	Various monks	Organized rallies, promoted Islamophobic propaganda
Ravana Balaya	Extremist faction	Linked to BBS	Participated in mob violence and intimidation
Sri Lanka Podujana Peramuna (SLPP)	Political party	**Mahinda Rajapaksa, Gotabaya Rajapaksa**	Accused of enabling or ignoring anti-Muslim violence during their tenure

Major Incidents of Anti-Muslim Violence

2013 Anti-Halal Campaign: Led by BBS, this campaign pressured Islamic clerics to withdraw halal certification, sparking attacks on Muslim businesses.

2014 Aluthgama Riots: Triggered by a BBS rally, mobs attacked Muslim homes and shops, resulting in deaths and mass displacement.

2018 Digana and Ampara Riots: False rumors and communal tensions led to widespread arson and looting of Muslim properties.

2019 Post-Easter Attacks: Following bombings by Islamist extremists, retaliatory violence targeted innocent Muslims. Hundreds of homes and businesses were destroyed.

Forced Cremation Policy (2020–2021): The government mandated cremation of COVID-19 victims, violating Islamic burial rites. The policy was reversed only after international pressure.

Legal Harassment: Laws like the **Prevention of Terrorism Act (PTA)** and **ICCPR Act** have been misused to detain Muslim activists, poets, and lawyers without trial.

Proposed Bans: Efforts to ban **niqabs** and **madrasas** reflect a broader agenda to suppress Muslim religious expression.

Consequences and the Path Forward

- **Erosion of Trust**: Muslims increasingly feel alienated from the state and fearful of their neighbors.
- **International Condemnation**: Human rights groups like Amnesty International and Human Rights Watch have called out Sri Lanka's failure to protect its Muslim citizens.

Need for Accountability:

- Investigate and prosecute perpetrators of communal violence.
- Repeal discriminatory laws and policies.
- Include Muslim voices in reconciliation and transitional justice mechanisms.

Reclaiming Unity Through Justice

Sri Lanka's future depends on its ability to confront the **ugly truths of communal politics** and dismantle the structures that enable **Islamophobia and violence**. The Muslim community's suffering—whether through **mass expulsions**, **mob attacks**, or **state-sanctioned di discrimination**—must be acknowledged, addressed, and remembered. Only then can Sri Lanka hope to build a society rooted in **pluralism, dignity, and peace**.

References
www.justiceforallcanada.org
asiacommune.org
en.wikipedia.org
www.amnesty.irg
www.hrw.org

69

Malays of Sri Lanka: A Forgotten and Politically Betrayed Community

I write not as a politician, but as a son of Sri Lanka. Let this chapter not be our elegy, but our anthem of resurgence. Let the Parliament hear our silence—and restore our voice.

The Malays of Sri Lanka, a vibrant yet numerically small ethnic group, have long been woven into the island's historical, cultural, and military tapestry. Despite their deep-rooted presence and contributions, they remain **politically marginalized**, struggling for recognition and representation in the national legislature. This essay explores their origins, historical role in Sri Lanka's governance, the erosion of their political voice, and the efforts of organizations like **COSLAM** to restore their rightful place in the country's democratic framework.

Dr. T.B. Jayah – The Malay National Hero

Historical Origins and Cultural Identity

The Sri Lankan Malays trace their ancestry to the **Malay Archipelago**, including present-day Indonesia, Malaysia, and Singapore. Their arrival in Sri Lanka spans centuries:

Ancient ties: Austronesian sailors reached Sri Lanka as early as **200 B.C.**, bringing Malayo-Polynesian languages and customs.

Colonial migration: During Dutch and British rule (1640–1948), Malays arrived as **soldiers, exiled nobles, and convicts**, many of whom settled permanently.

Cultural legacy: Malays enriched Sri Lankan society through cuisine (e.g., *watalappan*, *nasi goreng*), fashion (e.g., *sarong*, *songko*), and language. Their dialect, **Sri Lanka Malay (SLM)**, blends Malay, Sinhala, and Tamil.

Despite their assimilation, Malays preserved a distinct identity through **Islamic faith**, **linguistic heritage**, and **community institutions**.

Military Valor and Early Political Representation: Historically, Malays were celebrated as **warriors and administrators**:

Under Dutch and British rule, they formed elite military units like the **Ceylon Rifle Regiment** and later dominated the **colonial police force**.

In the early 20th century, Malays began entering **legislative bodies**, with notable figures including:

Dr. T.B. Jayah: First Malay lawmaker, served in the **Legislative Council (1924–1930)**, **State Council**, and **Parliament**, later becoming **High Commissioner to Pakistan**.

M.K. Saldin, Dr. M.P. Drahaman, B. Zahiere Lye, and **M.H. Amit**: Other prominent Malay parliamentarians and senators.

These leaders championed **education, labor rights, and minority inclusion**, but their presence in Parliament dwindled after the 1990s.

The Unsung Valor of Malay Officers in Sri Lanka's Eelam War

For over three decades, Sri Lanka was gripped by a brutal civil war between government forces and the Liberation Tigers of Tamil Eelam (LTTE). Amid the chaos and carnage, **Sri Lankan Malays—an ethnic minority with deep historical roots in the island—stood tall in service to the nation**, particularly within the ranks of the armed forces.

Leading from the Front

Malay officers were known for their **exceptional discipline, loyalty, and courage**, often serving in frontline combat roles. Despite their small numbers, they were disproportionately represented in leadership positions within the military. Many rose to the rank of **Major, Colonel, and even General**, commanding troops in some of the most volatile regions of the conflict.

- **Brigadier Tuan Nizam Muthaliff**, a highly respected intelligence officer, was assassinated in 2005—his death was a major blow to military intelligence operations.
- **Colonel Tuan Rizly Meedin**, another decorated Malay officer, was instrumental in counter-insurgency operations and was known for his strategic acumen.

- Countless others served in infantry, engineering, and logistics units, often in high-risk zones like Jaffna, Kilinochchi, and Mullaitivu.

Supreme Sacrifice

The war claimed the lives of many Malay servicemen, some of whom were posthumously honored for their bravery. Their sacrifices were not just military—they were deeply personal, as many left behind families and communities that mourned in silence.

- **Malay families across Sri Lanka**—from Colombo to Kandy—have stories of sons, brothers, and fathers who never returned.
- Their names may not always appear in mainstream narratives, but within the Malay community, they are remembered as **heroes who gave everything for the unity and sovereignty of Sri Lanka**.

A Legacy of Service

The Malay contribution to Sri Lanka's military history dates back centuries, with their ancestors serving in colonial regiments under the Dutch and British. The Eelam War was a continuation of that legacy—one marked by **duty, honor, and sacrifice**.

Today, Malay veterans and their families continue to advocate for recognition and remembrance. Memorials, oral histories, and community events help preserve their stories, ensuring that future generations understand the depth of their commitment.

Political Betrayal and Loss of Representation

Since **1993**, Malays have had **no representation in Parliament**, following the resignation of **M.H. Amit** to make way for Gamini Dissanayake. This absence has had profound consequences:

Loss of voice: Malays have been excluded from **constitutional reforms**, **budget allocations**, and **policy discussions** affecting minority rights

Misclassification: Malays are often grouped under the broader "Muslim" category, erasing their **ethnic distinctiveness**.

Demographic decline: Census data shows a **26.7% drop** in Malay population between 2001 and 2011, though community leaders dispute this figure, estimating **80,000 Malays** nationwide.

The lack of political representation has led to **cultural erosion**, **economic neglect**, and **social invisibility**.

(Pics: 2020 Presidential Candidate & COSLAM Chairman)

The Struggle for Parliamentary Representation

In response to decades of marginalization, Malays have mobilized through advocacy and civil society:

COSLAM (Conference of Sri Lankan Malays)

(T.K. Azoor - COSLAM Chairman)

Founded in **2000**, COSLAM aims to **unite Malays** and advocate for **Socio-Political Empowerment**.

It has made **formal appeals** to successive governments and parliamentary committees:

- **2002**: Resolution submitted to Minister G.L. Peiris.
- **2003 & 2013**: Delegations appeared before **Select Committees on Electoral Reforms**.

COSLAM argues that Malays, being **geographically scattered**, cannot win seats through direct elections and thus require **national list appointments**.

(Pic: Ahmed Azoor leading COSLAM Youth)

Launched in **2019**, this grassroots campaign demands the **restoration of a Malay MP and equal access to education, employment, and media**.

Leaders like **T.K. Azoor** have engaged with presidential candidates to secure commitments for Malay inclusion. Despite these efforts, **no Malay has entered Parliament since 1994**, and their appeals remain largely unheeded.

The Malays of Sri Lanka are not merely a forgotten community—they are a **betrayed one**, sidelined despite centuries of loyalty, service, and cultural contribution. Their struggle for parliamentary representation is not a demand for privilege, but a plea for **dignity, visibility, and justice**.

Restoring a **Malay seat in Parliament**, recognizing their **ethnic identity**, and supporting organizations like **COSLAM** are essential steps toward **inclusive governance**. In a nation that prides itself on diversity, the Malays deserve more than ceremonial acknowledgment—they deserve a **voice**.

The Legacy and Loss: A Malay's Case for Parliamentary Representation

(A cross section of COSLAM Malays)

Parliamentary representation for the Malays of Sri Lanka is not a recent or fanciful demand—it is a historical precedent rooted in our long-standing contributions to the nation. The late **Dr. T.B. Jayah**, a towering figure in our community, was appointed to the **State Council in 1936**, marking a turning point in Malay political visibility.

In **November 1944**, as the State Council debated the **Dominion Bill**—a crucial motion aimed at securing dominion status for Ceylon—Dr. Jayah made a **historic address**. At a time when the British Government hesitated, citing minority rights as a concern, Dr. Jayah declared unequivocally that **Muslims were committed to national freedom above communal interests**. His speech, widely acclaimed across political lines, was a key factor in propelling **Ceylon toward independence**. It remains a landmark moment of patriotism, solidarity, and principled leadership.

Following independence, other distinguished Malays continued to serve in **Parliament and the Senate**, championing national interests while giving voice to our community. Yet this momentum was abruptly halted. The constitutional reforms enacted under **President J.R. Jayewardene** dismantled the mechanism that ensured **ethnic minority representation**, leaving Malays politically orphaned and unheard.

This silence has persisted for over **25 years**. Despite their rich legacy, Malays have been **excluded from national governance**, relegated to symbolic participation while decisions that shape our futures unfold without our voice. And yet, our **contributions remain unparalleled** when measured proportionally to our population: in **defense and security**, **sports**, **medicine**, **education**, and **public service**, Malays have served with honor and excellence. We are **not known for financial exploitation or criminal enterprise**; we are known for **service, dignity, and loyalty**.

But their goodwill has been mistaken for passivity. Their **happy-go-lucky spirit**, once a source of pride, has made them easy to ignore. Political representation is not a privilege—it is a right. It is the cornerstone of democratic inclusion. It is long past time for our community to reclaim its seat at the table, not just as citizens, but as rightful contributors to the future of Sri Lanka.

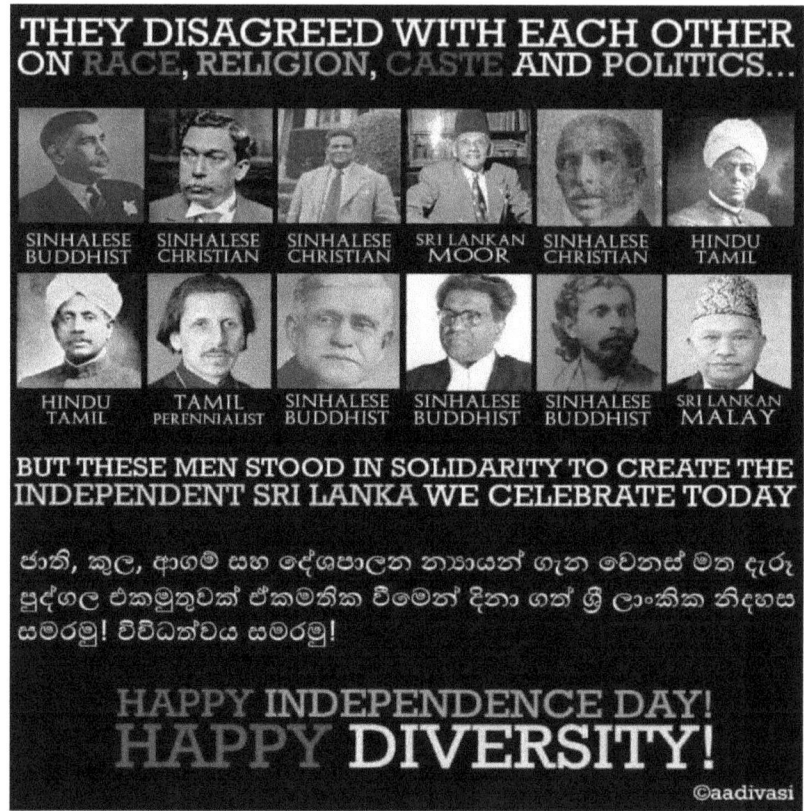

70

April 21, 2019 — The Morning Sri Lanka Trembled

The sun had barely risen when Sri Lanka plunged into one of its darkest days. Churches full of Easter worshippers and hotels alive with morning routines became scenes of carnage in an instant. The first blast tore through **Kochikade's St. Anthony's Shrine**—an explosion so violent it shattered stained glass and silenced prayers mid-hymn. Within the hour, more bombs ripped through the sanctity of **Zion Church in Batticaloa** and the opulence of luxury hotels in Colombo, scattering bodies, mangled pews, and twisted chandeliers. The country convulsed in disbelief. Radios and televisions echoed screams and sirens. Streets fell into stunned silence. The attacks, claimed by ISIS and carried out by local extremists, did more than kill innocents—they fractured the nation's sense of security and cast suspicion over an entire community already living on edge. What began as a sacred day of resurrection became a gruesome testament to hatred and the failure of intelligence systems meant to protect.

Prelude to Horror: April 21, 2019

It was a quiet Sunday morning. Families dressed in their finest gathered in churches across Sri Lanka to celebrate Easter — a day of resurrection, of hope. Tourists sipped coffee in luxury hotels, unaware that within minutes, their lives would be torn apart. At **8:45 a.m.**, the first explosion ripped through **St. Anthony's Shrine in Kochikade**, Colombo. Seconds later, **St. Sebastian's Church in Negombo** and **Zion Church in Batticaloa** were engulfed in flames and screams.

Simultaneously, suicide bombers detonated devices at **Shangri-La**, **Cinnamon Grand**, and **Kingsbury Hotels**, targeting breakfast buffets and lobbies. Two more blasts followed

— one at a **guesthouse in Dehiwala**, another during a **police raid in Dematagoda**, killing three officers.

By the end of the day, **270 people lay dead**, including **45 foreign nationals** and **over 50 children**. More than **500 were injured**, many permanently scarred.

Within hours, news outlets identified the attackers as **Islamist extremists linked to ISIS**, allegedly members of the **National Thowheed Jamath (NTJ)**. Panic swelled into suspicion, and suspicion bred hostility. All eyes turned toward the **Muslim community**, despite its overwhelming condemnation of the attacks. Hatred simmered beneath the shock, and communal retaliation seemed dangerously close.

A Voice of Grace Amid Chaos — Cardinal Malcolm Ranjith's Call for Peace After the Easter Attacks

In the immediate aftermath of the **Easter Sunday bombings on April 21, 2019**, Sri Lanka teetered on the edge of communal backlash. The horror of the attacks—targeting churches and hotels, killing over 250 people—sent shockwaves through the nation. Fear and grief quickly gave way to anger, and the potential for retaliatory violence loomed large, especially against the **Muslim community**, which was already vulnerable and deeply shaken.

One Man's Intervention — Cardinal Malcolm Ranjith's Defining Role

At the center of grief stood **Cardinal Malcolm Ranjith, Archbishop of Colombo**. His cathedral had just been desecrated. His flock had been slaughtered. And yet, his response carried **not vengeance, but grace**.

Rather than stoking fury, Cardinal Ranjith offered one of the most consequential messages of restraint in Sri Lanka's post-war history. He implored Christians and all Sri Lankans not to resort to violence or blame an entire community for the actions of a few.

"We do not seek revenge. We mourn in peace. We pray even for those who turned against us," he said from the altar, days after the massacre. "Let us not allow hatred to spread. Let us protect the sanctity of our nation."

Behind the scenes, the Cardinal **met with Muslim leaders**, embracing them in solidarity and pain. His message was clear: **do not let the attackers succeed in dividing us**. His voice — calm, courageous, unyielding — resonated across religious lines, defusing tension in areas like **Negombo** and **Batticaloa**, where emotions ran high.

Ripple Effects — How a Statement Saved Lives

Sri Lanka had suffered through decades of civil war and intercommunal violence. Retaliation was a familiar path, and political actors often let mob justice run unchecked. But this time, something different happened.

- **Mobs ready to riot paused**, hearing the voice of their spiritual leader.

- **Security forces intensified protection around mosques**, bolstered by the Cardinal's appeal for unity.
- **Muslim leaders publicly thanked the Cardinal**, joining hands in vigils and interfaith services.
- Even international leaders praised his **moral courage**, with Pope Francis referencing Sri Lanka's example in sermons on interfaith harmony.

According to government sources, Cardinal Ranjith's restraint **averted what could have become a second wave of bloodshed**, this time born from vengeance.

His public statements, marked by **calm, restraint, and spiritual clarity**, played a pivotal role in **preventing further bloodshed**. Rather than stoking division, he chose the path of **forgiveness and unity**, urging Christians not to retaliate and instead to uphold the teachings of Christ.

"We meditated on Christ's teachings and loved them, forgave them and had pity on them," Cardinal Ranjith said during a live-streamed Easter Mass shortly after the attacks. "We did not hate them and return them the violence. Resurrection is the complete rejection of selfishness."

Behind the scenes, Cardinal Ranjith also **met with Muslim leaders**, offering reassurance and solidarity. His actions helped **defuse tension**, especially in areas like Negombo and Batticaloa, where interfaith relations were fragile. According to Fr. Rohan Silva, director of Colombo's Centre for Society and Religion, the Cardinal's intervention **"saved bloodshed, the second bloodshed in the country after the massacre"**.

His leadership was not passive. He became a **vocal advocate for justice**, demanding an **independent international investigation** into the attacks and pressing the government to dismantle the "deep state" that allegedly obstructed accountability. Yet, he never allowed the pursuit of justice to devolve into vengeance.

President Anura Kumara Dissanayake later acknowledged that **"the cardinal's patience and calm nature prevented the major problems that could have occurred at that time"**, crediting him with helping maintain national stability during one of its most vulnerable moments.

A Malay Muslim's Perspective: From Suspicion to Survival

As a Muslim from Sri Lanka's Malay community, I remember those days with the clarity of pain. Suddenly, we were not neighbors. We were suspects. Doors closed quietly. Smiles faded. Even fellow citizens who once joined us for meals and festivals began to hesitate. My children asked why the world seemed different overnight.

*Then came Cardinal Ranjith's voice — not just in the churches, but on radios, on TV, in press conferences that played in every household. He spoke **not just to his flock**, but to the soul of the nation. His message reminded many that we were still one people.*

*That act of spiritual solidarity did not erase fear, but it saved lives. It allowed people like me to walk the streets without retaliation. It reminded Christians and Muslims alike that compassion is not weakness — it is the **strongest shield against chaos**. (Note by Author)*

Survivor Voices: Grief Etched in Flesh and Memory

(Pic) Daily Mail

Niranjalee Yasawaradana — A Mother Left Behind

Niranjalee lost her **husband and two daughters**, Nethmi and Vishmi, at **St. Sebastian's Church**. She survived but spent two weeks unconscious in a hospital. Today, she visits their graves every Saturday, kneeling before three crosses, whispering stories to the wind.

"I used to cook for them. Now I ask myself — for whom should I cook?" she told her counselor, Sr. Manoranji Murthy.

Her healing came slowly, through therapy, prayer, and the companionship of two dogs gifted to her to ease the silence.

Hasaru Shenal — A Son Reborn Through Faith

Hasaru was just a teenager when the blast at **St. Sebastian's** took his mother. He spent two weeks in intensive care, waking to a world without her.

"She was always smiling. I teach Sunday school now — for children like me who lost someone," he said, clutching a photo of his mother and another of **Pope Francis**, who prayed over him in Rome.

Sr. Sirima Opanayake — The Educator Who Lost Her Students

Seven students from her school died in the blast. She led months of counseling before classes resumed. A memorial hall now honors the children, and scholarships bear their names.

Timeline of Events and Investigations

DATE	EVENT
April 21, 2019	Coordinated suicide bombings at churches and hotels.
April 22–23	Arrests begin; curfews imposed; social media blocked.
April 25	ISIS claims responsibility; NTJ identified as local affiliate.
May 2019	Emergency laws passed; over 150 arrests made.
2020–2023	Investigations stall; survivors demand justice; Channel 4 documentary alleges deeper conspiracy.
January 2023	Supreme Court rules that President Sirisena and officials failed to act on intelligence; compensation ordered.
2024–2024.....	Investigations reopened; former intelligence chief and MP Pillayan arrested amid renewed scrutiny.

Despite early arrests, **only 25 suspects** have faced trial. Survivors filed **12 Fundamental Rights cases**, leading to a landmark ruling that **state officials failed to prevent the attacks**.

The **Channel 4 documentary (2023)** alleged links between **Sri Lankan Intelligence**, **political actors**, and the bombers — suggesting the attacks may have been used to engineer a security crisis that paved the way for **Gotabaya Rajapaksa's presidential win**.

The **Catholic Church**, led by **Cardinal Malcolm Ranjith**, continues to demand an **international inquiry**, refusing to let the tragedy be buried under bureaucracy.

Conclusion: A Nation Still Searching

Six years on, Sri Lanka remains haunted — not just by the lives lost, but by the **questions unanswered**. Survivors like Niranjalee and Hasaru carry their grief with grace, but they also carry a demand: **truth, accountability, and remembrance**.

This chapter is not just a record of violence. It is a testament to resilience. A call to ensure that **no community is scapegoated**, no victim forgotten, and no truth buried.

Personal Reflection

When Home Turns Hostile — A Farewell Etched in Pain

For a Malay Muslim born on the soil of Sri Lanka, leaving the country wasn't a choice lightly made—it was one born of sorrow, isolation, and a deep reckoning with the idea of belonging. The aftermath of the Easter Sunday attacks in April 2019 fractured more than buildings and lives—its broke communities, trust, and the fragile hope that coexistence could be revived.

In the days that followed, whispers turned into suspicion. Neighbours looked with wary eyes. Institutions tightened their grip. To be Muslim—especially visibly so—was to carry the weight of someone else's crime, to endure profiling, silence, and, worse, guilt by association.

I remember the week that followed. It felt as if the air thickened with fear and accusation. Security checks became interrogations. The mosques I once entered with peace became guarded gates. Even among colleagues and friends, a wall had arisen—unspoken, but undeniable.

Being Malay Muslim—distinct in language, dress, and tradition—only heightened the scrutiny. I was no longer just a citizen. I had become a suspect in the eyes of some, a stranger in the land I called home. Attempts to explain, to reach out, were often met with polite distance or thinly veiled mistrust.

Why I Chose to Leave

I did not leave Sri Lanka because I stopped loving it. I left because I could no longer breathe in its shadows. The emotional strain, the inability to thrive without fear, and the erosion of dignity eventually outweighed my desire to hold on.

My story is not one of betrayal. It is on one of survival. A testament to the inner conflict of being loyal to your homeland while realizing it no longer shelters your truth. I left behind memories, family roots, and a culture rich in warmth. But I carried with me a clarity forged in pain—the conviction that silence in the face of injustice is itself a violence.

Final Words

This book began as a witness's chronicle. It ends as a human's farewell. I leave not in bitterness, but in hope—that one day, Sri Lanka will be a place where being different is not dangerous, and where identity is embraced, not erased. Until then, I tell this story for those who remain. For those unheard. For those still hoping.

Rise of Alleged Extremist Muslim Groups in Sri Lanka

(2015–2019)

Between 2015 and 2019, Sri Lanka witnessed a troubling escalation in religious tensions, culminating in the **Easter Sunday bombings of April 21, 2019**. This period saw the emergence of **local Islamist extremist groups**, most notably **National Thowheed Jama'ath (NTJ)** and **Jamathe Millathe Ibrahim**, which were later banned under emergency laws following the attacks. Key Groups involved:

National Thowheed Jama'ath (NTJ): A radical Islamist group led by *Zahran Hashim*, known for promoting extremist ideologies and inciting violence.

Jamathe Millathe Ibrahim and **Vilayath As Seylani**: Lesser-known groups also linked to the Easter attacks and banned by the government.

Crimes Committed

1. **Easter Sunday Bombings (April 21, 2019)**

- **Targets**: Three churches (St. Anthony's Shrine, St. Sebastian's Church, Zion Church) and three luxury hotels (Shangri-La, Cinnamon Grand, Kingsbury).
- **Casualties**: Over **260 people killed**, including **five Americans**, and **500+ injured**.
- **Method**: Coordinated **suicide bombings** using **acetone peroxide-based explosives**.

2. **Radicalization and Weapon Stockpiling**

Authorities discovered **weapons caches** and **training camps** in the Eastern ⬚ Province linked to NTJ, but investigations were allegedly obstructed by political interference.

3. **Spread of Extremist Ideology**

- NTJ and affiliated groups were accused of promoting **Wahhabism**, a strict interpretation of Islam, and fostering **anti-Christian and anti-Buddhist sentiment**, particularly in the Eastern Province.

Evidence Presented - Intelligence and Surveillance

- **Prior warnings** were issued by foreign agencies and Sri Lankan intelligence as early as **April 4, 2019**, but were not acted upon effectively.
- **Video evidence**: Attackers were seen pledging allegiance to **ISIS leader Abu Bakr al-Baghdadi**, confirming ideological links.
- **FBI Affidavit (2020)**: Identified the attackers as members of "ISIS in Sri Lanka," with direct communication to ISIS leadership in Syria.

Arrests and Investigations

Over **1,000 individuals** were arrested under the **Prevention of Terrorism Act (PTA)**, though only a fraction remained in custody by year's end.

Weapons and explosives were found in homes and mosques linked to NTJ members.

Social media posts and literature were used as evidence of radicalization and incitement.

Masterminds Behind the Attacks

Zahran Hashim

- **Role**: Self-proclaimed leader of NTJ and **mastermind** of the Easter Sunday attacks.
- **Background**: Known for fiery sermons and extremist rhetoric; died in the Shangri-La hotel bombing.

Mohamed Naufer

- Alleged co-conspirator and recruiter; charged in the U.S. for involvement in the deaths of American citizens.

Ahmed Milhan Hayathu Mohamed

- Another key figure indicted by U.S. authorities for his role in the attacks.

Political Allegations

Some reports suggest **political interference** and **negligence** by officials in power during the attacks, including failure to act on intelligence.

Allegations against **Mohamed Ibrahim**, a wealthy businessman whose sons were suicide bombers, raised concerns about funding and support.

The period from 2015 to 2019 marked a dark chapter in Sri Lanka's post-war history, as **Islamist extremism** emerged in the form of NTJ and affiliated groups. The **Easter Sunday bombings** were the most devastating manifestation of this radicalization, with **Zahran Hashim** and his network identified as the key perpetrators. Despite substantial evidence and international collaboration, questions remain about **political accountability**, **intelligence failures**, and the **ideological roots** of extremism in the region.

At the time of writing, investigations ongoing to ascertain the "real masterminds" of the attacks.

71

Election by Fear — How the Easter Attacks Reshaped Sri Lanka's 2019 Political Landscape

Introduction: A Nation in Mourning, A Nation in Flux

April 21, 2019 — Easter Sunday — was meant to be a day of resurrection and celebration. Instead, it became a day of devastation. Suicide bombers targeted churches and luxury hotels, killing over **270 people** and injuring hundreds more. The attacks, claimed by **ISIS** and executed by members of the **National Thowheed Jamaath (NTJ)**, shattered Sri Lanka's sense of security and plunged the country into chaos.

But beyond the immediate horror, the bombings triggered a seismic shift in the nation's political trajectory. In the months that followed, fear became a campaign tool, and the promise of security became a rallying cry.

The **2019 Presidential and 2020 General Elections** were not just contests of policy— they were referendums on survival

Timeline of Events: From Tragedy to Turnaround

DATE	EVENT
April 21, 2019	Easter Sunday bombings kill 270+ people.
April–May 2019	Curfews imposed; Muslim community faces backlash; arrests begin.
June–August 2019	Investigations stall; intelligence failures exposed; political blame game intensifies.
August 11, 2019	SLPP officially nominates **Gotabaya Rajapaksa** as its presidential candidate.
September 26, 2019	UNP selects **Sajith Premadasa** as its candidate.
November 16, 2019	Presidential election held; Gotabaya wins with **52.25%** of the vote.
August 5, 2020	General election held; SLPP wins **landslide majority**.

The Political Narrative: Security as Strategy

The Easter attacks exposed deep fissures in the ruling coalition led by **President Maithripala Sirisena** and **Prime Minister Ranil Wickremesinghe**. Intelligence warnings from **India** had been ignored. The public was outraged. The government appeared paralyzed.

Into this vacuum stepped **Gotabaya Rajapaksa**, former Defence Secretary and brother of ex-President Mahinda Rajapaksa. His campaign was built on a single, potent promise: **"I will restore security."** The attacks gave him a platform tailor-made for his image as a wartime strategist and strongman.

Meanwhile, **Sajith Premadasa**, the UNP candidate, struggled to distance himself from the failures of the government he was part of. Despite support from minority communities, his campaign was overshadowed by Gotabaya's security-first rhetoric.

How the Easter Attack Plan Worked — Allegations and Investigations

While the NTJ and ISIS claimed responsibility, investigations revealed disturbing lapses:

- **Indian intelligence** had warned Sri Lankan authorities multiple times in April 2019, naming **Zahran Hashim** and detailing target locations.
- These warnings were **not acted upon**, allegedly due to political infighting between Sirisena and Wickremesinghe.
- Some reports suggest **state intelligence units** may have had prior knowledge but failed to intervene.
- A **Channel 4 documentary** and whistleblower testimony later alleged that elements within the security apparatus may have **enabled or manipulated** the attacks to create a climate of fear and facilitate Gotabaya's rise.

While these claims remain controversial and contested, they have fueled public suspicion and calls for an **independent international inquiry**.

Election Results and Aftermath

🏛 *2019 Presidential Election*

- **Gotabaya Rajapaksa (SLPP)**: 6,924,255 votes (52.25%)
- **Sajith Premadasa (UNP)**: 5,564,239 votes (41.99%)

Gotabaya's victory was swift and decisive. Within days, **Mahinda Rajapaksa** was appointed Prime Minister, consolidating the family's power.

2020 General Election

- **SLPP** won a **two-thirds majority**, enabling constitutional changes.
- The **19th Amendment**, which had curbed presidential powers, was rolled back.
- The **20th Amendment** restored sweeping executive authority to the President.

Legacy and Lingering Questions

The Easter attacks reshaped Sri Lanka's political landscape—but they also left behind a trail of unanswered questions:

- Why were intelligence warnings ignored?
- Who benefited most from the chaos?
- Was the tragedy exploited for political gain?

The **Supreme Court** later ruled that **President Sirisena and top officials** had failed in their duty to protect the public. Yet, deeper accountability remains elusive.

Conclusion: Democracy in the Shadow of Tragedy

The 2019 elections were not won by policy debates or economic plans. They were won in the shadow of a tragedy that shook the nation to its core. The Easter Sunday bombings became more than a terrorist attack—they became a political pivot point.

Sri Lanka's journey since then has been marked by **centralized power**, **constitutional reversals**, and **ongoing investigations**. The victims of Easter Sunday deserve justice. And the country deserves answers—not just about who bombed, but about who knew, who failed, and who gained.

72

The Corona Period in Sri Lanka: Missteps, Misgivings, and the Muslim Burial Controversy

The COVID-19 pandemic tested the resolve of nations across the globe. For Sri Lanka, the virus did more than bring illness—it unraveled trust, exposed systemic fragilities, and ignited a deeply emotional and divisive debate on dignity, rights, and identity.

A Nation on Edge

As COVID-19 arrived on Sri Lanka's shores, the government acted swiftly—imposing lockdowns, closing borders, and rolling out public health campaigns. Yet, beneath the surface, operational cracks widened:

- Hospitals were overwhelmed, especially outside Colombo.
- Public messaging was inconsistent, leading to confusion.
- Marginalized communities, particularly estate workers and urban poor, were disproportionately impacted by job losses and limited access to healthcare.

Amid these struggles, one policy in particular cast a long and painful shadow.

The Cremation Mandate: Pain Beyond the Pandemic

In March 2020, the Sri Lankan government issued a directive mandating cremation of all COVID-related deaths—arguing that burials could contaminate groundwater and spread the virus, despite WHO guidelines stating otherwise. This decision struck a raw nerve in the Muslim community, for whom burial is not just tradition—it is a sacred religious obligation.

The consequences were heartbreaking:

- Muslim families were forced to watch loved ones cremated, unable to perform final rites.
- Some refused to report deaths or seek hospital care out of fear.
- Protests erupted, both domestically and internationally, with human rights organizations condemning the policy.

Faith vs. Fear

The heart of the controversy was a conflict between science, policy, and faith:

- **Scientific Basis:** Multiple experts, including international virologists and Sri Lankan doctors, **stated burial posed no greater risk than cremation.**

- **Political Interpretation:** Critics accused the state of inflaming ethnic divisions under the guise of public health.
- **Religious Impact:** The Muslim population—already facing stigma post-Easter bombings—felt further isolated and targeted.

Resistance and Reversal

Despite pressure, the policy remained in place for over a year. During this time:

- Advocacy groups filed petitions and organized peaceful demonstrations.
- Religious leaders, both Muslim and non-Muslim, called for compassion and adherence to global standards.
- In February 2021, after global scrutiny and local unrest, the government reversed the cremation-only mandate.

The first COVID-19 burial took place in **Oddamavadi** in Eastern Sri Lanka, quietly—but symbolically—closing a painful chapter.

Beyond the statistics, the scars of this period linger:

- Families carry emotional trauma, knowing they could not honor loved ones.
- Trust between minority communities and the state remains fragile.
- The episode stands as a reminder: when policy dismisses dignity, even in crisis, it leaves wounds deeper than any virus.

Moving Forward

Sri Lanka's journey through COVID-19 is a mosaic of resilience, fear, and missed opportunities. The cremation controversy wasn't just about bodies—it was about belonging, belief, and the right to mourn in one's own way.

As the country rebuilds, there's a chance to do better:

- Strengthen public health systems for all.
- Engage communities in policy decisions.
- Preserve cultural and religious dignity—even in disaster.

Only then can healing begin—not just from a virus, but from the divisions it deepened.

73

The Strongman Who Stumbled —
Gotabaya Rajapaksa, Economic Collapse,
and the Aragalaya Uprising

"This is not just a cry for bread and fuel. It's a cry to be heard."
— A protester at GotaGoGama, July 2022

Aragalaya: People's Response To Rajapaksa-
Made Crisis - Colombo Telegraph

The Rise: A Nation's Gamble on Security and Strength

In **November 2019**, Sri Lanka elected **Gotabaya Rajapaksa** as its **8th executive president**, riding a wave of post-Easter attack fear and nationalist fervor. A former **Defence Secretary**, Gotabaya was hailed as the man who could restore order, revive the economy, and protect the nation from extremism. His military credentials and the legacy of his brother **Mahinda Rajapaksa**, credited with ending the civil war, gave him an aura of invincibility.

His campaign promised **discipline, development, and security**. He pledged to cut taxes, boost agriculture, and make Sri Lanka self-sufficient. The public, weary of political gridlock and shaken by terror, handed him a **decisive mandate**.

But beneath the surface of triumph, a storm was brewing.

The Fall Begins: Missteps and Miscalculations

Gotabaya's presidency quickly revealed troubling patterns:

- **Sweeping tax cuts** in 2020 slashed government revenue by nearly **30%**, weakening the fiscal base.
- A **sudden ban on chemical fertilizers** in April 2021, aimed at promoting organic farming, devastated crop yields and triggered food shortages.
- The **COVID-19 pandemic** crippled tourism and remittances, draining foreign reserves.
- The government printed money aggressively, ignoring IMF warnings, fueling **runaway inflation**.
- By early 2022, Sri Lanka was facing **fuel queues**, **blackouts**, and **medicine shortages**. The rupee collapsed. The country defaulted on its debt for the first time in history.

The once-promising presidency had become a symbol of **economic ruin and authoritarian drift**.

Aragalaya: The People's Struggle Ignites

(Pic: Daily FT)

In **March 2022**, spontaneous protests erupted across the island. Citizens from all walks of life—students, farmers, professionals, clergy—took to the streets. The movement, dubbed **Aragalaya** ("The Struggle"), was unprecedented in its **unity, creativity, and nonviolence**.

- Protesters camped at **Galle Face Green**, creating **GotaGoGama**—a symbolic village demanding the president's resignation.
- Slogans like **"Go Home Gota"** and **"Victory to the Struggle"** echoed nationwide.

- The movement transcended ethnic and religious divides, with Muslims, Tamils, and Sinhalese standing shoulder to shoulder.
- Despite curfews, tear gas, and intimidation, the protests grew stronger.

On **July 9, 2022**, demonstrators stormed the **Presidential Palace**. Gotabaya fled the country. On **July 14**, he resigned from Singapore, becoming the **first Sri Lankan president to step down mid-term**.

Aftermath: A Nation Reclaims Its Voice

The Aragalaya did more than oust a president—it **shattered the myth of invincibility** surrounding the Rajapaksa dynasty. It proved that **people power** could challenge entrenched authority.

Yet, the road ahead remains uncertain:

- **Ranil Wickremesinghe**, a seasoned politician, was elected president by Parliament on **July 20, 2022**, sparking mixed reactions.
- The economic crisis persists, with IMF negotiations and debt restructuring underway.
- The spirit of Aragalaya lives on, but many fear a return to **old political habits**.

A Reflection from Afar

From my new home in **Canada**, I watched these events unfold with a heavy heart. The land I once called home was burning—not just with fire, but with **rage, resilience, and hope**. The Aragalaya was not just a protest—it was a **rebirth**. A reminder that even in despair, **the people can rise**.

(Pic: Daily Mirror)

74

The Quiet Coup — Ranil Wickremesinghe and the Politics of Control

(Pic: nexttrravelsrilanka.com)

From Crisis to Command: The Rise of an Unelected President

In the wake of the **Aragalaya uprising**, Sri Lanka stood at a political crossroads. The mass protests of 2022 had ousted **Gotabaya Rajapaksa**, but the vacuum left behind was quickly filled by **Ranil Wickremesinghe**—a seasoned politician who had lost his own parliamentary seat in the 2020 election yet ascended to the presidency through a parliamentary vote. His rise was not through popular mandate, but through strategic maneuvering and alliance-building with remnants of the **SLPP**, the very party the people had revolted against.

Suppressing the Aragalaya: Emergency Powers and Tear Gas

Wickremesinghe's first major act as **Acting President** was to **crack down on the Aragalaya movement**. On **July 22, 2022**, he ordered the **military and police to forcibly evict protesters** from Galle Face Green, the symbolic heart of the uprising. Tear gas, water cannons, and baton charges replaced the chants of unity and resistance.

The **Supreme Court later ruled** that his use of emergency powers violated **fundamental rights**, branding the crackdown as **arbitrary and unconstitutional**.

He also vowed to **prevent any future Aragalayas**, threatening to deploy the military and impose emergency law if necessary. The message was clear: dissent would not be tolerated.

Managing the Economic Collapse: Austerity and IMF Strings

Wickremesinghe's economic strategy was built around securing an **IMF bailout**, which he achieved in **early 2023**. To meet IMF conditions, he implemented:

- **Tax hikes** and **removal of subsidies**, burdening the middle and working classes
- **Privatization of state-owned enterprises**
- **Cuts to welfare programs**, despite rising poverty and food insecurity

While these measures stabilized foreign reserves and reduced inflation, they also deepened **public hardship**. Critics labeled his approach **"authoritarian neoliberalism"**—a model where economic reforms are pushed through **without public consent**, and **protests are suppressed** to maintain control.

Democracy Deferred: The Postponement of Elections

One of the most controversial aspects of Wickremesinghe's rule was his **repeated postponement of elections**:

- **Local council elections**, scheduled for **March 2023**, were delayed indefinitely due to "lack of funds"
- The **Supreme Court ruled** that this violated citizens' **fundamental rights**, ordering the government to hold elections as soon as possible
- His party even proposed a **referendum to extend his term and delay presidential elections by two years**, sparking outrage across the political spectrum

These moves were widely seen as attempts to **avoid electoral accountability**, especially as public support for Wickremesinghe remained low.

The Good, the Bad, and the Ugly

ASPECT	ASSESSMENT
Economic Stabilization	✅ *Good*: Secured IMF deal, reduced inflation, restored fuel and electricity supplies
Democratic Governance	❌ *Bad*: Postponed elections, ruled guilty of violating rights
Crisis Management	⚠️ *Ugly*: Suppressed protests, used emergency powers, centralized authority

Members of Ranil Wickremesinghe's Cabinet (2022–2024)

After assuming the presidency in **July 2022**, Ranil Wickremesinghe formed a cabinet that blended **veteran politicians**, **technocrats**, and **loyalists from the SLPP** (Sri Lanka Podujana Peramuna). His government was a **minority coalition**, navigating both economic collapse and public dissent.

Here are some of the most prominent cabinet members during his tenure:

Top Leadership

Ranil Wickremesinghe (UNP)

President of Sri Lanka
Minister of Finance
Minister of Defence
Minister of Technology
Minister of Women, Child Affairs and Social Empowerment

Dinesh Gunawardena (SLPP)

Prime Minister
Minister of Public Administration, Home Affairs, Provincial Councils and Local Government

Key Ministers by Portfolio

MINISTER	PORTFOLIO(S)	PARTY AFFILIATION
Ali Sabry	Foreign Affairs	SLPP
Susil Premajayantha	Education	SLPP
Keheliya Rambukwella	Health, later Environment	SLPP
Wijeyadasa Rajapakshe	Justice, Prison Affairs, Constitutional Reforms	SLFP
Harin Fernando	Tourism, Sports & Youth Affairs	UNP
Manusha Nanayakkara	Labour and Foreign Employment	UNP
Douglas Devananda	Fisheries	EPDP
Bandula Gunawardena	Transport, Mass Media	SLPP
Ramesh Pathirana	Industries, Plantation, Health	SLPP
Mahinda Amaraweera	Agriculture, Wildlife	SLPP
Kanchana Wijesekera	Power and Energy	SLPP
Nimal Siripala de Silva	Ports, Shipping and Aviation	SLFP
Pavithra Wanniarachchi	Wildlife, Irrigation	SLPP
Jeevan Thondaman	Water Supply and Estate Infrastructure	CWC
Tiran Alles	Public Security	SLPP
Nalin Fernando	Trade, Commerce and Food Security	SLPP
Vidura Wickremanayake	Religious and Cultural Affairs	SLPP

This cabinet was marked by **continuity with Rajapaksa-era figures**, despite public calls for reform.

A Presidency of Paradox

Ranil Wickremesinghe's tenure was a study in contrasts. He brought **economic order**, *but at the cost of* **democratic disorder**. *He promised* **reform** *but ruled with* **repression**. *From afar, in the safety of Canada, I watched a nation once full of protest songs fall into a* **quiet compliance**—*not because the people were healed, but because they were exhausted.*

This chapter is not just about one man's rule. It is about how **crisis can be used to consolidate power**, *how* **democracy can be delayed**, *and how* **the voice of the people can be silenced—not with bullets, but with bureaucracy**.

"Ranil didn't silence the protests. He outlasted them. And in that silence, democracy lost its breath."
— Anonymous activist, Galle Face Green, August 2022

75

The Turning Tide — Sri Lanka's 2024 Presidential Election and the Mandate for Change

The run-up to the **2024 Presidential Election** in Sri Lanka was unlike any in recent memory. It followed years of economic collapse, mass protests, and political disillusionment. The **Aragalaya uprising of 2022** had ousted President Gotabaya Rajapaksa, and **Ranil Wickremesinghe**, appointed through Parliament, governed without a popular mandate. His tenure was marked by **austerity**, **election delays**, and **emergency crackdowns**, leaving the public yearning for accountability and reform.

The election, scheduled for **September 21, 2024**, was not just a contest for power—it was a **referendum on the future**. With **39 candidates**, the highest in Sri Lankan history, the ballot reflected a fractured political landscape and a desperate search for new leadership.

The Contenders: Familiar Faces, New Promises
Three candidates emerged as frontrunners:

Anura Kumara Dissanayake (Pic: britanica.com)

Anura Kumara Dissanayake (National People's Power – NPP): A leftist ⚡ firebrand and former JVP leader, Dissanayake campaigned on **anti-corruption**, **economic justice**, and

systemic reform. His manifesto promised **industrial revival**, **social protection**, and **truth and reconciliation**.

Sajith Premadasa (Pic: colombotelegraph.org)

Sajith Premadasa Samagi Jana Balawegaya – SJB): The Opposition Leader and son of former President Ranasinghe Premadasa, Sajith offered a **social democratic vision**, pledging **housing**, **education reform**, and **inclusive governance**.

Ranil Wickremasinghe (Pic: mawratanews.lk)

Ranil Wickremesinghe (Independent): The incumbent president ran without party backing, touting **economic stabilization**, **IMF compliance**, and **constitutional reform**. His campaign emphasized **discipline and continuity** but was haunted by his **undemocratic reputation** and **low public approval**.

Campaign Pulse: From Rallies to Reckonings

The campaign season was intense and unpredictable:

Dissanayake's rallies drew massive crowds, especially among youth and working-class voters disillusioned with traditional parties.

Premadasa's strategy focused on rural outreach and leveraging his father's legacy.

Wickremesinghe, despite his experience, struggled to energize voters and faced criticism for **postponing local elections** and **suppressing dissent**.

The **Election Commission**, under pressure, ensured a transparent process. Voting was conducted peacefully at over **13,000 polling stations**, with **79.46% turnout**—a testament to the public's hunger for change.

The Verdict: A Historic Realignment

For the first time in Sri Lankan history, **no candidate won an outright majority** in the first round:

CANDIDATE	PARTY/ALLIANCE	FIRST PREFERENCE	VOTES PERCENTAGE
Anura Kumara Dissanayake	NPP	5,634,915	42.31%
Sajith Premadasa	SJB	4,363,035	32.76%
Ranil Wickremesinghe	Independent	2,299,767	17.27%

With no majority, **second preference votes** were counted.

On **September 22**, **Anura Kumara Dissanayake** was declared the winner with **56% of the final tally**, becoming the **first third-party candidate** and **first left-wing leader** to be elected president.

Dissanayake's victory marked a **political earthquake**. It broke the dominance of the ⬚ **UNP** and **SLFP**, signaling a **generational shift**.

His inauguration on **September 23** was subdued—no firecrackers, no milk rice celebrations—reflecting both **hope and caution**.

His appointment of **Harini Amarasuriya** as Prime Minister, a respected academic and activist, suggested a commitment to **inclusive governance** and **truth-seeking**.

Yet, challenges loom:

- Can the NPP deliver on its promises without alienating global partners like the **IMF**, **India**, and **China**?
- Will the new administration confront **past human rights abuses**, including **enforced disappearances** and **war crimes**?
- Can it maintain unity in a deeply polarized society?

76

From Dominion to Democracy—Sri Lanka's Political Odyssey, 1948–2024

A Journey Through Seven Decades

Since gaining independence from British rule in 1948, **Sri Lanka's political trajectory** has been shaped by nationalism, ethnic tensions, civil war, economic fluctuations, and democratic resilience. The first few decades saw the rise of **post-colonial leadership**, followed by increasing polarization between Sinhala and Tamil communities, culminating in a brutal civil war that lasted nearly three decades.

The war's end in 2009 brought a brief sense of unity and reconstruction, but lingering grievances and authoritarian tendencies—particularly under the **Rajapaksa administrations**—stunted genuine reconciliation. Corruption, dynastic politics, and shortsighted economic policies widened the gap between the government and the governed.

The 2022 Crisis and Rise of the People

The **2022 Aragalaya movement**, a non-violent civilian protest that forced President Gotabaya Rajapaksa's resignation, was a landmark moment. It channeled decades of frustration into a united demand for change, proving the power of civic participation. It set the stage for political alternatives to emerge.

The 2024 Elections: A Democratic Reckoning

The **2024 General Elections** marked the culmination of this awakening. Following **Anura Kumara Dissanayake's** presidential win, the sweeping parliamentary victory of the **National People's Power (NPP)** shattered traditional allegiances. Voters across ethnic and regional lines chose reform over rhetoric.

Key aspects:

Largest majority since 1977 with 159 seats secured by NPP.
First-time MPs made up over two-thirds of Parliament.
Women and minorities gained historic levels of representation.
SLPP, once dominant, reduced to near-obscurity.

It wasn't just a shift in power—it was a shift in consciousness.

Reflections on the Evolution of Leadership

Throughout this political saga, leadership transitioned from the aristocratic elites of the 1950s to populist icons and technocrats. Leaders like **S.W.R.D. Bandaranaike, J.R. Jayewardene, Chandrika Kumaratunga**, and the Rajapaksas left indelible marks—both progressive and problematic. The newer generation, however, seems focused on transparency, equity, and technological modernization.

Sri Lanka in the Global Arena

Once caught in the Cold War crossfire and later tangled in regional diplomacy, Sri Lanka is now recalibrating its foreign policy. Dissanayake's administration pledges a non-aligned, economically pragmatic approach—cautiously balancing interests between China, India, and Western powers.

A Reflection from Exile

From my new home in **Canada**, I watched the election unfold with a mix of **hope and hesitation**. The land I left behind had finally spoken—not in rage, but in resolve. The people chose not just a president, but a **new possibility**. Whether this moment becomes a **milestone or a mirage**, only time will tell.

This book has traced Sri Lanka's turbulent yet tenacious march from colonial shackles to democratic renewal. The events of 2024 are not the climax, but a **beginning**—an invitation to redefine leadership, accountability, and citizen power. In this new Parliament sits not just elected officials, but the **hopes of a nation** ready to write its own story, not in the shadows of history, but under the bright light of possibility.

If the past 300 pages have shown anything, it's that **democracy is not a destination—it is a commitment**. And for the first time in decades, Sri Lanka seems poised to honor it.

"We were not born to inherit silence, but to shape tomorrow with our voices."
– Anonymous

This book is dedicated to **the dreamers, dissenters, and doers**—to every citizen who braved injustice, every youth who demanded better, and every soul who believed that democracy is not given but grown.

From the steps of **Temple Trees** to the crowded trains of **Jaffna**, from the whispers of history in **Galle Fort** to the chants on the streets of **Colombo**, this story belongs to all of Sri Lanka. May these 300 pages serve as a testament: that progress is never linear, that hope is not naive, and that renewal comes not from leaders alone, but from the courage of everyday people.

THE END

About the Author

Born in the misty highlands of Hatton in Sri Lanka, **Tuan B. Kamiss** grew up surrounded by rolling tea estates, vibrant culture, and the enduring rhythm of a country steeped in history. That early exposure to heritage and identity sparked a lifelong passion for storytelling—one rooted in truth, reflection, and the pursuit of understanding.

Now residing in Canada, Tuan continues to embrace writing not only as an art form but as a calling. His voice bridges continents and cultures, bringing Sri Lanka's rich and complex narratives to life for new generations of readers. Whether delving into the unsung contributions of communities or illuminating pivotal chapters of the past, his work seeks to preserve memory and stir thought.

Tuan has authored three distinguished books that document vital facets of Sri Lankan identity:

- *Malay Sport Personalities of Sri Lanka*
- *Malays in Uniform*
- *Sip of History: The Backbone of Ceylon Tea*

This fourth volume marks an ambitious and impassioned journey into Sri Lanka's post-independence political landscape—covering the nation's evolution from 1948 to 2024. In it, Tuan explores both triumphs and turmoil with historical clarity and personal insight, offering a powerful portrait of a nation striving to define itself.

Through his words, readers will find not only meticulous research but a heartfelt homage to his birthplace. His commitment to truth-telling and cultural preservation shines through each chapter.

When not writing, Tuan enjoys the quiet serenity of Canadian life, taking walks beneath vast prairie skies, sipping tea that reminds him of home, and engaging in reflective conversations about history, identity, and purpose.

Acknowledgements - Consolidated References

Author(s)	Title of Source	Publication Year	Type of Source	Notes/Chapter Referenced
K.M. De Silva	*A History of Sri Lanka*	1981	Book	Chapters 1 & 2 Post-independence Era
Jane Russell	*Politics and Education in Sri Lanka 1947–1976*	1982	Academic Publication	Chapter 3 – Education reforms
Various	*Hansard Reports – Parliament of Sri Lanka*	Various Years	Government Document	Chapters 4–10 – Parliamentary debates
A.J. Wilson	*The Break-Up of Sri Lanka: The Tamils' Fight for Justice*	1988	Book	Chapter 6 – Ethnic tensions
Newspaper Archives	*Daily News, Sunday Observer, The Island*	1948–2024	News Articles	Throughout – Political events timeline
S.J. Tambiah	*Levelling Crowds: Ethnonationalist Conflicts and Collective Violence in South Asia*	1996	Book	Chapter 7 – Civil unrest periods
Central Bank of Sri Lanka	*Annual Reports*	Various Years	Economic Data Report	Chapters 5 & 8 – Fiscal policy impacts
International Crisis Group	*Reports on Sri Lanka*	2000s–2020s	Research Reports	Chapters 9 & 10 – External perspectives
Personal Interviews	Various Sri Lankan political analysts	2021–2023	Primary Source	Chapter 11 – Contemporary reflections

Online References

Website Name	URL	Type pf Source	Notes/Chapter Referenced
Colombo Telegraph	colombotelegraph.com	Independent News Site	Political commentary and investigative journalism
Daily Mirror Sri Lanka	dailymirror.lk	News Outlet	Coverage of current affairs and political updates
Sunday Times Sri Lanka	sundaytimes.lk	News Outlet	Archival articles and opinion pieces
Groundviews	groundviews.org	Civic Media Platform	Human rights, governance, and reconciliation
Centre for Policy Alternatives	cpalanka.org	Research Institution	Policy analysis and constitutional matters
International Crisis Group	crisisgroup.org	Global Think Tank	Reports on conflict and political reform

www.ingramcontent.com/pod-product-compliance
Lightning Source LLC
Chambersburg PA
CBHW041136120626
46547CB00020B/3007